Anthony Martienssen was born in South Africa in 1919, and
educated at St John's College, Johannesburg, and St Catherine's
College, Cambridge. He has been on the editorial staff of
The Economist, and his publications include *Hitler and His Admirals*
and *Crime and the Police*.

QUEEN KATHERINE PARR

Anthony Martienssen

CARDINAL edition published in 1975
by Sphere Books Ltd
30/32 Gray's Inn Road, London WC1X 8JL

First published in Great Britain
by Martin Secker & Warburg Limited 1973
Copyright © Anthony Martienssen 1973

Set in Intertype Lectura

Printed in Great Britain by Cox & Wyman Ltd,
London, Reading and Fakenham

The more gentle a man, and the better a man is brought up, the more lowly and courteously he behaveth himself, the more villain, the more disdainful and fierce. Some times these vices come of dullness and lack of knowledge, and for this cause, good learning is called humanity.

If thou salute, and be not saluted back, ascribe it to negligence rather than contempt. If thou be spoken to unmannerly, attribute it to lack of good manners, or to nature, and not to malice or hatred. Be not so light as to be moved with the breath of a man's mouth.

— from *An Introduction to Wisdom*,
by Juan Luys Vives (1492–1540)

How one lives is so far distant from how one ought to live, that he who neglects what *is* done for what ought to be done, sooner effects his ruin than his preservation; for a man who wishes to act entirely up to his professions of virtue soon meets with what destroys him among so much that is evil.

— from *The Prince*,
by Nicolo Machiavelli (1469–1527)

ACKNOWLEDGMENTS

My most grateful thanks are due to the Essex County Library who procured vast numbers of books for me, including microfilms of rare sixteenth-century works, from all over the country, and whose efficient and friendly staff have been of great help in tracking down original sources and other material which I needed.

My thanks are also due to the National Portrait Gallery, London, for permission to reproduce the portrait of Katherine Parr.

Like most authors, I owe a considerable debt to my wife, not only for her help in the initial stages of research, but also for her forbearance in putting up with endless discussions in which the words 'Katherine Parr' occurred in almost every sentence.

Finally, I would like to thank my mother, Ruth Martienssen, but for whose unfailing optimism and aid in times of crisis this book might never have been written. In all gratitude, I dedicate this book to her.

PREFACE

Unfortunately for historians, Katherine Parr was never arrested so that her papers were never seized, and she is perhaps the least well documented of all the prominent people in the reign of Henry VIII. Her modern biographers must therefore rely mostly on circumstantial evidence to piece together the details of her life. This type of evidence is not necessarily any less valid than direct evidence – the fish-scale in the cat's bowl of milk is proof enough of who stole the fish – but it does present difficulties in that references to sources are not then sufficient to explain how one arrived at the fact stated. On the other hand, if every statement based on circumstantial evidence has to be explained, one would end up with more footnotes than text, which might please the student, but which would make tiresome reading for the general public for whom this book is primarily intended. Moreover, the voluminous collection of documents known as *Letters & Papers (Foreign & Domestic) of the Reign of Henry VIII* on which this and most other books about this period are based, is so well known to students of the period that separate references for every fact and quotation from this source have seemed to me to be superfluous. For these reasons, I have therefore confined references to sources to certain key points which I felt needed justification and to facts which are not contained either directly or by inference in *Letters & Papers*.

For the benefit of students, the main line of research which I followed was inspired by a report which Chapuys, the Spanish Ambassador, made from his retirement at Louvain at the end of Henry VIII's reign. In his report, Chapuys specifically mentions the activities of Katherine Parr and her ladies. Given this lead, it proved possible to trace these activities back through the documents and literature of the period even where the women were not mentioned by name. This theme was first picked up by Strype and outlined in his *Ecclesiastical Memorials*, but with the exception of researches into English Humanists, notably that by McConica, the theme was not followed up and hence many clues concerning Katherine Parr have been missed. The other major lead, contained in 'Household Accounts', was the fact that Katherine Parr's mother was continuously at Court from 1518 until her death in 1529. Other references make it clear that her children were with her, and this led to a number of significant deductions which are explained in the text of this book.

In addition to *Letters & Papers*, major contemporary references to Katherine Parr are to be found in her own writings, listed in the British Museum catalogue; Foxe's *Acts and Monuments* which was written some fifteen to twenty years after her death; Burnet's *History of the Reformation*; Strype's *Ecclesiastical Memorials* in which several important documents concerning Katherine are transcribed; Nichols' *Literary Remains of Edward VI*; and Agnes Strickland's *Queens of England* which, in spite of its Victorian romantic bias and many inaccuracies, does contain careful transcriptions of a number of letters and documents which are only summarised elsewhere. Other references are to be found in the reports of the Royal Commission on Historical Manuscripts, but nothing significant concerning Katherine Parr has so far emerged in reports published after the publication of *Letters & Papers*. I have also found the early County histories, particularly Whitaker's *History of Richmondshire*, useful for the documents they quote, but these sources need to be treated with some caution. Few of the many modern studies of the period contain more than a passing reference to Katherine Parr, and those few tend to limit themselves to the well-established events in which she was involved during her reign as Queen. For these sources, the student is referred to the many excellent bibliographies which modern studies of the period contain.

ANTHONY MARTIENSSEN

I Politics and Women

The marriage of Katherine Parr and Henry VIII in the summer of 1543 – his sixth and last wife, her third and penultimate husband – pleased everybody. Congratulations poured in from as far afield as Venice, Paris, and Brussels, and papists and anti-papists alike praised Henry for his choice. Katherine's father had been one of Henry's close friends, her mother had been a principal Lady-in-Waiting to Henry's first Queen, Catharine of Aragon, while she herself had been born and brought up in the full glare of Henry's Court. Here, then, was a Queen who was well known, a woman whose prudence, intelligence, and virtue offered great hopes of avoiding the unpleasant shocks which had come to be associated with Henry's matrimonial ventures. Only Henry, who never took a major step without a purpose, and a few of Katherine's intimate friends, knew of the power and ambition which her amiable manners concealed.

By this stage in history women had established an influential position in politics. For three-quarters of a century they had been steadily building up their political strength, determined to put their stamp on the new society that was emerging from the collapse of feudalism. The culmination of their work was to come in the next generation when women were to rule, either by right or in fact, not only over England but over half of Europe as well, for by then women had demonstrated beyond dispute their ability to take the lead in what was very much a man's world. Chance had played its part, but the intelligence and ambition needed to seize the chance when it came was cultivated, not accidental, and it was this capability which Henry had recognised in Katherine Parr.

The development of the political power of women in Tudor times had its origins in the Wars of the Roses during the preceding century. The prolonged absence of husbands on the battlefields left many women in charge of large estates, putting them in situations where decisions could no longer be deferred, but where a wrong judgment, caused by ignorance or inexperience, could jeopardise the fortunes of their families.

This led to an urgent demand for a much higher degree of learning and knowledge than was usual for women at that time, and first one anxious wife, then another, set about hiring tutors, ostensibly for their daughters but in reality for themselves. It so happened, however, that the majority of able tutors at that time were deeply imbued with what became known as the New Learning, and it was its inspiration and philosophy, instead of the traditional teaching of the Middle Ages, that the tutors passed on to their eager pupils.

The New Learning represented a clean break from the immediate past. Nothing, it taught, of what the Church or anybody else had said in the past few centuries should be taken for granted. Education was not the prerogative of the privileged clergy, but for all mankind, for it was only through education that man could rise above the beasts and become 'humane' – hence the name of 'The Humanities' for the subjects taught under the New Learning, and the name of 'Humanists' for its proponents. On questions of religion, ethics, and politics, the New Learning preached a doctrine of methodical research into the actual writings of the early Christian Fathers and the classical philosophers rather than reliance on the often stultifying canons of the Roman Church. On the question of future progress, the New Learning propounded a system of controlled investigation and experiment, untrammelled by superstition or religious dogma, and using the tools of astronomers, mathematicians, and doctors of medicine, to discover the true nature of the physical world. To fulfil this ambitious programme, more subjects should be studied in the universities: classical Greek, to avoid translators' distortions of the philosophers; Hebrew, to ensure a direct interpretation of the Bible; modern languages, mathematics, and the natural sciences, to meet the requirement to expand man's knowledge.

It was a far cry from elementary law and arithmetic, which was all that the anxious wives had thought to get from their tutors, and it opened up a new world of intellectual excitement which gave a new meaning to their lives. In England, led by such men as Linacre, Grocyn and Colet, and later by the two intellectual giants of the age, Erasmus and Sir Thomas More, the New Learning went on to preach that it was nonsense to think that the good life could only be lived in monasteries and nunneries. Such institutions, they said, might have been necessary havens of virtue and learning in the dark ages, but in this enlightened age they were no longer needed. Instead it was both possible and highly

12

desirable that the good life should be spread to town and village, to Court and government, indeed to all walks of life, however humble, however great.

It was a message which could not fail to reach the hearts and minds of women living in an age ravaged by war and plague, and gripped by the rapacious tentacles of a Church which had become corrupt. The first concrete action came from Margaret Beaufort, Henry VIII's grandmother.

The widow first of Edmund Tudor, Duke of Richmond, and later of Lord Stanley, Earl of Derby, Margaret Beaufort was a direct descendant of John of Gaunt. From her late husbands and from her father, the Earl of Somerset, she had inherited a fortune, and after her son, Henry VII, had seized the Crown at Bosworth in 1485, she took up the rôle of patroness of the New Learning. Tolerant, shrewd and now immensely rich, she financed a succession of thinkers and teachers, endowed new colleges at both Oxford and Cambridge, and brought her powerful influence to bear on the Court in the cause of reform. It was she who launched Caxton with his printing presses; founded, and firmly established, Christ's and St John's College, Cambridge, as leading seats of the New Learning in Europe; reformed the great monastery of Syon to make it a key centre of genuine religious scholarship; and set forth a host of famous men, including Erasmus, on their careers.

Even more important, Margaret Beaufort was a convinced believer in the duty of women to moderate the excesses and guide the destiny of the new bustling society which her son had begun to create. At that stage in history, women had begun to achieve a high degree of independence. They ran their own businesses, were accepted as members by many of the Craft Guilds, held property in their own right, and could follow almost any calling they chose. Only the professions, of which the most important at that time was the law, were officially closed to them, but even in the Law Courts, many a woman could and did plead her own cause as effectively as any attorney. True, they usually had to be wives or widows before they could enjoy their freedom, but they then tended to retain their maiden names as proof of their separate identity in business or public life.

In this atmosphere of independence, Margaret Beaufort gathered round her a circle of high-born ladies. She inspired them with her Humanist ideals, and through them she sought to spread her influence among the power-hungry men who had helped to put her son on the throne. It was uphill work. The boisterous, heavy-drinking, gambling crowd of courtiers did not take kindly to the women's efforts to civilise them, but gradually, by using the weapons of good-humoured wit and the penetrating insight into their affairs which the New Learning gave them, the women began to succeed. The drinking, gambling and frolics continued, but the rough edges were smoothed away, and by the turn of the century (1500) Erasmus was to write enthusiastically to a friend on the Continent that in no other Court in Europe was there so much wit and learning as in that of Henry VII. To emphasise the purity of her motives, Margaret Beaufort took the veil, but it was no ordinary nun that she became, for she remained at Court, and the robes of an abbess which she now affected were more a mark of feminine leadership than of religious seclusion.

By these means, Margaret Beaufort dominated her son's Court and laid the foundations of women's political power. And of the women she gathered around her, few admired her more than her close friend, Elizabeth Fitzhugh, the grandmother of Katherine Parr. Together with the rest of Margaret Beaufort's circle, Elizabeth passed the Humanist ideals on to the next generation of women, many of whom were from the same families, and so eventually to Katherine Parr's generation. Inevitably, there were to be some deviations and back-sliding, but it says much for the power of Margaret Beaufort's initiative that it continued almost unabated through three generations of women – and indeed beyond them, for Katherine Parr was to add her own drive and influence when she in turn came to take the lead at Court, and women were to remain in the ascendant until the end of the sixteenth century.

To ensure the continuity of her ideas for reform, Margaret Beaufort selected the members of the first Council of her grandson, Henry VIII, when he succeeded to the throne in 1509, and then died with what must have been a rare satisfaction at how much she had achieved. Good men launched in the pursuit of knowledge backed by solid research, a base established for a true Faith free from superstition and corruption, and the invention of printing financed to spread that knowledge and Faith easily and quickly to all mankind: these were the seeds she had planted and from which she prayed that the Utopia of which all men dream would grow and flourish.

After Margaret Beaufort's death, the role of patroness of the New Learning was taken over by Henry VIII's first wife, Catharine of Aragon. The Humanists had been as plentiful in the Spain of Catharine's childhood, before the days of the Inquisition, as they were in England, and to her pleasant surprise she found herself very much at home among the bright intellectuals who now thronged the English Court. Moreover, these were the days of Henry's youth, when he could out-ride, out-joust, out-gamble, and out-argue any man in the kingdom. 'You see me, you know me!' he roared, and the crowd yelled with admiration. But when it came to women, his tastes were unusual. Brought up in the society of the witty and learned women with whom his grandmother had filled the Court, he showed himself far more susceptible to the attractions of a lively woman's mind than to a beautiful figure, and throughout his life his greatest enjoyment was that of being surrounded by brilliant female intellectuals. He loved the swiftness of women's thought, and its apparent inconsequence, pitting his own exceptionally agile mind and breadth of learning against theirs, goading them on to extravagant arguments, and shouting with delight if he succeeded in trapping them with their own words. At that age, a pretty face and gentle manners meant little to him, and without at least a smattering of Latin and Greek, French and Italian, some knowledge of philosophy, the natural sciences, music, and the arts, a girl could make little headway in Court circles. The result was the acquisition by society women of an even higher standard of learning and intellectual ability than they already had. It made Catharine of Aragon's task of continuing Margaret Beaufort's policy that much easier.

Her first move was to persuade Henry to allow her to invite her best friend, Maria de Salinas, to leave Spain and join her in England. It may have been that she felt the need for the moral support of one of her own countrywomen in the English Court, but it is more likely that she was struck by the opportunity of repeating the success which she and Maria had enjoyed in their teens in the Spanish Court where, as a pair, they had easily outshone their contemporaries. Maria was a gay, brilliant, carefree woman, bold without being pert, at times impetuous, but never foolish. She served as a perfect foil to Catharine's cool intelligence and more solid qualities. Writing about the two women in 1514, the then Spanish Ambassador, Luis Caros, complained that Maria was 'the worst influence on the Queen'. They had been taught, he said, to forget Spain and everything Spanish in order to gain the love of the English. 'The consequence is,' he continued his report, 'that I can never make use in my negotiations of the influence which the Queen has in England, nor can I obtain through her the smallest advantage in any respect. I am treated by the English not as an ambassador, but like a bull at whom every one throws darts.'

Henry gave the two women every encouragement in their efforts to become anglicised. He insisted on calling Maria 'Mary', and in 1516 he arranged for her to marry the high-ranking William, Lord Willoughby, granting the bridal pair the substantial estates of Grimsthorpe in Lincolnshire as a wedding present. Subsequently, Henry named one of his new ships the *Mary Willoughby* in honour of the bride, and throughout her life, even during the tortuous drama of Catharine's divorce, Lady Willoughby was to remain assured of the King's protection. In 1519, the marriage produced a daughter, Katherine, who inherited her mother's gay and irrepressible nature, and who was to be to Katherine Parr what Lady Willoughby was to Catharine of Aragon.

The first of the principal English women who attended Catharine of Aragon was Henry VIII's elder sister, Mary, known as the French Queen, since her first marriage had been to Louis XII of France. Louis, however, had died three months after the wedding, and Mary had then married Henry VIII's boyhood companion, Charles Brandon, Duke of Suffolk. Mary, however, continued to be known as the French Queen, mainly to emphasise her royal status, but also to distinguish her from the other Marys at Court. The French Queen bore the Duke two daughters, the Ladies Eleanor and Frances, who were thus Henry VIII's nieces, and the second of whom was to become the mother of the unfortunate Lady Jane Grey. At a later date, Henry's third niece, Margaret Douglas, the daughter of his other sister, Margaret, by her second husband, the Earl of Angus, joined the French Queen's household, and together with Catharine of Aragon's daughter, Princess Mary, the four young girls formed the King's family at Court at that time. The French Queen was one of the more lovable Tudors, though she shared much of her brother's determination to have her own way. She adored her husband and she was clearly an excellent mother. In spite of being brought up by Margaret Beaufort, she was not a scholar, and, unlike the rest of Catharine of Aragon's circle, she tended to let her heart rule her head, but this endeared her to, rather than estranged her from, her more intellectual friends.

Next amongst Catharine of Aragon's attendants, there was Maud, Lady Parr, the wife of Elizabeth Fitzhugh's eldest son, Sir Thomas Parr. As the mother of Katherine Parr, the details of her life are treated more fully in later chapters, and all that needs to be said here is that, unlike the other women who divided their time between their homes and the Court, Lady Parr, from the time of the death of her husband in 1517 until her own death in 1529, was a permanent resident at Court with her three children. Highly educated and deeply influenced by her mother-in-law, her own mother having died while she was an infant, Lady Parr was in constant attendance upon Catharine of Aragon and was entrusted by Catharine with the organisation and control of the Court school which Catharine set up for the King's family and the daughters of her close friends, including Lady Parr's own daughters. It was to be from these schoolgirl companions that Katherine Parr later formed her own circle of women when she eventually became Queen.

The third English woman of importance was Jane, Lady Guildford, whose husband had been one of Henry VII's chief ministers and was selected by Margaret Beaufort to continue in office under Henry VIII. Lady Guildford was also an intellectual, and she shared with Lady Willoughby and Lady Parr the duties of principal Ladies-in-Waiting to the Queen. Apart from her close association with Catharine and the influence she exerted through her husband, Lady Guildford was responsible for taking into her household as a young boy John Dudley, the son of Edmund Dudley, Henry VII's detested tax collector, the execution of whom had been one of Henry VIII's first and most popular acts when he succeeded to the throne. John Dudley, who later married Lady Guildford's daughter, Joan, became a leading figure during the latter part of Henry VIII's reign and, as the Duke of Northumberland, was to dominate the reign of Edward VI, eventually losing his life as the instigator of the attempt to put Lady Jane Grey on the throne. Lady Guildford's daughter, who also attended the Court school, was herself, as Lady Dudley, to play a major part in Katherine Parr's bid for power. Finally, there was Lady Elizabeth Boleyn, the mother of Anne Boleyn.

In the early years of Henry's reign, Catharine's circle of women met with little opposition to their plans for reform. The struggle at that stage between the old Establishment and the Utopian 'alternative society' of the Humanists was, compared with what came later, a mild affair. Henry VIII began his reign with no doubt as to whose side he was on. His father had brought the old feudal nobility to its knees at Bosworth, and Henry continued his father's policy of encouraging the rise of new men from comparatively humble origins and, when the opportunity arose, of ridding the country of the few remaining Yorkists who had survived both Bosworth and the machinations of his father. At the same time he threw himself with characteristic fervour into the cause of the Humanists. It is difficult to judge how much he and his principal mentor at that time, Cardinal Wolsey, were imbued with genuine ideals, but both men, outwardly at least, made a great show of their support for the New Learning. Both poured money into the universities and the foundation of new schools; both applauded and rewarded notable achievements of the Humanists. Linacre got his College of Physicians, Colet his school of St Paul's, and Erasmus and Sir Thomas More were given a free hand in their biting and often bawdy satires on the old style of priests and religious teaching. In those early halcyon days, everything seemed in their favour.

During this period, Catharine of Aragon's rôle was one of consolidation rather than innovation. She and her ladies tended the seeds that Margaret Beaufort had planted, using their skill in handling men to protect the young Humanist growths from the power-game at Court. Being a generation younger than Margaret Beaufort, Catharine could not influence affairs as openly as the older woman had done, but within a few years she had won the respect and support of most of Henry's councillors. This was, however, still a time of youthful exuberance and fine ideas rather than of direct action.

Magnificent talk and grand designs were plentiful, but the actual work of reform was slow and unspectacular. What action there was tended to be focused on foreign affairs, the European subtleties of which challenged Henry's wits, and on some hit-and-run military campaigns in France. The rumblings of Lutheran thunder in Germany, the Low Countries, and even in France (where another great woman, Margaret of Angoulême, the French King's sister later to become the Queen of Navarre, had also felt the call of the Humanists), passed more or less unheeded in England, Henry wrote a book, which Luther scathingly pulled to pieces, criticising the German ideas, and the English Humanists continued to believe that reform could be gently organised from within the Establishment. The removal of an abbot here and there, the checking of one or two of the more outrageous abuses of landlord or priest, and above all the promulgation of vast numbers of books, printed in Gothic English instead of the traditional Latin, were felt to be enough to persuade people to see the light.

The Humanists, however, had reckoned without the baser elements of human nature. Henry's pleasure in lively, intelligent women had not passed unnoticed, and it was only the Spanish Ambassador who resented the remarkable influence which Catharine and her ladies exercised over the King. That this influence was wholly benevolent was immaterial. It was enough that Catharine had shown what a clever woman could do, and it was only a question of time before others would try to supplant her.

Such designs had little chance of success so long as Henry believed that his Queen would one day produce the male heir he wanted so much, but in this respect Catharine was singularly unfortunate. She conceived often enough, six live births in the first nine years of marriage, but, except for one child, all died within a few days or weeks of birth, and the one exception, born on 18 February 1516, was a girl. Henry had taken it well. He named the young princess after his sister, Mary, the French Queen, and London celebrated the christening for a week. But although it was not until 1525 that the doctors formally gave their opinion that Catharine, who was then in her fortieth year, would never bear another child, there are signs that it was in fact in 1518, not long after the birth of her last child, who lived but a few hours, that Catharine, and Henry, gave up hope of a male heir. Up to that time, compared with his contemporary monarchs on the Continent, Henry had been a model of virtue, but now his flirtations at Court became decidedly more pointed, and what had previously seemed but a faint hope of ensnaring him became a real possibility.

He was not caught easily. In 1519, one of Catharine's junior attendants, Elizabeth Blount, bore him a son, but though Henry was as proud as any father in the land, he made no attempt to set the mother up on her own. Instead, he found her a suitable husband, Gilbert Tailboys of Lincolnshire, and packed her off to the country, far from Court. He did take care of his son, however, naming him Henry Fitzroy, giving him a royal establishment, and eventually creating him Duke of Richmond and Somerset as a potential heir to the throne in the event of failure of the King's lawful issue.

When he was finally caught, it was as the result of a complex situation which gave the principal people concerned the opportunity they had been seeking. The elements of the situation were a mixture of foreign policy and foreign wars, the aims and achievements of which had become dangerously confused, economic and political troubles at home, a hardening of the attitude of the Humanists with more direct confrontation with the Church, the beginning of the polarisation of powerful English families into opposing camps, and the continued obsession of the King for a male heir, caused as much by the need to quench the ambitions of other claimants to the throne as by Henry's own desire to perpetuate his dynasty.

This complicated state of affairs developed from about 1519 through to about 1525, and a seemingly minor thread appearing in most events was Sir Thomas Boleyn. The Boleyns were merchant bankers, one of the new breed of men which the Tudors strongly supported as a counterbalance to the old feudal nobility. The fortunes of the family had been founded by Sir Thomas' grandfather, Sir Geoffrey Boleyn, who was Lord Mayor of London in 1457. Sir Thomas' father, Sir William, improved the family position by marrying the daughter of the Earl of Ormonde, while Sir Thomas himself spent his early years so effectively in trade that by the time Henry viii came to the throne in 1509, he was one of the wealthiest men in London. He appears in the record of Court events as early as 1511, when he was thirty-four years old, and from then on we find him employed on a number of missions for the King, both at home and abroad. He managed the Foreign Exchange in London and in Calais, led a detachment of troops in one or two of the French campaigns, assisted in the negotiations of treaties with the Low Countries, made the arrangements for the Field of Cloth of Gold, collected at some personal risk the taxes in Kent, won the reluctant support of his City friends for a twenty per cent tax, a 'benevolence', to be paid to the King, put up money for scholars, and, at his house in Durham Place in the Strand, one of the show buildings of London, entertained Sir Thomas More and the other leading men of his time on a prodigal scale.

Before all these events, Sir Thomas Boleyn had married the Lady Elizabeth Howard, sister of the 3rd Duke of Norfolk, thereby buying himself into the oldest noble family in England – the Howards could trace their descent in an unbroken line back to the year 970 AD – and also ensuring his acceptance in Court circles. It was probably through this connection that he was first able to catch the King's attention; his wealth and natural ability did the rest.

Sir Thomas Boleyn's wife bore him two daughters, Mary and Anne, and a son, George. Mother and daughters, though physically not very attractive, were much admired for their vivacity, learning, and outspoken wit. The son was both a gay young man about town and an active reformer within the Humanist movement, surprisingly religious, but also cool, intelligent, and openly ambitious.

Although both daughters occasionally accompanied their father on his missions abroad, Anne seems to have been his favourite, and she stayed with him in France for about three years during Sir Thomas' embassy preceding and immediately following the Field of Cloth of Gold in 1520. She was a frequent visitor at the French Court where she not only learnt French manners and customs, but where she also came very much under the influence of Francis I's sister, Margaret of Angoulême, who inspired her with the learning and ideals of the Humanists. She was only fourteen years old when she left France to return to England in 1521, but the reforming zeal which Anne had acquired from the French King's sister remained with her for the rest of her life. It gave her an inner intensity and sharpness of mind which, coupled with the sophistication she had learnt in the French Court, lent her a brilliance which outshone both her contemporaries and the older women in London society. Her first recorded appearance at Henry's Court was in March 1522, and it seems certain that either then, or very shortly afterwards, she became one of Queen Catharine's Maids-of-Honour.

Anne's elder sister, Mary, though apparently less of an intellectual than the rest of the family, made up for this deficiency by discreetly letting it be known that she was always prepared to continue an interesting religious or political discussion in bed. In 1520, when she was possibly not more than fifteen years old, she was married off to William Carey, a gentleman of the King's Privy Chamber, and shortly thereafter is believed to have become the King's mistress.[1] She bore three children, but no claim was ever made that any of them were sired by the King.

Throughout his life, Henry VIII made a special point of being generous to those who served him well, and during the critical years between 1519 and 1525, he showered grants and honours on Sir Thomas Boleyn – a reward, the unkind said, as much for his daughter Mary's services as for those of Sir Thomas himself. Early in 1522, Sir Thomas was appointed Treasurer of the Household and granted lands in Essex and Kent; in 1523, he was elected to the Order of the Garter, the highest Order of Knighthood; and finally, in 1525, at the end of this particular period, he was created Viscount Rochford at the same time as the King's illegitimate son, Henry Fitzroy, was made Duke of Richmond and Somerset.

With such great encouragement, the Boleyns would have been false to their stars if they had not from then onwards made a deliberate and concerted bid for the top. The Boleyns were a close-knit family, and young as the children then were – Anne was but eighteen, and her brother and sister were only a year or two older – there is little doubt that they participated in planning the family's future. Now that Mary Boleyn was married, Anne would have to be the bait to catch the King. Once the bait was taken, she was then to be the means for controlling Henry and establishing the male Boleyns in the top positions in the country. It was a star rôle and Anne was already groomed to play it. By 1527, it was known that she had succeeded, and towards the end of April or early in May that year the King informed Wolsey of his wish to have his marriage with Catharine of Aragon annulled. The grounds were that Catharine had been the widow of Henry's brother when she married Henry, and therefore the marriage was illegal. The Pope's dispensation for the marriage, Henry claimed, was invalid, because not even the Pope could go against the law of consanguinity so clearly defined by God in the Bible. The stage was set for the most famous divorce case in history.

At this point in time, Katherine Parr was a highly intelligent, observant young girl of thirteen. Brought up in Court where children, specially girls, were included in adult society at an early age, she had been, at least for the previous two or three years, as interested a witness of the spectacular rise of the Boleyns as everybody else. The parallel with her own family would not have escaped her: they were almost as wealthy, they could also command powerful support in the country, and as many would have thought, they were even closer to the King than the Boleyns. An eighteenth-century historian tells the story that while Katherine was still a child, her stars were read for her by an astrologer. He told her that she had 'all the eminent stars and planets in her house', and that she was 'born to sit in the highest seat of imperial majesty'. This extraordinary prophecy, later to be accurately fulfilled, went to her head, and when her mother used to call her to some domestic chore, she would say, 'My hands are ordained to touch crowns and sceptres, not needles and spindles.'[2] If the story is true, one might well suppose that even before her teens Katherine had already conceived the idea that she might one day follow in Anne Boleyn's footsteps. For the moment, there was no question of any such illustrious fate, for Katherine was then already either betrothed or actually married to her first husband.

NOTES

1 Many years later, Sir George Throgmorton, one of Katherine Parr's uncles, giving evidence in his own defence for protesting against the divorce of Catharine of Aragon, described an interview he had had with Henry: 'And I told your Grace I feared if ye did marry Queen Anne your conscience would be more troubled, for it is thought ye have meddled with both the mother and the sister. And his Grace said "Never with the mother." And my Lord Privy Seal [Thomas Cromwell] standing by said "Nor never with the sister either, and therefore put that out of your mind."'

2 Strype, in his *Ecclesiastical Memorials*. Strype relates that he found the story written in the margin of a sixteenth-century edition of Bale's *Centuries*.

2 Birth and Upbringing

Katherine Parr came from a family which had risen to wealth and power through the traditional methods of military service and lucrative marriages. Six generations before Katherine was born, the family was established as lords of the manor of Parr in Lancashire, where Sir John de Parre ruled over a modest estate. In 1383, his son, Sir William de Parre, married an heiress, Elizabeth de Roos, whose family held the barony of Kendal in Westmorland, and through whom Sir William inherited Kendal Castle and a quarter of the barony, becoming known as Sir William de Parre of Kendal. Sir William's grandson, Sir Thomas Parre, improved the family fortunes still further by marrying into the powerful family of Tunstall of Thurland Castle, Lancashire. (The Tunstalls later moved to Tunstall in Richmondshire in the North Riding of Yorkshire.) Sir Thomas Parre took up arms and mustered a body of some one hundred archers on the side of the Yorkists during the Wars of the Roses, serving as Deputy-Lieutenant and subsequently as Sheriff of Westmorland. He was attainted in 1459 during the reign of Henry VI, but lived long enough to see the Earl of Warwick place the young Edward IV on the throne, and to have his attainder reversed. He died in 1464, leaving three sons and two daughters. His youngest son was killed at Barnet in 1471, and his second son married the daughter of Sir John Yonge, a Lord Mayor of London. His eldest son, Sir William Parr of Kendal, was Katherine Parr's grandfather.

An intellectual as well as a soldier, Sir William Parr was thirty years old when he succeeded his father, and it was he who brought the Parr family to the forefront of the political scene. His father had introduced him to Warwick and to Edward IV, and he won the confidence of both men to such an extent that Warwick employed him as his spokesman in the abortive negotiations which preceded the brief return of Henry VI to the throne. In 1471, however, when Edward IV returned from exile, Sir William Parr abandoned Warwick and met the King at Nottingham, raising his standard at the King's side and riding with him to victory at Barnet. He was well rewarded, receiving the Order of the Garter, more land, and an appointment as Comptroller of the Household in Edward's court.

Sir William's change of parties at that critical moment had shown a cool judgment of the balance of forces, but his next move was a risk in which he had to gamble as much on his own powers of persuasion as on the accuracy of his reading of Edward's position in the country. His first wife, the widow of one Thomas Colt of Roydon, Essex, had died in 1473, and now, in order to put his family in a position where it would not matter who succeeded Edward IV, he sought the King's permission to marry into one of the foremost houses on the Lancastrian side, that of the Lord Fitzhugh. This family, apart from having a pedigree which stretched back through their ancestors, the Marmions, to the days of the Norman Conquest, was probably the most powerful family and largest landowner in the North of England. The Lords Fitzhugh had served the past three Lancastrian Kings, Henry IV, Henry V, and Henry VI, with outstanding distinction and had been rewarded with high positions in government. It can be assumed that Sir William Parr represented to Edward IV the desirability of a truce with at least one of the prominent leaders of the Lancastrians, and to the Lord Fitzhugh he would have put forward the material advantages to be gained from having a son-in-law at the Yorkist Court. Both succumbed to his persuasions, and he was given as his bride Elizabeth Fitzhugh, the youngest daughter of the family.

The marriage had other advantages for the Parrs. Elizabeth's mother was Alice Neville, the daughter of Richard, Earl of Salisbury, and sister to the Earl of Warwick. It was, therefore, a double alliance, taking in the southern branch of the extensive Neville family in addition to the Fitzhughs. Since his bride had little hope of inheriting anything from her family, Sir William Parr could not have had much thought at that time of anything but political gain from the marriage, but, as it happened, the Fitzhugh line failed in 1513 and Sir William's eldest son, Sir Thomas Parr, who was Katherine Parr's father, inherited half the enormous Fitzhugh estates.

After this highly successful marriage, Sir William Parr consolidated his position. In addition to his duties at Court, he was Sheriff of Cumberland from 1473 to 1483 and, ever willing to be of service to his King, negotiated a settlement in Scotland for breaches of the truce in 1479. Finally, in 1483, he topped a distinguished career by obtaining the position of Chief of the Commission for exercising the office of Constable of England. That same year he officiated at the funeral of Edward IV, but died shortly afterwards at the comparatively early age of forty-nine. He was buried in a marble monument in Kendal Church, the last of the Parrs to be buried there and almost certainly the last of the Parrs ever to spend much time in Kendal Castle.

Sir William left no children by his first wife, but by Elizabeth Fitzhugh he had two sons, Thomas and William, and two daughters, Alice and Anne. The eldest child could not have been more than nine years old when Sir William died, and for their sake as much as for her own protection, Elizabeth Fitzhugh then took as her second husband Nicholas Vaux, who later became Lord Vaux of Harrowden in Northamptonshire. It was at Harrowden that she brought up her young family of Parrs in addition to the three children, all girls, which she bore Lord Vaux.

Elizabeth Fitzhugh was a remarkable woman and deserves special attention in her own right as well as for being the grandmother of Katherine Parr. As already stated, she was one of the first generation of women to be persuaded by the New Learning, and she seems to have been a close acquaintance of Henry VIII's grandmother, Margaret Beaufort. The names of the tutors whom she employed to teach her children are not known, but that they were effective is indicated by the success of both her sons. The elder, Thomas Parr, was knighted and 'pricked' as Sheriff of Northamptonshire in 1509, and shortly thereafter was appointed a Knight of the Body to Henry VIII who had just succeeded to the throne. The appointment to such a position at that time required the approval of Margaret Beaufort, and though Margaret Beaufort might have been influenced by her friendship with Elizabeth Fitzhugh, she was noted for insisting on high academic qualifications as well as administrative ability for senior positions at Court. Sir Thomas' younger brother, William Parr, was also favoured. He was knighted in France in 1513, and later, in about 1523, he was put in charge of the establishment which Henry had set up for his illegitimate son, the Duke of Richmond and Somerset, at that time his only potential male heir.

Next to their education, Elizabeth Fitzhugh's main concern for her children was to ensure that they made good marriages. Settling in Northamptonshire, which was thenceforth to be the principal home of the Parr family when they were not at Court, had been a happy choice.

Halfway between North and South, it was fairly neutral in politics and embraced a number of prosperous landowners who could be expected to welcome alliances with a family so well placed as the Parr children. Elizabeth Fitzhugh was not disappointed, and for all but two daughters, Alice Parr and Joan Vaux, the latter of whom became a nun at Deptford, she made singularly successful marriage arrangements. Sir Thomas Parr, who had inherited his father's title to Kendal, was betrothed to the heiress Maud Greene, the daughter of Sir Thomas Greene of Boughton and Green's Norton, who had large estates in several parts of the county. They were married in 1508 when, according to Baker's *History of Northamptonshire*, Maud Greene was thirteen years old. Sir William Parr was married to another Northamptonshire heiress, Mary Salisbury, the daughter of Sir William Salisbury of Horton, and Anne Parr was married to the wealthy Thomas Cheyney of Irthlingborough, also in Northamptonshire. One of the two remaining Vaux daughters was married to Francis Lord Lovell, and the other to Marmaduke Constable. All the Vaux daughters, however, died without issue.

With the ending of the Fitzhugh line in 1513 when Sir Thomas Parr added his half-share of their vast estates to his already very substantial possessions, the stage was set for him to follow a career at least as notable as his father's had been. He and his cousin, Cuthbert Tunstall, an outstanding scholar and one of the ablest men of Henry's reign, were among the King's inner circle of friends and, through his many inheritances, he commanded powerful family alliances in the North of England, which could be of great value to the King. (The blunt Northerners, with their direct, simple reactions to complicated matters, alarmed Southern Englishmen then as much as they do today. It was the only area of England which Henry never fully understood, and of which he was always, if but slightly, afraid.) Unfortunately, on 11 November 1517, before Sir Thomas Parr was able to make any further progress, he was struck down by a sudden illness and died at his London house in Blackfriars. He was buried in the church at Blackfriars,[1] leaving behind him his wife, Maud, and three infant children, Katherine, Anne and William.

There are no records from which the dates and places of birth of Katherine Parr and her brother and sister can be reliably determined. The available evidence makes it clear that Katherine was older than her sister, and that she may have been the eldest child. Correspondence between Lady Parr and Lord Darce (see p. 39) also indicates that in 1523 Katherine was probably nine years old. The evidence about her brother, William Parr, is conflicting, but with some caution it is assumed here that Katherine was born in 1514, her sister in 1515, and her brother in 1516.[2] The place or places of the three children's birth must also be a matter for conjecture, but Kendal Castle, which is preferred by Strickland and other Northern historians, seems an improbable choice. Sir Thomas Parr and his wife spent most of their life in London and at Court; when not there they were more likely to join their relatives and friends in Northamptonshire, where Sir Thomas owned a number of fine houses, than to go as far as Westmorland. Sir Thomas certainly visited Kendal from time to time, on his own and the King's business, and he might once or twice have taken his wife with him, but he would not have risked the long and difficult journey if his wife were pregnant. It seems more likely, therefore, that Katherine Parr was born in her father's house in Blackfriars in London.

Maud Parr was only twenty-two years old when her husband died, but she did not risk jeopardising the huge inheritance she now held in trust for her children by taking a second husband. She was already one of Queen Catharine's principal Ladies-in-Waiting and, as a result of the King's high regard for her and the Parr family, she was allowed to retain her place at Court where she was one of the very few people to be allocated rooms on a permanent basis.[3] Though her two colleagues at Court, Lady Willoughby and Lady Guildford, also kept up their London houses, her brother-in-law, Sir William Parr of Horton, appears to have taken over her late husband's house in Blackfriars, and she is recorded as having lodgings at Court for every year from 1518 until her death in 1529.[4] From this and the fact that she was in constant attendance upon the Queen, going with her on the annual Progresses, waiting on her at the Field of Cloth of Gold and other major occasions, one may deduce that almost all her life was spent at Court. Since she also had a reputation, according to a letter from Lord Dacre to Lord Scrope (see p. 42), for having the best school for children that Lord Dacre knew of, one may also deduce that Maud Parr's other main function at Court was the administration of the Royal nursery. In this way, she was able to ensure that her children would receive the same education and upbringing as the King's own family. Indeed, when her son, William Parr, grew too old to remain with the girls, he was sent off to join the King's illegitimate son, the Duke of Richmond, at King's College, Cambridge, where the two boys were put in the charge of two outstanding English scholars, Richard Croke, a leading authority on Greek, and John Palsgrave, whose speciality was French.[5]

Lady Parr did not suffer much from widowhood. She had friends enough to help her. On the male side the most important help she had was from her husband's great friend, Cuthbert Tunstall, who was then Master of the Rolls, and who shared with Sir Thomas More the reputation of being one of the more brilliant stars in a brilliant Court. Cuthbert Tunstall and Sir Thomas Parr had been closely related, both through their fathers' line and through the Fitzhughs, and when Sir Thomas Parr died, Cuthbert Tunstall took Lady Parr and her children under his special care.

He was a remarkable man. Said at one time to have been the illegitimate son of his father, Thomas Tunstall of Thurland Castle, he ran away from home while still a boy and was found working in the kitchens of Sir Thomas Holland. He was sent home and subsequently entered Oxford University in about 1491, but left shortly afterwards to join King's Hall (later merged with Trinity College), Cambridge. From Cambridge, he went on to the University of Padua where he took his doctorate in law. An outstanding example of the New Learning, he was proficient in Greek, Hebrew, mathematics, and civil law, and was an intimate member of Sir Thomas More's circle. He entered the Church in 1506, and in 1511 became Chancellor to the Archbishop of Canterbury (Warham), in which post he attracted the attention of the King who employed him on diplomatic missions. In 1516, he was appointed Master of the Rolls, and in 1522 became Bishop of London, where he remained until 1530, when he was transferred to the Bishopric of Durham. He later became President of the Council of the North (while still retaining the Bishopric of Durham), and throughout Henry's reign served as one of the King's most trusted and influential advisers.

Notably free from greed and personal ambition which dominated so many of his fellow bishops, Cuthbert Tunstall's watchword on religious matters was 'invincible moderation'. He was a strong, independent man, of sound judgment and with a pleasing sense of humour, scrupulously honest, and the most respected churchman of his time. What was rare, if not unique, in that age, he was a man without any serious enemies. Maud Parr could hardly have had a better friend.

On the female side Lady Parr was equally well placed. In Catharine of Aragon, Lady Willoughby, Lady Guildford and the French Queen she had friends of exceptional intelligence and strength of character who, for the first few years of her widowhood, were well able to protect her from the feminine intrigue at Court. In her own right, or through Cuthbert Tunstall, she had the additional support of Sir Thomas More's wife and three daughters, that redoubtable enclave of feminine learning and gaiety whose intellectual parties were renowned throughout Europe. Whether she was also friendly with the Boleyn family is not known, but she was rich, intelligent, and backed by powerful forces in the North, and the Boleyns are not likely to have neglected her.

Lady Parr, therefore, had little to fear. Moreover, being a woman, she did not have to indulge in the lavish extravagance which Henry expected of his wealthier subjects, and which kept so many of them in debt. The patrimony of her children was in fact safer in her hands than it would have been had her husband not died and, like most women, she guarded her wealth with care, grudging any expense which seemed unnecessary or for which she could not see some profitable return for her children or herself.

The children were fortunate in that their education started at a time when a major reform of teaching methods was just being introduced. Instead of having their lessons beaten into them by rod and birch, strong efforts were made to hold their interest by less drastic means. As Sir Thomas Elyot put it a few years later (in his book published in 1531), the children's teachers should be 'of much affability and patience', and the children themselves should not be 'enforced by violence to learn, but according to the counsel of Quintillian, to be sweetly allured thereto with praises and such pretty gifts as children delight in. And their first letters to be painted and limned in a pleasant manner: wherein children of gentle courage have much delectation.' The old grammars and reading books, with their long lists and incomprehensible rules, were replaced by books designed specially to catch the child's attention; examples taken from interesting or amusing stories were added, and gay illustrations became the rule rather than the exception. The birch remained as the most effective known means of punishment, but its use was reserved for wilful wrong-doings, rudeness, or disobedience.

From 1523 onwards, the principal tutor at the royal school at Court was Juan Luys Vives, a brilliant Humanist scholar who later came to enjoy the same international fame as Erasmus and Sir Thomas More. Vives was born in Valencia in Spain, but he left Spain when he was barely twenty and enrolled as a student at the University of Paris. After some two or three years in Paris, he moved on to the University of Bruges where he obtained his doctorate and where he first began to make a name for himself as a teacher. At Bruges, Vives met Sir Thomas More during one of Sir Thomas' diplomatic visits to the Low Countries. A firm friendship developed between the two intellectuals, and Sir Thomas More subsequently introduced Vives to Catharine of Aragon during a State visit which she and Henry made to Brussels after the Field of Cloth of Gold. Vives then dedicated one of his earliest books, *The Education of a Christian Woman*, to Catharine who was so impressed by it that she invited him to come to England. Wolsey intervened, and tried to entice the young Spaniard to join his college at Oxford, but Catharine persuaded Henry that he would be better employed as tutor to Princess Mary and the other girls at Court.

Katherine Parr was nine years old, and Princess Mary was seven, when Vives took over their education. They were joined in the royal school by the daughters of the French Queen, and by Katherine Parr's sister, Anne. Katherine Willoughby and Joan Guildford, the daughters of Lady Parr's fellow Ladies-in-Waiting, were then about four years old and did not join the older girls until some two or three years later.

Katherine Parr had been taught to read and write, most probably by her mother, at the age of three or four. Latin, and possibly French, was introduced under a qualified tutor at about the age of seven and, when Vives took over, Katherine was already familiar with the simpler classics and could plod her way through the New Testament in Latin.

Vives, however, transformed the little school. He was, according to Sir Thomas More, the best teacher in the whole of Europe, and his books on education, written some years later, became the standard guide for liberal schools and universities for several generations. He was but thirty-one years old when he joined the Court, with an infectious enthusiasm for his work and that gallant combination of beautiful manners and the gift of telling stories which made Spanish noblemen so very welcome to the ladies in Henry's Court. Fortunately for the peace of mind of the mothers, he was very obviously happily married to a delightful Belgian wife. Among his many qualifications, he had made a special study of the education of girls and young women, believing not so much in the equality of women as in the need for them to acquire a depth of wisdom which would enable them to make the best of their natural advantages and to overcome the frailties of their sex. His objective, as he wrote, was for women 'to be instructed altogether in that part of philosophy which taketh upon it to inform and teach and amend the conditions of living'.[6]

Learning, in his opinion, was the cure for all evils, for, as he wrote: 'The study of learning is such a thing that it occupieth one's mind wholly, and lifteth it up unto the knowledge of most goodly matters, and plucketh it from the remembrance of such things as be foul.'

He classified women into three main groups – maids, wives, and widows – and he was concerned that each group should understand the problems and benefits of the others. The facts of life, in the broadest meaning of the phrase, should be as well understood by the young girl as by the elderly widow. He was also very much concerned that women should understand men, whether as lovers, husbands, or simply people with whom they had to have dealings, partly in order not to be duped by men, partly, in the case of wives, so that they would have a better chance of a happy marriage, and partly in order to learn how to control men without being too obvious about it.

His teaching methods were such that the children were kept in a continual state of delighted expectation, knowing that each day would bring some new and dramatic story, sometimes deliciously horrifying, sometimes bitingly satirical, with which Vives always pointed his lessons and precepts. His examples, however, were all taken from history or the Bible or from the classical philosophers, and fairy-tales were banned. Children brought up on vain and trifling fables will, he said, when they grow older 'have such childish and tender stomachs that they cannot abide to hear anything serious or wise, and will delight only in books of silly stories which be neither true nor likely'. He loved children but, as his advice to the young mother shows, he also believed in discipline, though in his own case this was achieved by exciting their interest and respect rather than by the birch:

Let the mother beware that she does not weaken her children's bodies, intelligence or virtue, with wanton and dainty bringing up. I have seen very few men come to great proof of learning, ability or virtue, that had been softly brought up. Nor can children's bodies grow into their natural state if they be enfeebled by

32

delicate keeping. Let the mother be unsparing in her love for her children, as is right, but yet let them hide their love, lest the children become emboldened to do whatever they like. Nor should her love stop her from punishing her children for their vices, nor from strengthening their minds and bodies by firm bringing up.

In case his young audience might have been somewhat sceptical about this reference to themselves, he followed this particular precept up with the example of Agrippina, mother of the Emperor Nero, who once asked soothsayers whether or not her son would become Emperor. 'Yea,' they told her, 'but he shall kill his mother.' 'Let him kill her,' she said, 'as long as he may be Emperor.' And so it happened, but, as Vives pointed out, 'Agrippina would not gladly have been killed, and repented her foolish wish.'

To drive his point home, he added another example, more typical of the stories with which he held Katherine Parr and her friends captive:

> There is also a tale of a young man, who when he was led to be put to death, desired to speak with his mother. When she came, he laid his mouth to her ear, and bit it off. The bystanders rebuked him, calling him not only a thief, but also accursed for so treating his mother. 'This is her reward,' he replied, 'for how she brought me up. For if she had corrected me for stealing a book at school, which was my first theft, I would not then have gone on to the wicked deeds that brought me here. But she cherished me, and kissed me for my doing.'

Vives, however, was an idealist through and through, and he summed up his views on the upbringing of children in the following passage taken from the same chapter as the preceding quotations:

> The Stoic philosophers say that nature has bred in us a certain fire, or spirit, of that same justice which God put into the first father of mankind, and that that little fire, if it might grow within us, would bring us to the perfection of happiness and virtue. Howbeit, so they say, when that fire begins to flame up a little, it not only lacks fuel, but is quenched with contrary blasts of corrupt opinions and judgements. Fathers and mothers, schoolmasters, friends, kinsfolk and the common people, all do what they can to overwhelm that little fire as soon as it begins to appear. But all these are they who hold riches in high regard, who seek power, worship pomp, and give themselves up to the pursuit of pleasure. They tread poverty underfoot and mock simple minds. They suspect loyalty and hate learning, and all virtue they call folly. They abhor and despise those good things I spoke of before, and no man applies himself to them. Why else, I pray you, even though the good nature of mankind is itself more inclined to virtue than to vice, do we have so many fools and wicked men, and so few who are good and wise? A

good wife, therefore, shall withstand these corrupted opinions and nourish that little fire in her children so that it becomes a great flame.

Through most of his teaching Vives sought practical reasons for being good rather than bad. On virginity, after pointing out that 'a maid should not be proud because no man hath touched her body, if many men have pierced her mind', he goes on to describe the lot of a girl who thinks nothing of losing her virginity. She will become the subject of idle gossip, men who might have made good husbands will avoid her, her parents will suffer from the slur on the way they have brought her up, and she 'shall be ever vexed with the scourge of her own conscience'. She will become afraid to look anybody in the face. 'If anybody speak softly, she shall think they speak of her. If she hear talk about loose women, she shall think it meant for her. The same pain have wicked men, but women fare worse, because they be more timorous of nature and their offences be reckoned fouler.'

Romantic love, according to Vives, was to be feared by women more than anything else. 'It confounds and blinds her wit and reason, so that she shall not see or know what is done, but suffers herself to be wholly led and drawn at love's pleasure.' It made a woman, he said, hasty, foolhardy, full of servile flattery, unmeet for everything and, in the end, unmeet for love itself. It was also the main weapon used by men to trap women:

This affliction of love strikes everyone, but specially women. Therefore they need to take the more care that it should not steal upon them. For mostly it comes unawares, when the woman neither cares nor minds what is happening, and receives it as a sweet and pleasant thing, not knowing what and how perilous a poison lies hidden under that pleasant face. Therefore a woman should specially resist the first occasion of its coming, which thing Ovid, the master of love, himself doth counsel. Let her not listen to the lover, no more than she would to an enchanter or sorcerer. For he comes pleasantly and flattering, first praising the maid, showing her how he is taken with the love of her beauty, and that he must die for her love. For these lovers know well enough the vainglorious minds of many that delight in their own praises, wherewith they may be caught, as a poacher beguiles birds. He calls the maid fair, proper, witty, well-spoken, and of gentle blood, whereas she is perhaps none of these things. But she, like a fool, is too glad to hear these lies, and thinks she is indeed what he says.

He paints a grim fate for those who succumb, and wonders how it happens that so many young women 'willingly drown themselves in this great sea of wretchedness, from which come so many brothels and so many harlots, yea, and from honest families, too'. It was the cause why, in every city, so many young women lay poxed and scabbed in the hospitals, why so many, pale and sick, went a-begging.

It was strong meat for an audience of seven- to nine-year-old girls, but, for all its faults, the Tudor age was singularly free from prudery and humbug, and it is safe to assume that Katherine and her friends lapped it up without a blush. On the subject of finding a good husband, he was equally uncompromising. Those who spent their time gadding about and showing themselves off were mad if they thought that that was the way to catch a man's attention. They should hear, he said, what men say about them afterwards among themselves:

> As for eloquent maids, that is to say, great babblers, men think they are likely to be shrews, and that he who marries such a one shall think he has married a serpent, not a wife. Young men may praise to her face the maid that is full of talk and a jolly dancer, and they will call her who is full of merry conceits and pleasantries well mannered and well brought up. But they say this only to have her at their pleasure, not to marry her, for they all believe they can quickly obtain their pleasure of such a one.

The best husbands, he advised, were obtained by those who never set out to tempt men and who kept their reputations free from blemish. He was also adamant that only men, not women, should ever marry for love:

> Young women have said that they could not love, nor find it in their heart to marry, someone whom they did not know before, and whom they did not love. But if the maid will only marry a man because she is already used to his love, she is not very different from a mistress who for like cause loves her lover. She spends the love (which ought to be kept until after the wedding) before her marriage, and so it is said: 'They that marry for love, shall spend their life in sorrow.'

As an idealist and a Humanist, Vives himself avoided the power-game, but for those women who were obliged to become involved in it, he had this to say:

> Howbeit, if she needs must come to court for affairs of business, and in order that her cause will be treated most favourably by the judges, let her have but feeble attorneys, or none at all. For then the judges themselves will take care of

her affairs, and will often withstand the most powerful defenders and advocates. For naturally we hate them that have great power and riches, and help them that have but little, putting down those who exalt themselves, and supporting those who be humble and lowly. In all manner of conflicts, as the wise man [Solomon] says, the greater shall seem to do the wrong, yea, even though he be most wronged against, lest he should do some other wrong.

But this was only in the case of those who were known to be good and upright men; there were others who were subtle and wanton, corrupt, and open to bribes. According to Vives, a woman in such cases had insuperable problems:

These [corrupt judges] should doubtless be punished, but the Law, as Solomon says, is like a cobweb: it takes all the little beasts, but lets the great ones alone. If the woman knows her judges or advocates to be such men as these, which she would well enough from the name they have among the people, she should eschew them and flee, suffering the loss of her property and putting herself in jeopardy, if needs be. And the same I would she should do from all that be wanton and vicious.

Interspersed with the slices of real life and moral precepts, Vives slipped in the main part of his teaching. This could be divided roughly into two parts: first came the tools for acquiring knowledge – ancient and modern languages, logic, rhetoric, some mathematics and music – and then, once these had been sufficiently mastered, the critical study of the great philosophers, historians and religious teachers. Although Vives had little time for priests, he was a convinced believer in the need for a universal Church to spread the doctrine of Christ, and since such an organisation already existed in the Catholic Church he remained, as did Erasmus and Sir Thomas More, a Catholic to the end of his life. His religious teaching, however, was firmly that of the Humanists, based on the actual words of Christ and the early Christian Fathers, and eschewing superstition and elaborate ritual; it effectively transcended religious boundaries, and had it not been for the thorny questions of the celibacy of the priesthood and validity of the sacraments, questions which Vives did not discuss, this teaching would have been as acceptable to Luther as to the Pope.

The acquisition of so much learning was hard work for the young girls but, by the time Katherine Parr was twelve, she was as well educated as a junior university lecturer would be today. Plutarch was her favourite author, but she was thoroughly familiar with all the classic writers and knew large portions of the Bible by heart. In spite of so much school work, however, the girls did have time for some relaxation. In the case of Katherine Parr and Princess Mary, their greatest pleasure was riding, and few days passed without an hour or two spent in the saddle. Both girls became expert horsewomen, and Katherine Parr, probably encouraged by her country-loving uncle, Sir William Parr of Horton, also acquired a keen interest in hunting. She had her own pack of greyhounds and became a skilled shot with the cross-bow, unusual tastes for an intellectual, but ones that were much in keeping with ancient royal traditions. It was part of the upbringing of a princess, and for Lady Parr nothing less than the upbringing of a princess would do for her elder daughter.

All in all, the children had a happy childhood. Their lessons were as pleasurable as their pastimes and, although they were not spoilt, they were surrounded by comfort and cheerful affection. It was something that they all cherished, and the memory of those happy days was to form a bond between the girls at the royal school which endured for the rest of their lives.

NOTES

1 A memorial tablet was also erected to him in Kendal Church (Whitaker).
2 The order of the names as given in Sir Thomas Parr's will.
3 *Letters & Papers* III. Nos. 491, 528, 577, etc. (Household Expenses).
4 *Letters & Papers* III. No. 2486.
5 Nichols, *Literary Remains of Edward VI.*
6 This, and all other succeeding quotations and examples of Vives in the following pages are taken from *De Institutione foeminae christianae*, first published in Latin in 1523, and in English in 1528.

3 Marriage Arrangements

In the sixteenth century, however, potential heiresses were not allowed to enjoy their childhood for long. Until they were firmly betrothed in marriage, their wealth – and private happiness – was at considerable risk as a result of the custom of trading in wardships. Anyone who owned the wardship of a child had the right to arrange the marriage of that child, which meant in effect the right to dispose of the child's property. Wardships, therefore, had a real money value related to the size of the ward's inheritance, and over the centuries the custom had arisen of buying and selling wardships as a means of raising ready money, often regardless of the welfare of the child. In an age when death was alarmingly sudden, responsible parents therefore tried to insure against the risk of the wardship of their children passing into unsuitable hands by making firm contracts of marriage for them at as early an age as possible.[1]

By law, such marriages could not be consummated until the child, in the case of girls, was twelve years old, or, in the case of boys, fourteen years old, but the engagement contract, called the betrothal, was binding in law and needed the full procedure of divorce before it could be annulled. The child marriages which resulted from these betrothals were not, however, always as bad as they sounded, for in many cases the child bride or groom would remain in the care of one or other of the sets of parents until a more suitable age for the actual consummation – carnal copulation was the phrase used – had been reached. This was usually fourteen for the girls and sixteen for the boys.

In Katherine Parr's case, her mother began the search for a husband for her as soon as she was nine years old. Katherine's direct inheritance from her father was £800 (worth about £20,000 now), which was not very large in proportion to the family estate, but on the other hand only her brother stood between her and the Parr estates, which made her potentially one of the richest matches in the land.

In 1523, when Lady Parr's search began, there were no suitable matches at Court, and she looked to the North for a good alliance for her daughter. She invoked the aid of her cousin by marriage, Thomas, Lord Dacre, whose mother had been Elizabeth Fitzhugh's sister, Alice. The first attempt at an agreement was with Henry, Lord Scrope of Bolton, for a marriage between Katherine and Lord Scrope's son and heir. The negotiations were eventually broken off, but the following correspondence, taken from Whitaker's *History of Richmondshire*, is given in full, both for the clues it contains about Katherine and her mother, and as an illustration of such marriage negotiations:

Maud, Lady Parr to Thomas, Lord Dacre:
Most honourable and my very good Lord,

I heartily recommend me unto you. Where it pleased you at your last being here to take pain in the matter in consideration of marriage between Lord Scrope's son and my daughter Katherine, for the which I heartily thank you; at which time I thought the matter in good furtherance. Howbeit, I perceive that my said Lord Scrope is not agreeable to the consideration, as more plainly may appear unto you by certain articles sent to me from my said lord, the copy of which articles I send you herein enclosed. My Lord's pleasure is to have a full answer from me before Lammas next coming [1 August], wherefore it may please you to be so good to have this matter in your remembrance, for I perceive well this matter is not like to take effect except by your help. The jointure is little, for 1,100 marks which I will not pass, and my said lord will not repay after marriage had, and 200 marks must needs be repaid if my daughter dies before the age of 16 years, or else I should break M. Parr's will, which I should be loth to do; and there can be no perfect marriage until my lord's son comes to the age of 14, and my daughter to the age of 12, before which time if the marriage should take none effect, or be dissolved, either by death, wardship, disagreement, or otherwise, which may be before that time, notwithstanding marriage solemnised, repayment must needs be had of the whole, or else I might fortune to pay my money for nothing. As for the day of payment, I am content with the first day, but the residue of his days of payment be too short for me.

Glad I would be to have the matter go forth if might be conveniently; if it please you to call to remembrance the occasion before you at Greenwich was that I should pay at your desire 1,100 marks, whereof 100 marks in hand, and every year after 100 marks, which is as much as I can spare, as you know; and for that, my daughter is to have 100 marks jointure, whereof 50 marks I to have for her finding [maintenance] until they are able to lie together, and then they to have the whole 100 marks, and repayment to be had if the marriage take no effect.

My lord, it may please you to take so much pain as to help to conclude this matter if it will be; and if you see any default on my part I shall be ordered as ye shall deem good, as knoweth Jh'u, who preserve your good lordship.

Written at the Rye (Greenwich), the 14th day of July,

My lord, it may please your lordship to give credence to this bearer.

Your cousin,
Maud Parre

A copy of the articles proposed by Lord Scrope was enclosed:

First, the said Lord Scrope is content for 1100 marks of money to give a £40 feoffment [trust], whereof £10 to be taken yearly for the finding of the said Katherine Parre, daughter of the said Lady Maud Parre, and the residue of the said feoffment to enter to him when the said Lord Scrope's son and heir shall be come to the age of 18 years, and after the death of the said Lord Scrope to make the feoffment a further 100 marks.

Item. If the Lady Parre will pay 1200 marks in money the feoffment to be £100 after the death of the said Lord Scrope, so that the whole feoffment remain in the said lord's hands to his said son and heir come to the age of 18 years.

Item. Of the aforesaid 1100 marks, 600 marks to be paid at the signing of the indentures of covenant, and 500 marks to be paid in the two years next following by even portions. And if the said Lady Parre will pay 1200 marks, 600 marks to be paid at the signing of the indentures of covenant, and 600 marks to be paid in the two years next following in even portions.

Item. The said Lord Scrope will not agree to repay no money after the marriage is solemnised and executed, nor to enter into no covenant especially for the governance of the children during the nonage of them.

Lord Dacre replied as follows:

Madame,

In right hearty manner I recommend me unto you, and by the hand of your servant, bearer hereof, I have received your writing, dated at Rye the 14th day of this instant month of July, and to me delivered yesternight, together with a copy of certain articles to you sent from my Lord Scrope touching the marriage to be had between his son and your daughter Katherine, by the contents whereof I do perceive ye think that the said matter in communication of marriage, which ye thought had been in good furtherance, is like to go back, by reason that my said Lord Scrope is not agreeable to such communication as was had of the same at my last being with you, for even so and many causes specified in your said letter and articles at length.

Cousin, since my departure from you I assure you I was not two nights together at mine own house, by reason whereof I had never leisure to labour in these matters. And I do think, seeing my Lord Scrope cannot be content with the communications that was had at my last being with you, which was thought reasonable to me, and as I perceive semblably [according] to his counsel, that this matter cannot be brought to no perfect end without mutual communication to be had with my said lord, either by myself, my son, or my brother. Wherefore, as soon as conveniently any of us may be spared this matter shall be laboured,

40

trusting verily that I shall bring it to a good point, and as I shall do therein ye shall be advertised [informed] at length. I have promised of my said lord, and of my daughter, his wife, that they shall not marry their son without my consent, which they shall not have to no person but unto you; and undoubtedly my said lord must needs have some money, and he has nothing to make it of but only the marriage of his said son, wherefore my full counsel is, that ye be not overhasty, but suffer [wait], and finally ye shall be well assured that I shall do in this matter, or in any other that is or may be either pleasure, profit, or surety, to you or my said cousin, your daughter, that lieth in my power.

At Newcastle, the penultimate day of July, 15th year of Henry VIII [1523]

Lady Maud Parre, who was now on Progress with the King, replied thus:

Right honourable and my singular good lord,

I recommend me unto you: I have received your letter dated at Newcastle the penultimate day of July, and by the same I perceive your pleasure, and also what pain ye intend to take in the matter between my Lord Scrope and me, for the which I heartily thank you.

The Lord Scrope said to a servant of mine that he would no longer drive time in that matter with me, but he would be at large, and take his best advantage as with the Lord Treasurer, which had made motions to be in communication with him.[2] Therefore it may please you at your convenient leisure to have this matter in your remembrance, and thus I am always bold to put your lordship to pains and business, which I pray God I may some part defray, which should not be failed if it lieth in my power, by the grace of Jh'u, who preserve your good Lordship.

Written at Easthampstead [Berkshire], this 22nd day of August.

Your . . . . . .

Maud Parre

Lord Dacre let the matter rest for some months, but then received a letter from Lord Scrope, his son-in-law, asking his advice, and replied as follows:

My Lord and son,

I recommend me unto you in right hearty manner, and by the hand of your servant, bringer hereof yesterday, I received your writing dated the 10th day of this instant month, I understanding thereby that for such communications as has been had and moved between my Lady Parr and you by your counsels concerning the marriage of your son and mine according to the tenour thereof, ye have now sent with your servant, this said bringer, the articles of the same, wherein ye desire that ye may know my answer in writing; and, further, that ye would be sorry for any such considerations that any long drive were made therein, as further your said writing purporteth.

41

My Lord, your son and heir is the greatest jewel that ye can have, seeing that he must present your own person after your death, unto whom I pray God lend long years. And if ye be disposed to marry him before he come to full age, when he may have som [property] himself, I cannot see, without [unless] that ye would marry him to one heir of land which would be right costly, that ye can marry him to so good stock as my Lady Parr, for divers considerations. First, in remembring the wisdom of my said Lady, and the good wise stock of the Greenes whereof she is come, and also the wise stock of the Parrs of Kendal, for all of which men do look when they do marry their child, to the wisdom of the blood of that they do marry with. I speak not of the possibilities of my Lady Parr's daughter, who has but one child between her, and 800 marks [pounds?] land to inherit thereof. Such possibilities doth oftentimes fall, and I speak it because of the possibility that befell unto myself by my marriage, and therefore, in mine opinion, the same is to be regarded.

My Lord, to declare unto you truly, I assure you your copy of articles containing your demands, which ye have now sent, and my Lady's demands, is so far asunder that in manner it is impossible that ever ye shall agree in that behalf; wherefor, if ye can be content to go groundly to work [to start again], and go to a short conclusion, I think it best that ye go after the common course of marriage, that is to say, to give 100 marks jointure for the payment of 1100 marks, that is to say, 400 or 500 marks to be paid at the making of the covenant, and 100 yearly, unto such time as the sum be fully grown, the one child to be in the keeping of my said lady; and if it fortune the said persons one or other of them to die before carnal copulation had betwixt them, or before the age of consent, then the sum received to be repaid at such days and after such form as it was delivered, without [unless] new marriage may be had with the young child, for I think it is not convenient [right] nor profitable that 100 marks should go out yearly of your land to so young a person as my said Lady's eldest daughter, if it fortune, as God defend, that your said son and mine should die.

And thus, my Lord, I assure you this is the effect of my opinions; and if ye can thus be content, the matter shall shortly take effect. Also, I think it good, but I would not have it comprised in the covenant, that during the time of three years, by which time my said son and yours will come to [the age of] consent, that he should be with my said Lady, if she keep her widowhood, and ye to find him clothing and a servant to wait upon him, and she to find him meat and drink, for I assure you he mought learn with her as well as in any place that I know, as well nurture [upbringing], as French and other languages, which meseems were a commodious thing for him.

At Morpeth, the 17th day of December, 15th yr. of H.VIII [1523]

In spite of Lord Dacre's friendly intervention, however, neither party could agree to the other's terms. Lady Parr informed Lord Dacre:

Right honourable and my singular good lord,

I heartily recommend me unto you, thanking you of your manifold pains taken between my Lord Scrope and me, and concerning the same, I have received your letters, and my Lord Scrope's also, and right well perceive the contents of the same; wherein I have taken advice of my Lord of London [Cuthbert Tunstall] and divers other of my husband's friends and mine, who think that my said Lord Scrope's offer, as well concerning the jointure as the repayment of my money, is so little and so far from the customs of the country, and his demand is so great and so large of me, with short payment, that my said friends will in no wise that I shall meddle with the said bargain after my Lord Scrope's offer and demand.

My Lord, seeing this matter hath been so long in cogitation, I am right sorry on my part it cannot take effect, for in good faith hitherto I never had communication for no marriage to her for that I would have been so glad should have come forward as this, or else I would not have made so large offers for the furtherance of the same as I have. My Lord, I beseech you to be good lord unto my cousin, the bearer, in such cause as he hath to do in your parts, that the rather through your good help he may obtain his right of such things as his father gave him in his bequest, the which shall be hard for him to obtain without your favour. And thus the Holy Ghost preserve your good Lordship to his pleasure.

Your......
Maud Parre

From the Court at Greenwich, this 15th day of March [1524]

Lord Dacre's reply, which ended the matter, first repeats the first part of Lady Parr's letter as confirmation that it was correctly understood, and then continues:

Madame, for my part I am sorry that ye be thus converted in this matter, seeing the labour I have made in it, which was most for the strength of my friendship for my said cousin, your daughter, assuring you that ye shall not marry your daughter in any place that had been so good and comfortable to my said cousin, your daughter. And concerning Lord Scrope's demands, he demanded nothing but it that ye were content without the meddling of any person to give, which was 1100 marks, and concerning his offer, which was 100 marks jointure, it is not far from the custom of the country, for from the highest degree unto the lowest it is custom and is used always for every 100 marks of money ten marks jointure. But, finally, Madame, seeing that ye are thus minded, whereat I am sorry as nature constraineth me, as it doth please you in this business so shall it please me. And thus heartily fare ye well.

At Morpeth, the 25th day of May, the 16th year [1524]

Katherine, in fact, was well out of the match. As Lord Dacre had pointed out, the Scrope family lacked funds, and the bad feelings which the negotiations had generated would not have made her life with them any easier. It was not easy, however, to find suitable alternatives. From the point of view of the Parr family, Katherine had to be married to a peer or the son and heir of a peer; nothing less would do – a sentiment which Katherine herself fully endorsed. On the other hand, there was at that time a total of only about forty peers in the country, and the majority of these and their eldest sons were already either married or betrothed. But Lady Maud Parr and her friends continued the search, and finally came up with the elderly widower, Edward, Lord Borough of Gainsborough in Lincolnshire. The Borough family were related to the Parrs through the Fitzhughs and, like the Parrs, had good connections at Court. Although they were not as wealthy as the Parrs, they were comfortably endowed with land in Yorkshire as well as in Lincolnshire and, through his first wife, Anne Cobham, the heiress of Sir Thomas Cobham, Lord Borough had also acquired a number of estates in Kent.

From the material point of view, therefore, it was a good match, but from the personal aspect Katherine Parr might have had some qualms. When the marriage was solemnised, probably in 1526, she was but twelve years old, while her husband, who had succeeded to his father's title in 1495–6, was almost certainly in his late fifties or early sixties, with adult children who, according to Strickland, were at least fourteen years older than his bride.

It is unlikely, however, that Katherine joined her husband immediately after her marriage. The Parr household and their relatives and friends were much influenced by Humanist teaching, and twelve-year-old girls were not expected to fulfil their marriage vows to sixty-year-old men as soon as the wedding ceremony was over. It is much more probable, therefore, that Katherine remained with her mother for another year or two, enjoying the title of 'Lady Borough' and doubtless using its authority to the discomfort of her companions and the annoyance of her family. Her education, however, continued unabated, and there was no real change in her way of life at least until after her thirteenth birthday.

When Katherine did go to Gainsborough, probably towards the end of 1527, she needed a degree of poise unusual in a girl of thirteen or fourteen. Gainsborough was a baronial hall, and such establishments had in those days a staff of upwards of a hundred people. They were largely self-contained, supplying their own food, brewing their own beer, weaving their own cloth, making their own wagons and ploughs, and building their own cottages and barns. The administration was usually in the hands of a steward, but the lady of the house had a heavy responsibility. 'She needed,' to quote Mitchell and Leys from *A History of the English People*, 'remarkable qualities of organising ability, independence of judgment, resolution, and physical endurance, to meet the necessities of her daily life as well as emergencies caused by war, local food shortages, or belligerent neighbours. In her husband's absence she might have to withstand a siege, or bargain with intruders too powerful to be ejected, dismiss a knavish attorney, or combat the dishonesty of her bailiff or cook. She must be ready to entertain unexpected guests at any time with the strictly limited resources at her disposal, to be a good wife and companion to her husband, and to bear him children at frequent intervals.'

Katherine was later to have to do all these things and much more besides, but at Gainsborough her life was comparatively tranquil. Most of the domestic responsibility was taken by a housekeeper, and her main duties were to please her husband and to help him entertain their guests. At times things were dull compared with the sparkle of Henry's Court, but the novelty of her position and the need to learn the many aspects of running a large estate kept boredom at bay.

Lady Parr did not seek a husband for her younger daughter, Anne. The cost of a good match for one whose chances of inheritance were slight would have been too high, and Maud Parr clearly decided that Anne's legacy from her father, which was the same as her sister's, £800, would be more profitably employed in supporting her in a career at Court. In spite of the gathering momentum of the Boleyn bid for power, Lady Parr managed to retain her influence with the King and, as indicated in her will, she persuaded him, at a price, to help her with her remaining children, and through him secured the position of Maid-of-Honour for Anne.

The 'Waiting Gentlewomen', as the Maids- and Ladies-in-Waiting were called, were Court officials rather than personal servants. Their tasks were concerned with supervising the domestic side of the Queen's Household and with officiating at Court functions. Since they were in daily contact with the King and Queen, and with members of the Council, and were also frequently called upon to entertain ambassadors and other important visitors from abroad, they were selected with care, and their appointment owed little to the Queen's own choice. The Queen, like other senior people at Court, could and did nominate candidates, but the King made the final selection.

The Maids and Ladies were chosen in the first place for their learning and their discretion, but Henry believed firmly in the value of experience, and seldom considered anybody of use to him until he or she had been two of three years in his service. One result of this policy was that the appointments had a high degree of permanence, and though Queens came and went the Waiting Gentlewomen stayed on. Mrs Stoner, for example, was appointed 'Mother of the Maids' early in Catharine of Aragon's reign and held that position throughout the reigns of all Henry's wives. Margery Horsham, known familiarly to everyone at Court as 'Madge,' served as Lady-in-Waiting also to all six Queens, and this in spite of her apparently close friendship with Anne Boleyn. Anne Parr was to become another example. For those who were able to keep out of politics, therefore, it was a secure and valuable position, similar today to that of a civil servant, and for those who cared to run the risk of politics it offered the most effective way for a woman to influence public affairs. Needless to say, these positions at Court were fiercely competed for by the daughters, and sometimes the wives, of most of the well-born or wealthy families in the land.

Next to a good marriage, it was the best that Lady Parr could do for her younger daughter. It put Anne directly under the King's care and in a position where she would later be able to mediate for the family or herself, should the need arise. It also put her in a position sufficiently prominent for her to be able to make her own match if she should ever choose to do so. There was some danger for a young girl in the free society of Henry's Court, but Anne had been brought up in it since she was an infant and would have known its ways better than most of her contemporaries.

Lady Parr's son, William, should not have presented any problems. He was the chosen companion for the King's son and the heir to a fortune, and Lady Parr could justifiably hope for great things for him: a high position at Court, elevation to the peerage (not yet achieved by any Parr), and a choice of brides from among the best families in the country. His marriage was her only real concern, but there was no need for haste, and arrangements could easily have been left until he reached his majority. Towards the end of 1528, however, having received an offer which she felt was too good to be turned down, Lady Parr once more threw herself into the battle of marriage negotiations and did everything in her power to get the best possible terms for her son, even to the extent of putting herself in financial debt to the King.

The chosen match was with Anne Bourchier, the only child and heiress of Henry Bourchier, Earl of Essex. Anne Bourchier was also a close relative and contingent heiress of the Countess of Oxford. The combination of the Parr estates with those of the Earl of Essex, plus the possibility of a third share in the estates of the Countess of Oxford, held out the chance for young William Parr to become a landowner on the scale of the great dukedoms of earlier centuries, and Lady Parr's anxiety to complete the agreement can be well understood.

The terms were settled early in 1529, and on 20 May in that year, Maud Parr died. She was still only in her mid-thirties, and had dedicated the whole of her adult life to the interests of her children. By the time she died, she had succeeded in placing all of them in positions from which, even though they were still barely adolescent, they had an advantage over the rest of their generation which would have been difficult to equal, let alone surpass. In addition, she had imbued them with high ideals, and given them a superlative education, shared only by the King's own children and those of the King's closest friends. Although her character was possibly marred by a sharp manner and an over-serious mind, few women could have done better for their families.

A few months after Maud Parr's death, in September or October of 1529, Katherine's husband, Lord Borough, died,[3] and Katherine's stay at Gainsborough came to an end. It would seem that she had been of considerable comfort to her elderly husband, for she inherited from him the estates in Kent that had previously belonged to his first wife, Anne Cobham.

A more important outcome of Katherine's stay at Gainsborough, however, was the development of her friendship with the youngest daughter of the Askew family who lived at Stallingborough, some thirty miles from Gainsborough. The Askews were distant relatives, and their family history was similar to, if not so spectacular as, that of the Parrs. The family came from Ayscough (the original spelling of Askew) near Bedale in the North Riding of Yorkshire, and had migrated south, much as the Parrs had done, through a combination of profitable marriages and successful government service. One ancestor of the family was the Bishop of Salisbury, Confessor to Henry vi, who had been killed by the followers of Jack Cade in 1450. Another had been Chief Justice of the Common Pleas, also under Henry vi. The present head of the family was Sir William Askew, a former Sheriff of Lincoln who had been knighted by Henry VIII in France in 1513. He had three sons and three daughters, the youngest of whom, Anne, was eight or nine years old when Katherine first arrived at Gainsborough.

With all the authority of a married woman, the fourteen-year-old Katherine took Anne under her wing and introduced her to the pleasures and excitements of the lessons she had learnt under Vives. At this stage in her life, Katherine was undoubtedly a prig, and she obviously delighted in the opportunity to play the part of guide and tutor to her youthful protégée, showing off the learning and, more particularly, the special brand of Humanist irony which she had begun to develop. But the effect on Anne was devastating. Katherine became to her an object of adoration, an example of learning and wit which struck her as being everything that a girl could aspire to. It gave her an overwhelming ambition to follow in Katherine's footsteps and sowed the seeds of a discontent with her lot which eventually led her to the stake, and which very nearly cost Katherine her life. But this is to anticipate events by nearly twenty years, and much was to happen before that fateful crisis arose.

NOTES

1 R. J. Mitchell and M. D. R. Leys, *A History of the English People* (Longmans, 1950).
2 This was Sir Thomas Boleyn, presumably offering Anne as a bride for Lord Scrope's son, but that, too, came to nothing.
3 His son and heir, Thomas Borough, had assumed the title at the opening of Parliament on 3 November 1529.

4   Hawks and Doves

The three years of Katherine Parr's life after she left Gainsborough are unrecorded. Strickland reports a legend that she spent the time with a kinswoman, Catharine Neville, the widow of Sir Walter Strickland, at the Strickland family seat, Sizergh Castle, Kendal, but the evidence for this is unreliable and there is no mention of Katherine Parr among the Strickland family papers which are still preserved in the muniment room of the castle. Katherine Parr was then only fifteen years old, and she is more likely to have gone back to her more immediate family. She might have stayed with one of her many relatives in Northamptonshire, or she might have gone to the Parr house, now owned by her uncle, in Blackfriars. Circumstantial evidence, however, plus certain oblique references in her 'confession', *The Lamentation of a Sinner*, indicate that she had a familiarity with the dramatic events which occured during that period, a familiarity which would be more probably obtained at Court than anywhere else. It has therefore been assumed that she spent these years with her sister, Anne Parr, at Court, where her sister was now one of the King's wards and where she herself was what is known as a 'King's widow', a status which put her under the King's personal protection and which meant that she would require the King's permission to make a second marriage.

Katherine, however, was in no hurry to marry again. At fifteen, she lacked the brilliance and sophistication which Anne Boleyn had shown at the same age, and her most powerful allies besides the King, Cuthbert Tunstall and her uncle, Sir William Parr of Horton, either of whom might have sought a new match for her, were now absent from Court: Tunstall had taken up his appointment as Bishop of Durham, and her uncle was occupied with the care of the King's illegitimate son, the Duke of Richmond, and Katherine's brother, William, in their establishment at York. Katherine therefore decided instead to make her mark by acquiring a reputation for scholarship and virtue.

She later confessed that she was proud of her righteousness and of

49

the fact that she was 'none adulterer, nor fornicator, and so forth'. She had taken Vives' advice to heart:

> It does not become a widow to dress up and paint herself, for she should not be seen to seek any marriage bargain, but on the contrary to refuse any that are offered. She should not only speak such words as shall show her to be chaste and honest, but also as shall impress her hearers with her learning, and amend their ways by the example of her living.

In the same confession, however, she admits that she also loved wealth and luxury, and that she coveted to rule over men. The picture that emerges is thus something more subtle than that of a self-righteous fifteen-year-old girl making a great show of her piety and virtue.

She now had property of her own, separately from the Parr estates, and a favoured position at Court. Her title of Lady Borough, her family, and her independence made her a minor personage; her youth, if not her looks, made her physically attractive. It was a heady position for a young girl. As she was to prove much later in her life, she was by no means impervious to the magnetism of bold young courtiers, and she must have hankered after the uninhibited life of her contemporaries. But prudence prevailed, and she remained studiously aloof from the lively goings-on at Court, preferring the company, as Vives had recommended, of serious-minded older men. In this way, she preserved her virtue, but at the same time she cultivated the flattering respect of influential councillors who saw in her a wisdom and strength of character far beyond her years.

Katherine and her sister indeed needed all the support at Court they could find, for the success of Anne Boleyn and her family had practically destroyed the protective circle of Catharine of Aragon's ladies. In a sense, the French Queen was to blame. In the summer of 1527, when she had first heard of Henry's intention to divorce Catharine, the French Queen had told her brother in no uncertain terms what she thought of his behaviour and had flounced out of Court, taking her two daughters with her. She retired to her home at Westhorpe, near Bury St Edmunds, and refused to return to Court until her brother should come to his senses. It was a fine gesture, but it deprived the remaining Ladies-in-Waiting of her powerful support and, although they remained at their posts with Catharine, they ceased to have any further influence on the course of events.

Apart from this much weakened position of her late mother's friends, Katherine Parr also found, when she returned to Court in the autumn of 1529, that more of her former school friends besides the French Queen's daughters were no longer there. Lady Willoughby, whose husband had died in 1526, had run into debt and had sold the wardship of her daughter to the French Queen's husband, the Duke of Suffolk, in order to solve her money problems. As a result, the nine-year-old Katherine Willoughby was now another resident at Westhorpe. Some months later, the French Queen had again intervened in the case of the King's third niece, Margaret Douglas. Anne Boleyn had befriended the young exile from Scotland, but the French Queen had objected strongly. No one, she said, had a better right than she to take care of her sister's daughter, and she insisted that Margaret, too, should join her growing household.

Of Katherine Parr's friends, this left Princess Mary, Joan Guildford, and Katherine's sister, Anne, still at Court. Their normally high spirits were very much subdued by Princess Mary's misery at the treatment of her mother, and later evidence shows that it was at this time that Katherine Parr took the lead in trying to comfort the Princess. It reinforced the earlier bond of their school days together and earned Katherine the unhappy young woman's lasting gratitude. But not long after Katherine's return to Court, Henry sent Mary away to a small establishment of her own at Beaulieu, now called New Hall, near Boreham in Essex, and Katherine did not see her again until her enforced reconciliation with her father in 1536.

The three remaining girls were then joined by a newcomer, Joan Champernown, who came from a well-known Devonshire family. Joan was about thirteen years old, the only really pretty girl in Katherine Parr's circle, but her beauty was combined with a bright intelligence which quickly endeared her to the others. They were not the only girls at Court – Jane Seymour, who had been introduced by her brother, Sir Edward Seymour, who was then an officer of the Household, was another who joined the Court at about that time – but Katherine Parr and her friends formed a small group apart from the rest.

The girls would have seemed unusually adult to modern eyes, but in those days teenagers knew nothing of the generation gap. They mixed freely with their elders, and their gay chatter and shining eyes were one of the major attractions at Court. They were not looked upon as children – Katherine Parr, after all, was a widow at fifteen, and there was nothing extraordinary in the fact – and though their legal responsibilities were limited, they were expected to be, and for the most part were, conscious participants in the adult world in which they lived. Admittedly, their influence was normally slight, and they could be cowed by parental or other authority, but by the time a girl at Court had reached her teens, she was in a position to be able to play her part, small though it might be, in the power game.

The situation at Court when Katherine Parr came back centred round the divorce proceedings against the Queen. The sympathies of Katherine and her friends were all with Catharine of Aragon, but there was little they could do to help her and, under Katherine's guidance, they carefully avoided any direct involvement in the dispute. In this, Katherine was again influenced by the example of the girls' former tutor, Vives.

Vives had been asked by the Queen to serve as one of her counsel in the initial inquiries into the legality of her marriage. Vives had duly appeared on her behalf, but at the end of the hearing he had been arrested and sent to prison. His release was secured six weeks later, but the experience unnerved him, and he sought Henry's permission to take his wife on a visit to Belgium. The permission was granted on condition that he returned to England three months later. Vives fulfilled his promise and came back, but without his wife. This was early in 1528. He then heard that he was again accused of treason and fled the country, never to return. From his sanctuary in Bruges, he wrote of his feelings to a friend:

Who can blame me, that I listened to a miserable and afflicted woman? that I soothed her by discourse and consolation? She, a Queen born from such a race, and whose parents, I tremble to remember, were formerly my natural princes, and of such virtue that she seems least of all worthy of misfortune. In the course of time the thing went on, and reached the disputation and examination of the cause. What was concluded was not known. The Queen was unable to ascertain what his royal majesty had decreed in this behalf; for it was concealed from all excepting a very few; only report and common opinion was noised abroad that the cause was remitted to the Pope. Then the Queen commanded me to go to the Emperor's orator [ambassador], and to ask him, on her behalf, to write to request the Emperor that he would deal with the Pope, that she might not be condemned in ignorance (a thing indeed most just); but that she might be heard before His Holiness decided on her cause. The orator promised to do so; but whether he did it, whether the Emperor received the letters – in fact, of the whole or what was done we are as yet ignorant. Who does not admire and respect the moderation of the Queen? In an affair in which other women would have raised heaven and earth, and filled all with clamour and tumult, she merely seeks from her sister's son to obtain from the judge that she may not be condemned unheard.

This is the sum of all about which the Queen and I conversed, nor will more be found. Nor did I intermeddle with other things, because I interfere not willingly in the affairs of princes . . . .[1]

It is not known whether Katherine Parr saw this letter or not, but Lady Willoughby was in attendance upon the Queen, and she would certainly have told the girls what had happened to their tutor. The story must have affected them deeply, but at the same time it was a practical demonstration of the danger they would be in if they too interfered in the affairs of princes, and for the rest of that unhappy drama they remained impotent spectators on the sidelines.

The further events of Henry VIII's divorce from Catharine of Aragon are too well known to need repeating here. However, when Katherine Parr became Queen, she put into practice the lessons she had learnt from her predecessors, and an account of those aspects of Anne Boleyn's bid for power which influenced Katherine Parr is relevant to a better understanding of Katherine Parr's actions when she eventually became Queen.

The two women were outwardly very different. Where Anne Boleyn would be gay and vivacious, Katherine Parr would be gently amused; where Anne Boleyn would explode with anger at some stupid mistake, Katherine would quietly try to correct what was wrong. Katherine seldom approached an obstacle directly, whereas Anne would charge straight at it. Anne's weapons were scathing sarcasm or open abuse; Katherine's were an air of superior knowledge backed by the ironical wit of the intellectual – which usually passed over its victim's head.

Yet Katherine and Anne had more in common than is generally realised: both were excessively ambitious, both were deeply imbued with Humanist ideals and the spirit of reform, both had the interests of their families very much at heart, and, although in Katherine Parr's case the steel was sheathed in velvet, both were ruthless in their determination to achieve their objectives. Moreover, most of the dominant men in Katherine Parr's reign were, with one exception, the same as in Anne Boleyn's, and even that one exception, Thomas Cromwell, was to be the subject of Katherine Parr's special attention before she became Queen. Katherine Parr's tactics were to be very different from Anne Boleyn's, but there is little doubt that those tactics were chosen mainly as a direct consequence of her knowledge of where Anne Boleyn had gone wrong.

The first and most important aspect of the affair from Katherine Parr's point of view was Henry's motive. Those at Court who pictured Henry as an infatuated monarch who was prepared to sacrifice his honour and turn his kingdom upside down all for the sake of an intriguing woman were clearly wrong. With no standing army, no centrally directed police force to support him, Henry's power depended almost wholly on his ability to convince his subjects not only that their welfare was his foremost and ever present concern, but also that he, and he alone, was fit to be their King. This made him extremely sensitive to public opinion. It did not stop him from indulging in his pleasures, which his more high-spirited subjects in any case admired, but it did stop him from taking unnecessary risks with either his kingdom or his authority. Furthermore, his bluff heartiness concealed a brilliant far-seeing mind coupled with a devious subtlety in carrying out his plans which made it impossible for all except those who knew him very well indeed to discover his real intentions. If he appeared to have been trapped by a clever woman, it was only because this is what he wanted the world to think.

Sometime in 1529 Thomas Cromwell put Machiavelli's book *The Prince* into Henry's hands, extolling its virtues as the greatest book on the art of practical government that he had ever read. From that day on, *The Prince* was never far from Henry's reach, and it is in *The Prince* that the secret of Henry's methods and motives is to be found. (Reginald Pole, one of Sir Thomas More's circle, reporting this fact in a famous letter to Charles v, stated that Cromwell had also tried to persuade More and him to study *The Prince*, but that they had rejected it as being the work of the Devil.)

The Prince was written between 1513 and 1518 while Nicolo Machiavelli, a Florentine diplomat, was in enforced retirement. It is a book which could hardly be more different from the works of the Humanists, for it takes people as they are, not as they perhaps should be. It does not seek to improve or change people, but only how to control them. Men, the author points out, are the dupes of their simplicity and greed; they will not look at things as they really are, but as they wish them to be – and are ruined. 'A Prince,' he adds, 'so long as he keeps his subjects united and loyal, ought not to mind the reproach of cruelty; because with a few examples he will be more merciful than those who, through too much mercy, allow disorders to arise, from which follow murder and robbery; for these injure the whole people, whilst those executions which originate with a Prince offend a few individuals only.' It was a precept which Henry was to follow faithfully for the rest of his life.

One other precept of *The Prince*, however, struck Henry even more forcibly:

> And it ought to be remembered that there is nothing more difficult to take in hand, more perilous to conduct, or more uncertain of its success, than to take the lead in the introduction of a new order of things, because the innovator has for enemies all those who have done well under the old conditions, and lukewarm defenders in those who may do well under the new. This coolness arises partly from fear of opponents, who have the laws on their side, and partly from the incredulity of men, who do not readily believe in new things until they have had a long experience of them. Thus it happens that whenever those who are hostile have the opportunity, they attack like partisans, whilst the others defend lukewarmly, in such wise that the Prince is endangered along with them.
>
> It is necessary, therefore, if we desire to discuss this matter thoroughly, to inquire whether these innovators can rely on themselves or have to depend on others: that is to say, whether, in order to consummate their enterprise, have they to use prayers, or can they use force? In the first instance, they always succeed badly and never compass anything; but when they can rely on themselves and use force, then they are rarely endangered.
>
> Hence it is that all armed prophets have conquered, and the unarmed ones have been destroyed.

Henry had only to look at the history of the church to prove the truth of Machiavelli's statement. If the Church had not become militant, it could never have succeeded. Moreover, its persecutions of heretics, its crusades, its support of wars by countries against each other, had given it bloodier hands than any other power in Europe. Yet the majority of mankind was agreed that, even though it might now be corrupt, it had been both holy and good.

From such reasoning, it was but a short step to realise that the ideals of the Humanists and the statecraft of Machiavelli, apparently so different, were in fact complementary: the one was the means to the other. By 1529, Henry's year of decision, it had already become clear that the tactics of men like Erasmus, Sir Thomas More, Vives, and Reginald Pole, for promoting a gentle reform from within, to be achieved by satire and the honest preaching of God's Word, had no hope of success. The common people, except in parts of London, remained firmly wedded to the superstitious rites – and payments – imposed by Rome. Political trickery, backed by force, would have to be used to make them see the light, and the shudders of the older school of Humanists, already shocked by Luther's violence in Germany, would have to be ignored. However, guided by yet another of Machiavelli's precepts, Henry was careful, as far as the common people were concerned, to avoid being directly involved, and to retain his image as the Father of his People – in Machiavelli's words 'altogether merciful, trustworthy, humane, upright and religious'. Hence his pretence of having been trapped by Anne Boleyn: if anything went wrong he could always blame her.

And in many other ways Anne Boleyn was the answer to Henry's prayer. By putting her forward as a potential Queen instead of merely as another mistress, Henry was able to force a confrontation with the Church on grounds which challenged the Pope's authority without revealing his main motive, which, in addition to promoting Humanism, was to transfer the Church's huge wealth and power to the State. Next, Anne, her family and her reforming friends, formed an ideal focal point for the creation of a party of hawks, initially to support, but later to replace, Sir Thomas More and his friends, who were essentially doves. Sir Thomas More had been outstandingly clever in Parliament, outwitting Wolsey and defeating the opposition, but at the end of every conflict he had shown the intellectual's preference for compromise rather than outright victory, and to Henry compromise with an enemy was the same as defeat. He now needed people who would be prepared to carry the attack on the Church through to the kill, and Anne, with so much to gain from success, was a natural leader for the operation. Finally, there was the need to establish the succession of his dynasty on a firmer basis than on one daughter, whose health was suspect, and on one illegitimate son. Once again, Anne suited his requirements well: her breeding on her mother's side, the Howards, was impeccable; there was no doubt about her intelligence and strength of character; and marriage with her would not entail any awkward foreign entanglements.

Nevertheless, Henry did not act precipitately. Although it was in May 1527 that he had first asked Wolsey to investigate the possibilities of getting a divorce from Catharine of Aragon, it was not until the summer of 1529 that he put Anne in charge of a small team at her father's house at Durham Place in London with the task of breaking the power of the Pope in England and completing the divorce proceedings. The main members of the team, apart from Anne's family, were Thomas Cranmer (later to become Archbishop of Canterbury), Thomas Cromwell (later, Lord Privy Seal), and Stephen Gardiner (later, the Bishop of Winchester).

The team at Durham Place came into being mainly as the result of a chance meeting between Cranmer and Gardiner in an inn near Waltham in Essex. At that meeting, Cranmer had put forward the idea that the King might get better results in the religious dispute over the divorce if he were to appeal to the universities of Europe for their opinions on the right of the Pope to overrule the Bible rather than to plead his case at the Vatican. Gardiner, who had known Cranmer at Cambridge, passed the idea on to Henry. In the discussions with Henry and his Council which then took place, Cranmer showed himself to be skilful in debate, persuasive in argument and, above all, uncompromising – except to the King. Where Henry was concerned, Cranmer made it clear that to him the King was the final arbiter in all affairs, God's as well as man's. He would put his own opinion fearlessly, but if Henry disagreed then Cranmer would defer to his judgment (unlike Gardiner who would continue to argue) and subsequently defend the King's opinion as adroitly as he had previously argued against it. No man could have suited Henry better, and towards the end of August 1529, Henry asked the Boleyns to take Cranmer in as a lodger so that he could prepare the brief for the universities within easy reach of the Court. That then led to consultations with Gardiner and Cromwell at Durham Place (for Henry did not want to be involved openly at Court), and so the team was formed.

Cranmer stayed some months at Durham Place on this first visit, and returned for several more visits between his missions to the Continent. During these periods which went on for some three years, Cranmer, Cromwell, and Gardiner, under Anne's guidance (directed by the King in the background), created the hard core of doctrine and policy which was to become the English version of the Reformation. Gardiner subsequently turned against Cranmer and Cromwell, but at that stage all three men were united to serve Henry's wishes. All three were later to play major rôles in the life of Katherine Parr, and the relationships, tactics, and philosophies which they developed at Durham Place had much to do with their subsequent attitudes to Katherine Parr.

Of the three men, Thomas Cranmer was the least like a hawk. When he first met Anne Boleyn, he was about forty years old and very much a Cambridge don. Learning was almost a fetish with him, and even during the busiest parts of his life he would spend the first two or three hours each day reading and keeping himself informed of recent developments through an extensive correspondence with his academic friends at home and abroad. Outwardly, he was always soothing and calm, though he was not above showing a cold anger at the 'mumpsimus' of ignorant priests gabbling through Latin prayers which were as meaningless to them as they were to their congregations. He was abstemious in his living and careful about his health. He rose at five in the morning and usually went to bed at nine in the evening, spending, when possible, an hour or two each afternoon in the open air, hawking, shooting with both long- and cross-bow, or just riding.

Cranmer liked women and respected their intelligence. While he was still an undergraduate, and before he entered the Church, he nearly wrecked his career by marrying the daughter of an innkeeper. Fortunately for him, his wife died not long after their marriage and he was able to resume the celibate state required of those who wished to teach in the universities or enter the priesthood. But the taste for marriage remained, and towards the end of the Durham Place period, in 1532, he was one of the first to take advantage of the Humanist doctrine that celibacy was a matter of personal choice, unconnected with religion, and he took as his second wife a German girl of good family, Margaret, the niece of Osiander, a leader of the German Protestants. The marriage was a well-kept secret, known only to Henry and possibly to Anne Boleyn, but in those days it marked him out as a man of courage and a convinced anti-Papist.

Anne Boleyn took Cranmer more into her confidence than any of the others, and a deep, though strictly platonic, friendship developed between them. Cranmer became chaplain to the Boleyn family and, after Anne's marriage to the King, he moved to Court as her personal chaplain and as her chief, if unofficial, adviser, a position which he continued to hold even after his elevation to the See of Canterbury. It was from Cranmer that Anne acquired the theological knowledge to back her Humanist ideals; it was also through Cranmer that she built up the coterie of religious reformers, notably Hugh Latimer and Nicholas Shaxton, the Bishops of Worcester and Salisbury respectively, whom she called 'My bishops', and whom Katherine Parr, too, later took under her wing.

The most complex character of the Durham Place team was Thomas Cromwell. The liberal historian H. A. L. Fisher has described him as 'sly, cruel, greedy, yet not without the witty and agreeable converse of a man of the world'. Immensely energetic, Cromwell did most of the work of the team. His particular skill lay in his ability to manipulate Parliament, not only to secure favourable votes, but also to frame the legislation with which to clothe their plans in irrefutable legal form. He hated the nobility, and later, when his power became almost absolute, he never lost an opportunity to make them grovel before him. He never hesitated to kick down those who had helped him, nor ever forgot a wrong, imagined or real.

Yet both Cranmer and Anne Boleyn regarded him as a firm and pleasant friend. In their eyes politics was a dirty business, and the fact that Cromwell had to do the dirty work, and apparently did it with wry good humour, enhanced rather than decreased their respect for him. There was no doubt in their minds that he had a genuine and deep-seated concern for the Humanist cause. He gave freely of his patronage to numerous writers and scholars, and though much of this was part of the programme of propaganda which the Durham Place team had framed, it was through his sympathy and understanding that the scholars drew their inspiration.

Cromwell's attitude to women was another point in his favour. He was uninhibited in his desires; but at the same time he stood out as the champion of women's causes. His correspondence is full of letters from women asking for his help or thanking him for his efforts on their behalf, particularly in matrimonial cases, in which he was singularly successful in winning financial support from husbands for deserted wives or in protecting them against cruelty. In a number of cases, his activities on behalf of women were in order to use their complaints as a means for ruining their husbands, but this seldom worried the women concerned, and they remained ever grateful to their champion.

Stephen Gardiner, the last of the main members of the Durham Place team, was the antithesis of Cranmer and the aristocratic complement to Cromwell. Where Cranmer was mild and reasonable, he was sharp and didactic; where Cromwell would fawn with mock humility, he was openly contemptuous. Some mystery surrounds his birth. He was reputed to be the son of a clothworker in Bury St Edmunds, but there was a story current at one time that he was the son of Henry VII's sister, Helen, and Henry VIII once referred to him as 'nobly born'. Some three or four years younger than Cranmer, he read both civil and canon law at Trinity Hall, Cambridge. His outstanding academic ability, which was to become widely known abroad as well as in England, combined with an exceptionally strong personality gained him rapid promotion, and in 1525 he was elected Master of his college. At about the same time he met the Duke of Norfolk, with whom he formed a lasting if uneasy alliance, and through him he was introduced to Wolsey. Like Cromwell, he became a member of Wolsey's staff, and was employed almost immediately on diplomatic missions to France and the Vatican. During these missions, he showed a toughness in negotiations which earned him the King's admiration, and in July 1529, just before Wolsey's fall, Henry took him away from Wolsey and made him Secretary to the Council. He rose steadily in Henry's favour, mainly as the result of his diplomatic ability, and in 1531 he was appointed Bishop of Winchester.

Gardiner's attitude to women was that of St Paul: they might be seen, but they should not be heard. He treated most women as ignorant wantons, fit only for bed when the fancy took him, and he usually kept a temporary mistress in his house. As he said of himself, however, he was no hypocrite, and he made no secret of his opinions or his conduct. As a result he was very unpopular with the women at Court, but this seldom worried him and he made no attempt to play the courtier or to win their favours.

His principal task in the team was to advise on diplomatic tactics to prevent the Pope from mounting a crusade on Henry when the time should come to break with Rome. In this field he was in his element, and he took a chess-master's pleasure in working out the moves and counter-moves, but pride, ambition, and his uncompromising stand against Cranmer and Cromwell on points of theology made him an unsatisfactory partner. Henry kept a close watch on the situation, and it was probably then that he began to see the advantages of having a Council divided against itself which he was later deliberately to foster, but for the moment unity was all important, and Henry saw to it that Gardiner stayed in line with his main policies.

The strategy formed by the Durham Place team and its consequences provided a further object lesson for Katherine Parr, for, although the breach with Rome was a long-accomplished fact when she became Queen, Humanism had by then suffered a severe rebuff, and its revival, together with the defeat of the anti-reformers, was to be one of Katherine's main achievements. In carrying this out, Katherine was to be constantly reminded by Cranmer and Gardiner, who were to repeat under her rule the same rôles they now played under Anne Boleyn, of the successes and failures of the Durham Place plans in broadly similar circumstances.

The strategy proposed by Anne and her colleagues to Henry had a number of prongs: first, a Parliament to pass the Acts necessary to secure the secession from Rome and the dissolution of the monasteries – to be controlled by Cromwell assisted by Anne's brother, Lord Rochford; secondly, a Convocation to bring the bishops and clergy to heel – to be managed by Cranmer; thirdly, diplomatic missions to Germany to secure the support of the Protestants (Cranmer), to France and Spain to keep those countries guessing (Gardiner), and to Rome to lull the Pope (Anne's father, the Earl of Wiltshire); fourthly, an intense and widespread propaganda by books and broadsheets to convince the people of the need for reform – to be directed by Anne, Cromwell, and Cranmer; and finally, the mailed fist in the form of persecutions of heretics and traitors, which was outwardly Cromwell's responsibility, but which was in fact controlled by Henry who personally decided who should or should not suffer.

But before anything could be done, Wolsey had to be got out of the way. It would clearly be a popular move, and early in October 1529 Henry approved a writ of *praemunire* against him. Two weeks later, he surrendered the Great Seal. Anne took it upon herself to write in Henry's name as well as her own to tell him why:

My Lord,
   Though you are a man of great understanding, you cannot avoid being censured by everybody for having drawn upon yourself the hatred of a King who has raised you to the highest degree to which the greatest ambition of a man seeking his fortune can aspire. I cannot comprehend, and the King still less, how your reverend Lordship, after having allured us by so many fine promises about divorce, can have repented of your purpose, and how you could have done what you have, in order to hinder the consummation of it. What then is your mode of proceeding? You quarrelled with the Queen to favour me at the time when I was less advanced in the King's good graces; and after having therein given me the strongest marks of your affection, your Lordship abandons my interests to em-

61

brace those of the Queen. I acknowledge that I have put much confidence in your professions and promises, in which I find myself deceived.

But, for the future, I shall rely on nothing but the protection of Heaven and the love of my dear King, which alone will be able to set right again those plans which you have broken and spoiled, and to place me in that happy situation which God wills, the King so much wishes, and which will be entirely to the advantage of the Kingdom. The wrong you have done me has caused me much sorrow; but I feel infinitely more in seeing myself betrayed by a man who pretended to enter into my interests only to discover the secrets of my heart. I acknowledge that, believing you sincere, I have been too precipitate in my confidence; it is this which has induced, and still induces me, to keep more moderation in avenging myself, not being able to forget that I *have* been

Your servant,

Anne Boleyn[2]

Katherine Parr is unlikely to have seen this letter, but she and her friends did see and hear Anne Boleyn gloating in public over the fall of her enemy. Although almost everyone at Court was delighted that Wolsey had at last paid the penalty for his arrogance and greed, Anne's gloating was a bad mistake. It was unnecessary, and it raised fears about who would be her next victim, thereby sowing the seeds of opposition among people who would otherwise have remained neutral. Katherine Parr's handling of the same sort of situation eleven years later shows that she took note of Anne's mistake and was warned.

The next lesson for Katherine Parr concerned the conflict between the doves and the hawks. By skilful political play, the doves were not at first disturbed by the hawks. This was achieved mainly by the way in which Sir Thomas More was initially treated. Much to More's surprise, Henry appointed him Lord Chancellor in place of Wolsey, an almost unheard-of honour for the post was traditionally filled by the most senior churchman in the land, and Sir Thomas More, though deeply religious, was not even a priest. Further, Anne's father, the Earl of Wiltshire, made a great point of continuing his friendship with Sir Thomas More and his circle, among other things commissioning Erasmus to write a number of books to exemplify the Humanist doctrine. As a result, Sir Thomas More was put in the position of being regarded as an associate member of the Durham Place team, and his presence did much to dispel the alarm of the doves. The political moves in Parliament, the diplomatic missions, the propaganda, even the first wave of burnings, so long as they had the tacit support of Sir Thomas More, thus did nothing more than mildly upset the older Humanists.

In the spring of 1532, however, one of the main prongs of the Durham Place strategy, namely the submission of the clergy to the Common Law from which they had hitherto been exempt, came to a head, and Sir Thomas More rebelled. He objected as a matter of principle to the State control of the Church, and he refused to countenance Cranmer's moves in Convocation. Gardiner, who also objected, but on the more worldly grounds that it would weaken his power as a bishop, slipped out of Henry's control and joined More in his protest. The two men lobbied the bishops and successfully persuaded them to reject Cranmer's proposals. Cranmer appealed to Cromwell for help. Cromwell and Anne's brother, Lord Rochford, responded by packing Parliament and leading the Commons in full cry against the priests. On 15 May 1532 the clergy surrendered, and on the following day Sir Thomas More resigned from his position as Lord Chancellor. Two days later, Gardiner was dismissed from his post as Secretary to the Council and was replaced by Cromwell, who, until then, had been officially only a Clerk of the Council.

Event followed event in rapid succession. In August, Archbishop Warham died and Henry appointed Cranmer in his place. Since the Pope's approval of the appointment was necessary if there was to be no doubt about his authority, Cranmer went to Rome and won an unexpected success by obtaining the required Bull elevating him to the See of Canterbury. On his return, he summoned Catharine of Aragon to a special court at Dunstable where he declared that her marriage to Henry was null and void, that Henry was and had been a bachelor, and that therefore Princess Mary was a bastard. Meanwhile, in January 1533, in the knowledge that Anne was pregnant, Henry and Anne were secretly married. After publishing the Dunstable verdict Cranmer set his seal upon the marriage, and in June Anne was crowned Queen. In July, the Pope excommunicated Henry; in September, Anne gave birth to a daughter, the Princess Elizabeth; and in January 1534 the final Act of Parliament, prohibiting all appeals to the Pope, completed the secession from Rome.

The whole plan had taken a little more than three years to complete. Its execution had been brilliantly successful, and the Boleyns, Cromwell, and Cranmer had reason to congratulate themselves.

From Katherine Parr's point of view, the lesson in politics was noted, but one of the main consequences was the removal of Catharine of

Aragon, the heroine of her childhood, from the political scene. The ex-Queen was sent to Kimbolton Castle in Huntingdonshire where she was kept a virtual prisoner. Her ladies were dismissed, visits were strictly controlled, and she was allowed only a small domestic staff for company. That something like this would happen had been obvious for several months, but the actual event shocked Katherine into action. Henry's regard for her, her family, and her young friends, was as firm as ever, and none of them had anything to fear, but whereas the others were quite willing to continue in their posts at Court under the new Queen, Katherine decided to get out, if she could.

Her motives, as always, were complex. Apart from the emotional shock of Catharine of Aragon's dismissal, there was the realisation that Anne Boleyn had no intention whatsoever of allowing any other woman to have any political influence at Court. Her Maids-of-Honour and Ladies-in-Waiting might applaud and admire, but there would be short shrift for any woman who tried to interfere, even as a supporter, with the Council or with 'her' bishops. Let them by all means indulge in love affairs and gay pastimes, but let them put out of their minds any thoughts of continuing the intellectual traditions of Margaret Beaufort and Catharine of Aragon. This had been the route by which she had risen to power, and she was determined that no one should follow in her footsteps. Such suppression of women was in fact to contribute to Anne's downfall, but all that Katherine Parr could see at the time was that it would make Court life intolerable for her.

There was also the question of religion. In her 'confession', Katherine states that during her youth she held 'wrong opinions', meaning that, like Sir Thomas More, she believed at that time that Humanism belonged within the established Church, whose fundamental beliefs and rites should not be changed. It was clear that the reform movement sponsored by Anne Boleyn was to be something much more radical, and that Katherine would run the risk of being caught up in the religious conflict if she remained at Court.

It seems likely that, at this juncture, Katherine consulted her childhood guardian and 'uncle', Cuthbert Tunstall, from whom she had derived these beliefs and on whose guidance she had learnt to rely. Cuthbert Tunstall had the answer. A close neighbour and friend in the North, the new Lord Latimer, a forty-year-old widower with two young children, was in search of a wife. It would be a good match for Katherine, and would put her under the protection of the powerful Northern families to many of whom she was, as a Parr, already related. The King gave his blessing, the marriage contract was agreed, and sometime before the end of 1533 – the exact date is not recorded – Katherine celebrated her second wedding, to become Lady Latimer of Snape Hall, Richmondshire.

NOTES

1 Wood, *Letters of Illustrious Ladies*.
2 Wood, *Letters of Illustrious Ladies*.

5   Lady Latimer

Katherine Parr's second husband, John Neville, Lord Latimer, was the eldest son in a family of thirteen children. He had succeeded to the title on the death of his father towards the end of 1530, and he is recorded as having first taken his seat as a peer in Parliament on 16 January 1531. Before that date, he had, as Sir John Neville, been an occasional visitor at Court as one of the King's honorary bodyguard, the Gentlemen Pensioners, and he had served in the French wars. His branch of the Neville family was descended from the earls of Westmorland, on whom successive Kings of England had depended for the defence of the borders against Scotland. In the previous century, the then Earl of Westmorland, Ralph Neville, had obtained the lands and barony of a certain Lord Latimer who had died childless and without any other heirs. These lands and the title of Lord Latimer were then bestowed on one of the Earl of Westmorland's younger sons; the new Lord Latimer was the third holder of the title after that younger son.

The new Lord Latimer had been married twice before he married Katherine Parr. His first wife, whom he married in 1518, was Elizabeth Musgrave, the daughter of a well-known Border family. She died some three or four years later, and Lord Latimer then married Dorothy de Vere, the sister of the 14th Earl of Oxford. Lady Dorothy bore him a son, John, and a daughter, Margaret, before she, too, died in 1526–7. By the time Lord Latimer married Katherine, therefore, he had been a widower for some six years, and his children were between seven and ten years old. He himself was about forty-two, and Katherine was nineteen.

It is not known whether Lord Latimer knew the Parr family before he took his seat in Parliament, but he was a distant relative through the Fitzhugh line, and besides Cuthbert Tunstall, who was both a neighbour and a friend, he had several other acquaintances in common with Katherine and her family. Moreover Parliament sat for many months in 1531 and assembled again, after a short recess, for a further long session. Lord Latimer, therefore, is certain to have met Katherine at Court functions during these sessions even if he had not known the Parrs before, and this paved the way for the match between them.

Lord Latimer was a wealthy man. His main estates surrounded Great Tanfield, near Bedale, in the North Riding of Yorkshire (known also as Richmondshire), and included Snape Hall, a magnificent semi-fortified castle standing on the brow of a hill which the Earl of Westmorland's younger son was said to have built over the ruins of a Norman keep. Lord Latimer also had substantial lands in Worcestershire, where he had another fine house, Wyke Hall, which he preferred to Snape, and yet more land in Buckinghamshire. In addition to these country estates, at about the time of his marriage to Katherine Parr, he bought an impressive mansion in the grounds of the Charterhouse in London, and it was almost certainly to the Charterhouse that he first took his young bride.

From the material point of view, therefore, it was an excellent match for Katherine. The marriage settlement ensured her a comfortable income while her husband was alive and, if she should outlive him, would leave her a rich woman. On Lord Latimer's side, he stood to benefit from Katherine's contingent interest in the Parr estates: if her brother should die before she did, and without children, Katherine would inherit the whole of the Parr fortune which would then become the joint property of herself and her husband. In spite of the fact that Katherine's brother had just married Anne Bourchier, the sole heiress of the Earl of Essex, and was then only seventeen years old, Katherine's contingent interest was a more material factor in the marriage agreement than it would be today when early deaths are less common. Katherine's influence at Court was possibly even more important to Lord Latimer. In marrying him, Katherine might have wished to escape from Court intrigues, but the fact remained that she and her family stood very high indeed in the King's favour, and in the prevailing uncertainty of the times her help could be of the utmost value to Latimer, even to the point, as it proved to be, of saving his life.

Katherine was now fully grown. Tall, slim, with auburn hair and an oval, almost pointed face, marred a little by upward slanting eyes, a firm nose, and tiny mouth, she made up for her somewhat severe appearance by an open, friendly manner which at once put people at their ease. Her marriage to Lord Latimer was not a love match, but there is little doubt that the pair were genuinely fond of each other. Her quiet ways and gentle wit, mixed with an occasional outburst of shrewd irony, made her an interesting as well as a comfortable companion to her husband. She particularly pleased him by the special, affectionate interest she took in his children, quickly winning their love – in the case of his daughter, it was close to adoration – and personally supervising their education and upbringing. Although she had spent most of her life in the South, Katherine was a Northerner by birth, and for her part, she found comfort in John Latimer's unemotional forthright attitude in comparison with the elaborate web-spinning of the Southerners. At the same time he was highly educated, and Katherine was delighted to find that he appreciated her intellectual sallies and enjoyed a lively debate as much as she did.

Without being unusually religious, Lord Latimer held orthodox views, but he also felt it necessary to pay Cromwell a 'fee' of £40 a year (equal today to about £1,000), ostensibly to protect his landed interests in the courts, but which he hoped would cover him as well against anti-Papists. He was a conscientious landlord with a keen sense of duty towards his tenants, who looked up to him, sometimes to his discomfort, as their natural leader in any conflict with London or other outside authorities. If he had a fault in Katherine's eyes, it was lack of political ambition and a desire to avoid trouble, but this only became important to Katherine several years later. For the moment, she heartily echoed his wish for seclusion and supported his policy of preferring appeasement to conflict.

Although they both preferred to live in Worcestershire rather than in Yorkshire, Lord Latimer had military and judicial duties in his Yorkshire barony which obliged him, when he was not attending Parliament in London, to spend most of his time at Snape, and Snape Hall thus now became Katherine's principal home. At Gainsborough she had been a cosseted child bride, but now she was the real lady of the house and carried the full authority and responsibilities of her position. She had a household staff of seventy, whose daily work she had to organise and control, and she also had a number of her husband's numerous brothers and their families as more or less permanent guests. Outside her household responsibilities, she was expected to play her part by her husband's side, sharing with him the social obligations of high rank and the patronage and charity expected of the wealthy. Moreover, Richmondshire was an affluent area containing an unusually high proportion of noble houses, and the Lady Latimer was expected to be a leader of that noble society. These were major tasks for a young woman of nineteen, but Katherine tackled them with zest and greatly enjoyed her new rôle in life.

The year 1533 saw other major changes in Katherine Parr's circle of friends. In July, one month after Anne Boleyn's coronation, the French Queen died. Her two daughters and her step-daughters were by then married and off her hands, leaving only Margaret Douglas and Katherine Willoughby of the original group of girls at Westhorpe. With the French Queen out of the way, Anne Boleyn had little difficulty in persuading Margaret Douglas to rejoin her at Court, which left Katherine Willoughby on her own. The French Queen's husband, the Duke of Suffolk, whose ward Katherine was, had previously arranged for Katherine to marry his son, the Earl of Lincoln, when he should come of age – he was four years younger than Katherine – but now, unexpectedly finding himself a widower, the Duke decided to marry his young ward himself. The marriage took place some six weeks after the French Queen's death, when Katherine Willoughby was fourteen years old, and the Duke was forty-nine.

To some the Duke of Suffolk was all brawn and no brains, but in fact he possessed a great fund of natural wit which enabled him easily and good-humouredly to side-step the few political attempts which were made to bring him down. He was a born leader of men, an able administrator, and far and away the most popular man in England. He had been brought up with Henry VIII as a result of the gratitude of Henry VII to his father who had been killed while bearing the King's standard at Bosworth. As boys, the young Henry and he had done everything together, outvying each other in acts of daring, and as friendly rivals in endless jousting and shooting matches. At Henry's coronation feast, he had ridden round the tables on a white charger, shouting encouragement to the new King and cheering on the revellers. He enjoyed the King's complete confidence, and he was said to be the only man that Henry VIII ever loved.

But it was in his marital exploits that the Duke of Suffolk both shocked and titillated the Court. He was one of those rare men whom women, however intelligent or high-minded they might be, found impossible to resist. The French Queen had been his third wife. Henry had sent him to fetch her back from France after the death of her first husband, Louis XII, but knowing his sister's infatuation for the Duke, he had made the Duke promise not to do anything to encourage her until they got back to England. The French Queen, however, could not wait. As soon as the Duke arrived, she told him that she was sure that Henry had another match in mind for her, and that she would tear herself to pieces rather than let that happen. 'She wept, I never saw woman so weep,' Suffolk reported later. The French Queen takes up the tale: 'Whereunto I put my Lord of Suffolk in choice whether he would accomplish the marriage in four days, or else he should never enjoy me.' Suffolk gave in, and the pair were promptly married on French soil. At first the affair caused a storm at Court and the couple did not dare to return, but the details soon became known, and the Duke of Suffolk was generally praised for his gallant conduct. Henry relented – his anger had never seemed very real – and, after obliging his sister to pay him a third of what she had received in France, he allowed the Duke and his doting royal bride to come home.

The marriage was popularly supposed to have been a love match, which made Suffolk's fourth marriage to Katherine Willoughby, coming so soon as it did after the death of the French Queen, all the more shocking to the public. Nor did the fact that the Duke had stolen his own son's bride-to-be help matters. But within a fortnight the scandal was eclipsed by the news that Anne Boleyn had given birth to the Princess Elizabeth, and the Duke was allowed to enjoy his latest marriage in peace.

Katherine Willoughby was thus now Katherine, Duchess of Suffolk. Apart from the Queen and the King's own family, she ranked second only to the Duchess of Norfolk among the ladies at Court, but this did not strike her as being of any great importance. She had a gay, devil-may-care attitude to life and, judging from Suffolk's previous experiences at the hands of women, it is more than likely that, though Katherine was only fourteen at the time, it was she, not Suffolk, who was the pursuer, and it was the man, not his rank, that she wanted. Almost exactly a year after her marriage, she bore him a son, Henry, and less than a year after that, a second son, Charles.

In other respects, the marriage seems to have been equally happy. Katherine had 'the stomach of a man': she was as fearless as her husband and shared his easy-going philosophy. Like the rest of her contemporaries, she was exceptionally well educated, but she carried her learning lightly, and she was as ready to mock pretension as she was to praise honesty. Her insight into the true characters of people was a byword, and many a pompous courtier came to dread the rapier-sharp wit with which she would thrust home her observations. Like her husband she was careless about money and, in spite of Henry's grants of lands and offices to the Duke and her own not inconsiderable inheritance, the ducal pair were seldom out of debt. Part at least was due to their generosity, the Duke's four daughters – two by the French Queen, and two by his second wife, Anne Browne – being a continual drain on their resources. All had married well, but time and again they appealed to their father for help and were not often refused. In one way or another, however, Katherine and her husband managed to survive. On one occasion, they found some jewels which the French Queen had smuggled out of France and which they sold to Cromwell, and once or twice Henry took pity on them and came to their rescue.

The Duchess of Suffolk avoided the Court as much as she could during the first few years of her marriage. Her sympathies, like those of her mother, Lady Willoughby, were firmly on the side of Catharine of Aragon, and she had no wish to be obliged to honour Anne Boleyn. Her pregnancies, and later a rumour of the plague at Westhorpe (to which she had now succeeded the French Queen as lady of the house), gave her sufficient excuses to absent herself, but at the same time she paid fairly frequent visits to London, to her mother's house in the Barbican where both her sons were born, and to the Duke's new house in Southwark.

It seems certain that these visits to London coincided with Katherine Parr's visits when she accompanied her husband on his summonses to Parliament, for it was during this period that the indissoluble friendship between the two women first began to flourish. They had known each other at the Court school, but in those days the five-year gap in their ages had put them in different groups, and the Duchess of Suffolk had been much too young to share the life of the older girls. However, now that both were married and carrying the responsibilities of great houses, the gap in their ages had become insignificant.

In some ways it was an attraction of opposites. Katherine Parr was usually serious, always prudent, and secretly ambitious, while the Duchess of Suffolk was gay, a little wild, and clearly content with her position in life. But each woman was exceptionally intelligent, each

71

admired in the other the qualities she felt she lacked, and both knew that as a pair they might be invincible. They were also drawn together by their common feelings about the current situation at Court. Both considered that Catharine of Aragon and Princess Mary had been shockingly treated, but neither was prepared to ally herself to the Papists who were now trying to make the ex-Queen and her daughter a rallying point for their cause. It was not a question of religion, since neither woman had made up her mind at this stage on points of doctrine, but a question of foreign interference in English affairs. Anne Boleyn might be a usurper, but this did not give the Pope, the Emperor or the French King the right to tell the English people what they should or should not do about it. It was an attitude which set them apart from both the new Humanists and the Roman Catholics, and which united the two young women in a small, isolated group of their own.

The rest of their former circle at Court — Katherine Parr's sister, Anne, Joan Guildford, and Joan Champernown — were not so inhibited by their previous attachment to Princess Mary and her mother. No marriage arrangements were in the offing for any of the three girls, and the alternative to remaining at Court in the service of the new Queen would have been banishment to what they considered the dull backwoods of their country homes. As the King's ward, Anne Parr had no choice, even if she had wanted to leave, but as it was, all three girls accepted their new mistress with professional cheerfulness and suitable tokens of loyalty, and continued in their rôles as Maids-of-Honour at Court.

The lip-service, however, soon changed to genuine homage. Anne Boleyn had scant time for other women, but etiquette required that she should spend a good part of each day in the company of her 'waiting gentlewomen', and since she disdained small talk, much of her conversation concerned her political opinions and religious beliefs. The girls were struck by her brilliance and, with no effort on Anne's part, they succumbed to the spell of her personality. In particular, they were infected by Anne Boleyn's enthusiasm for the Humanist cause and by her condemnation of the false images, pagan rites, and faked miracles which, they believed, then corrupted the Church of Rome. As a result, all three girls — Joan Champernown, perhaps, more than the others — became ardent supporters of the New Faith, that is, of a simple belief in the Gospels, as expounded by Erasmus and unpolluted by superstition or worldly considerations. It was, however, the religion of the hawks rather than of the doves that the girls now acquired and, following Anne's direct example, their ardour was expressed more in abuse of Rome than in terms of love and charity to their neighbours. Later, they were to settle down to a more feminine and adult approach to religion, but, for the moment, they embraced Anne's teaching with all the idealism of their adolescence and, in spite of Anne's indifference to them as individuals, they became her fervent admirers.

The conversion of the girls was aptly timed for, although the Act forbidding appeals to the Pope had formally completed the secession from Rome, Henry decided later on in 1534 to put the loyalty of his subjects to the test by forcing another Act through Parliament requiring all subjects to take an oath acknowledging him not only as Head of the State, but also as Supreme Head of the Church of England. Those who refused were to be declared guilty of treason and to suffer a traitor's death – to be hanged, cut down while still alive, disembowelled, and quartered.

The majority of citizens, including Katherine Parr, her husband, family, and friends, complied with the Act, but several hundreds of devout Roman Catholics refused, and a reign of terror ensued, the worst that had so far been known in English history. Throughout the next twelve months, huge crowds witnessed gruesome executions almost weekly in London and the larger county towns, the most pitiable case being that of the Carthusian monks from the Charterhouse in London, some of whom must have been personally friendly with Katherine Parr and her husband whose London house was situated in their grounds.

The Humanists were appalled at the slaughter but, with two notable exceptions, they could see no reason why the oath should not be taken. The two exceptions were Sir Thomas More and John Fisher, the Bishop of Rochester.

At first Henry accepted that it would be too dangerous to execute two such universally admired men, and their sentences were commuted to perpetual imprisonment instead. In April 1535, however, the very strong adverse reaction at home and abroad to the martyrdom of the Carthusians decided Henry to demonstrate his determination to rule the Church by insisting that More and Fisher should take the oath. For three months, Cranmer, Cromwell, and the new Lord Chancellor, Sir

Thomas Audeley, reasoned with the two men. More's family, particularly his daughter, Margaret Roper, added their persuasions, stating that they could not understand why More should stick on a point which in their eyes was of small significance compared with the opportunity they now had of promoting their ideas for reform. But neither More nor Fisher would budge from the stand they had taken.

They might still have been saved, for Cranmer devised a new wording of the oath which the two men might have accepted, but towards the end of May the Pope offered a Cardinal's hat to Fisher. Cromwell was sent to get his reaction. Fisher, now a tired old man, replied that unworthy though he was for such an offer, he would accept the hat. Henry exploded, 'What,' he roared, 'is he yet so lusty? Well, let the Pope send him a hat when he will; but I will provide that whensoever it cometh, he shall wear it on his shoulders, for head he shall have none to set it on.' Fisher's fate was sealed, and he was beheaded on 22 June 1535. On the scaffold, Fisher told the vast crowd to love and obey their King, who was good by nature, but had been deceived by bad advisers.

For the first time, the angry public reactions to the executions began to worry Henry, and he ordered one more attempt to be made to persuade Sir Thomas More to conform. Cranmer took the lead, pointing out to More that he, More, had openly declared that he did not object to others taking the oath: why, then, should More object to taking it himself? More prevaricated, but stubbornly held to his opinion, and the judicial commission had no option but to find him guilty. He was executed quickly, on 6 July, and without being allowed to make the traditional speech from the scaffold, but like Fisher, he too told his gaolers that it was not the King, but the King's councillors who were responsible for the terrible events of the past year. The message was duly passed on to the people. It also showed Henry the way to extricate himself from blame without impairing his authority or surrendering his objectives.

Henry kept his plans to himself, but during his annual summer Progress he called on the Seymour family at their home, Wolf Hall, in Wiltshire, and there showed himself to be much attracted by Sir Edward Seymour's sister, Jane Seymour. Probably only Cromwell sensed what was coming. He knew his master better than anybody else, and he too must have been apprehensive about the mood of the people. A scapegoat was essential, and by his too obvious attentions to Jane Seymour, Henry was hinting that Anne Boleyn might suit the rôle. From the beginning, everybody had considered that she had trapped Henry; public opinion was certain that she exercised an overpowering influence over him; and there was no secret about the leading part she had played in the breach with Rome and the reform movement. It would take the minimum of effort to persuade the people that she was the evil adviser to whom Fisher and More had referred. But Cromwell was also in danger, and he set about making sure that he would not be implicated. A whispering campaign was started that Anne had bewitched Henry, and Cromwell pointedly began avoiding her presence. By the end of that year, 1535, rumours were rife of impending trouble for Anne and her family.

Two things delayed matters. The first was that Anne was once more pregnant, and Henry did not care to risk losing the chance of a male heir. Secondly, as long as Catharine of Aragon was still alive, Henry could not easily repudiate Anne without reopening the divorce question. On 7 January 1536 Catharine died, and towards the end of the same month Anne had a miscarriage. The two events put an end to any hope of Anne's survival as Queen.

The lesson for Katherine Parr in Anne Boleyn's downfall lay primarily in Anne's neglect of women's power. By holding herself so aloof from those women who might have been able to help her, Anne lost what opportunity she might have had of rallying support at Court. Worse still, she had antagonised a number of her Ladies-in-Waiting (as distinct from the Maids, who thought so highly of her), so that when Cromwell began looking for suitable legal grounds to bring her down, he had little difficulty in finding highborn women who were prepared to tell tales about her. The Countess of Worcester, who, without her husband's knowledge, had borrowed £100 (worth today about £2,500) from Anne, passed on her suspicions about Anne and the Court musician, Mark Smeton, and it was Anne's sister-in-law, Lady Rochford, who hinted at Anne's possible incestuous relations with her brother, Lady Rochford's husband. These were all the leads Cromwell needed, and by the end of April he had collected a confession of adultery with the Queen from Smeton, and *prima facie* evidence implicating three other men, plus the trump card of the charge of incest with her brother. All were arrested after the May Day celebrations and, on 2 May, Anne and her brother were imprisoned in the Tower.

One other aspect of the affair, unknown to Katherine, was significant. This was Cranmer's reaction when he heard of Anne Boleyn's arrest. His letter to Henry has often been quoted, but it bears quoting again here because he was also to become Katherine's guide on religious matters, and his attitude to her was governed by his experience with Anne Boleyn. Cranmer's lack of political sense and strict avoidance of gossip had kept him wholly in the dark about what had been going on at Court, so that Anne's arrest came as a profound shock to him. The letter, written the day after Anne's imprisonment, begins with a long, rambling prologue in which he exhorts Henry to acknowledge God's will and not to blame himself for what has happened. Cranmer continues:

> And I am in such perplexity that my mind is clean amazed; for I never had better opinion in woman that I had in her; which maketh me to think that she should not be culpable. And again [on the other hand], I think your Highness would not have gone so far, except she had surely been culpable. Now I think your Grace best knoweth that next unto your Grace I was most bound unto her of all creatures living. Wherefore I most humbly beseech your Grace to suffer me in that which both God's law, nature and also her kindness biddeth me unto, that is, that I may, with your Grace's favour, wish and pray for her that she may declare herself unculpable and innocent. And if she be found culpable ... I repute him not your Grace's faithful servant and subject, nor true to the realm, that would not desire the offence without mercy to be punished to the example of all other. And as I loved her not a little for the love which I judged her to bear towards God and His Gospel, so, if she be proved culpable, there is not one that loveth God and His Gospel that ever will favour her, but must hate her above all other.

On 15 May 1536, Anne and her brother stood separate trials, presided over by their uncle, the Duke of Norfolk. Each made an excellent defence, and in Lord Rochford's case, spectators laid bets in court that he would be freed. However, both were found guilty. Rochford was executed on 17 May, and Anne two days later. The day before Anne was executed, Henry divorced her, and Princess Elizabeth was declared illegitimate.

The Spanish Ambassador, Eustace Chapuys, to whom historians owe so much for his witty and accurate accounts of events in England, was present at Anne's execution. He adds the details that she was accompanied by four young ladies who, after her speech from the scaffold, stripped her of her short mantle furred with ermine, and that after the execution, the young ladies, although very distressed, refused to allow any man to touch her. One of them covered her head with a white cloth while the others took her body, and the whole was then carried into the church nearest the Tower of London.

The identities of the young ladies are not reported but, from their devotion, it is possible that they comprised Katherine Parr's sister and her friends. If so, their loyalty may not have been so deep as it seemed, for, one month later, they were all back at Court in the service of Jane Seymour, whom Henry had secretly married the day after Anne's execution.

Much of what Katherine Parr learnt from Anne Boleyn's downfall only came home to her several years later. At the time her only reaction was as far as possible to avoid being involved with any of the parties concerned. The news of Anne's arrest does not seem to have reached Snape, where Katherine and Lord Latimer were then staying, until about a week after the event. This was unusual, for news from London normally reached the North within two days, particularly when, as in this case, it also carried an urgent summons to all peers to attend Parliament for the trial. The apparent delay may have been because Katherine and her husband at first wondered whether they could avoid being involved by pretending ignorance of the affair, but on second thoughts they decided to play for time instead, and Lord Latimer sent the following letter to Cromwell.

> It is reported here that the Lords shall be sent for to come up [to Parliament] shortly. I beg you will have me excused by reason of business in Worcestershire. I have been at every prorogation and session of the last Parliament since it began, which has been very painful and chargeable to me.
> From Snape, in the north parts of Yorkshire. 12th May, 1536.
>
> John Lord Latimer

By the time Cromwell got this letter the trial was over, but the Latimers were not allowed to escape their duty, and they were ordered to be in London by 8 June when Parliament was to meet again for the proclamation of Jane Seymour as the new Queen. This second summons, however, was not so unwelcome as the first. Katherine had known Jane Seymour when they were both at Court during the three years immediately preceding Katherine's marriage to Lord Latimer, and she was curious to see how the new Queen would conduct herself.

Chapuys, for one, was not impressed.

> She is of middle stature, [he reported] and no great beauty, so fair that one

would call her pale than otherwise. She is over 25 years old. I leave you to judge whether, being English and having long frequented the Court, she is likely to have had any scruples about anticipating the knowledge of what matrimony means. Perhaps the King will be only too glad to be so far relieved from trouble. Also according to the account given of him by the concubine [Anne Boleyn], he has neither vigour nor virtue; and besides he may make a condition in the marriage that she be a virgin, and when he has a mind to divorce her he will find enough of witnesses. The said Seymour is not a woman of great wit, but she may have good understanding. It is said she inclines to be proud and haughty. She bears great love and reverence to the Princess [Mary]. I know not if honours will make her change hereafter ...

Katherine's judgment is unrecorded, but she and the Duchess of Suffolk, with whom she joined forces in London, are likely to have echoed Chapuys' opinion. Here was no intellectual, no leader of women to re-establish their influence at Court, and the question in everyone's mind was why had the King chosen her to be his new Queen. The answer lay first in the very fact of her insignificance. After Anne Boleyn's excess of activity, Henry needed to reassure his people that he would not be 'trapped' by such a woman again. He had achieved his two principal objectives: he now had control of the Church, and one month before Anne Boleyn's execution, Parliament had passed the first Act dissolving the monasteries and allocating their possessions to the King. He could therefore afford to be magnanimous, and by choosing the quiet, mouse-like Jane Seymour to be Queen, he sought to convince his subjects that the reign of terror – which was now attributed wholly to Anne Boleyn's wicked influence – was over, and that he was once more the benevolent Father of his People.

A second reason was to be found in Jane Seymour's family. Her eldest brother, Sir Edward Seymour, was a man of exceptional intelligence and executive ability. He had been at Court for several years, but it was only during the past eighteen months or so that Henry had begun to appreciate his outstanding talents. He had need of such men, and though this was not in itself sufficient reason for him to marry Seymour's sister, it was an added incentive. The family of whomsoever he married was bound to benefit from the royal alliance; in choosing the Seymour family, Henry would at least get some return for those benefits in the form of the services of Sir Edward Seymour. There was also a promising younger brother, Sir Thomas Seymour, but he had yet to prove himself.

Interesting though these speculations were to Katherine and the Duchess of Suffolk, their main concern lay in the fact reported by Chapuys, namely Jane Seymour's interest in Princess Mary. Of all their former circle at Court, Princess Mary alone remained ostracised and uncared for. Now, if ever, during the feasting and general rejoicing which accompanied the proclamation of Jane Seymour as Queen, was the time to help the Princess, and it was with this in mind that Katherine and the Duchess of Suffolk paid their respects to the new Queen.

As it happened, their intentions had already been anticipated by Chapuys, who, acting on behalf of Princess Mary's cousin, Charles v, Emperor of Spain, had approached Cromwell on the subject of the Princess' release almost as soon as he had heard that Anne Boleyn was in the Tower. His efforts had resulted in a number of visits by Cromwell and other councillors to Beaulieu to test out Princess Mary's willingness to accept the conditions which Henry had laid down for her return to Court. These were that she should acknowledge that Henry was the Supreme Head of the Church of England, and that his divorce from her mother was legal. This meant that she should admit that she was a bastard, with no rights to the Crown, and that she should deny the authority of the Pope. At the first few meetings, Mary flatly refused to do anything of the sort, and her obstinacy provoked some of the councillors to say 'that if she was their daughter, they would beat her and knock her head so violently against the wall that they would make it as soft as baked apples'. Chapuys then tried to speak to Jane Seymour, hoping that she might persuade the King to moderate his conditions, but Henry allowed him only a few minutes of introductory pleasantries with Jane, fearing that in her inexperience she might make some diplomatic gaffe. The ground, then, had been partially prepared when Katherine and the Duchess of Suffolk made their first appearances. Though Chapuys does not report the fact, there seems little doubt that the two women acted in collusion with him, either directly or through the Duchess' mother, Lady Willoughby, whom Chapuys knew well. They also briefed their women friends at Court, and the women then made a concerted effort to get Henry to change his terms. The result was unfortunate. Chapuys reports that the King 'grew desperate with anger', and ordered inquiries to be made 'into certain ladies who were thought to be supporting the Princess's cause'. All that could be proved, however, was that one of them, Lady Husey, had once called Mary 'Princess' a few months before. Lady Husey claimed that it was just a slip of the tongue, but she was sent to the Tower, and it was some weeks before she was released. This was enough to stop Katherine and the Duchess, and all they could now do was to add their persuasions to Mary to conform to the King's wishes. Anything would be better than perpetual imprisonment, and nobody could tell what might happen in the future.

Mary wrote to Chapuys for advice. He told her that nothing would make the King change his mind, and that she should submit to all that she had been asked to do. Her conscience need not be troubled, he consoled her, since the submission would be made under force, and God regarded more the intent than the deed. Mary then subscribed to the articles, writing them out in her own hand at Cromwell's dictation, and as soon as the news arrived at Court 'incredible joy was shown'. Arrangements were promptly made for a secret reunion between father and daughter, and on 6 July 1536 Henry and his new Queen met Mary at Hackney. Queen Jane gave her a splendid diamond, and Henry gave her a thousand crowns in cash 'for her little pleasures'.

'She is now very happy,' Chapuys concluded his report to Charles v, 'especially on account of the goodwill that Cromwell bears her in the promotion of her affairs. She has also desired me to write to your Majesty's ambassador in Rome to procure a secret absolution from the Pope, otherwise her conscience could not be at perfect ease.'

Katherine Parr and the Duchess of Suffolk were equally pleased for their old schoolfriend's sake. Neither woman, at that stage, was particularly religious, and Mary's submission seemed to them to be a small price to pay for freedom. Only one sour voice was raised, and that was from Katherine's brother's father-in-law, the Earl of Essex, who commented that the affair had been 'a game' which would one day cost a lot of people their heads for all the injurious language used against the Princess.

Three days before Mary's secret meeting with her father at Hackney, the social festivities in celebration of the new Queen reached their peak with a triple wedding in which Lord Latimer's cousin, the Earl of Westmorland, married off his son and heir, his eldest daughter, and another younger daughter, respectively to the Earl of Rutland's eldest daughter, the Earl of Oxford's son and heir, and the Earl of Rutland's son and heir.

Katherine Parr, the Duchess of Suffolk, Katherine's sister and her friends, indeed everyone who was anyone was there. It was a magnificent occasion, and after the ceremony, the chronicler, Wriothesley, reports:

> There was a great dinner, and divers great dishes and delicate meats with subtleties, and divers manner of instruments playing at the same, which were too long to express; and after dinner the King's Grace came thither in a mask, riding from York Place, with 11 more with him, whereof the King and 7 more with him wore garments after the Turkish fashion, richly embroidered with gold, with Turkish hats of black velvet and white feathers on their heads and visors on their faces, and four others were arrayed in purple sarcenet, like Turks, which were as their pages, and so they danced with the ladies a good while; and then the King put off his visor and showed himself; and then the King had a great banquet of 40 dishes, wherein was divers subtleties and meats, which was a goodly sight to behold. The banquet ended, the King with his company departed thence, and rode again to York Place in their masks and garments as they had come.

But a month of continual feasting and revels was bound to have its moral casualties among the women at Court. Most were discreetly concealed, but the King's niece, Margaret Douglas, who had been the Duchess of Suffolk's remaining companion at Westhorpe before the death of the French Queen, made no secret of her affair with Lord Thomas Howard, a brother of the Duke of Norfolk. She set the Court agog by claiming that she and her lover were engaged to be married.

The Lady Margaret was then eighteen years old. According to the French Ambassador who had high standards, she was 'beautiful and highly esteemed here'. Henry treated her more like a favourite daughter than a niece, and now that both Princess Elizabeth and Princess Mary had been declared illegitimate, she was indeed in line for the English throne. Apart from this fact, which made any proposed marriages for her a political issue, her choice of a Howard so soon after Anne Boleyn's disgrace was foolish to say the least, and Henry's affection turned to furious anger. The betrothal was immediately annulled, and on 8 July she and her lover were sent to the Tower. An Act was rushed through Parliament making it treason to espouse, or to attempt to espouse, any member of the King's immediate family without his consent given under the Great Seal, and Lord Thomas Howard was then sentenced under this Act to life imprisonment.

A few weeks later, Henry relented slightly and had Margaret Douglas transferred from the Tower to the greater comfort of the monastery at Syon. But her troubles were not over, for it was discovered that she had taken two of Lord Thomas Howard's servants with her. Cromwell, on behalf of the King, demanded an explanation. In her letter answering the charges, Margaret declared that she had done it only 'for the poverty I saw them in, and for no cause else', and went on to complain about how few servants she now had: 'but a gentleman and a groom that keeps my apparel, and another that keeps my chamber, and a chaplain that was with me always in the Court.' Her letter ends:

> And, my Lord, as for resort [company], I promise you I have none except it be gentlewomen that come to see me, nor never had since I came hither; for if any resort of men had come, it should neither have become me to have seen them, nor yet to have kept them company, being a maid as I am. Now, my Lord, I beseech you to be so good as to get my poor servants their wages; and thus I pray Our Lord to preserve you body and soul.
>
> By her that has trust in you,
> Margaret Douglas

Lord Thomas died in the Tower of an ague fifteen months later (October 1537), and Margaret Douglas was then released and restored to favour at Court.

Parliament was dissolved on 18 July 1536, and a few days later Katherine Parr and Lord Latimer returned to Snape Hall. He at least was glad to get away from the political quicksands at Court, and it is recorded that before he left London, he paid his taxes, presumably to ensure that he would be left undisturbed in his Yorkshire retreat.

Katherine, however, did have regrets. It had been an exciting six weeks, and her first tentative efforts with the Duchess of Suffolk to play politics in Princess Mary's case had opened up a view of possibilities which had hitherto been but vague dreams. There was a new atmosphere at Court, a tingling in the air of big things about to happen, and Katherine wanted to be there to play her part. Had she realised what those things were to be, she might have had second thoughts, but all she knew at the time was that major changes were pending, and she envied the position of her brother and sister close to the King and high in his favour. Katherine was a dutiful wife, however, and she could not remain in London while Lord Latimer went north. She therefore contented herself before she left with trying to involve her husband more in the political world of the North Country, in spite of his reluctance to be involved, and a note among Cromwell's memoranda for that period lists Lord Latimer as a possible member of the Duke of Richmond's Council which governed the North of England in the King's name, and of which Katherine's uncle, Sir William Parr of Horton, was a prominent member. The Duke of Richmond died at the end of July, however, and the Council was temporarily dissolved. Nevertheless, Katherine did succeed in obtaining the minor appointment of Lord Latimer as one of three peers nominated to assist at the forthcoming sessions of the York assizes. It was not very much, but it was a beginning from which other more important functions could emerge, and on that optimistic note, Katherine took her place at her husband's side on the long journey back to Snape.

One other important chain of events had its beginning during that eventful summer. This concerned Anne Askew, Katherine's protégée from her Gainsborough days. According to Anne's biographer, Mary Stirling, Katherine Parr introduced Anne at Court before the latter's marriage, which dates the introduction as having occurred during that summer when Anne was sixteen years old. Anne Askew was a lively, attractive girl, and the attention she received in the brilliant surroundings of the Court was a revelation after the dull platitudes of her remote Lincolnshire home. She had ambitions to become a Maid-of-Honour, ambitions which might well have been realised, for her family was well connected and Katherine Parr's support will have counted for much. Unfortunately, after Anne had only been at Court for a month or two, her elder sister, Martha, who had been engaged to be married to one Thomas Kyme, a big Lincolnshire landowner, died, and Anne's father, Sir William Askew, loath to lose such a profitable alliance for his family, forced Anne to come back home and take her sister's place as Thomas Kyme's bride. It was a tragically unhappy marriage. Thomas Kyme was a solid, unimaginative country squire, with no time for learning, and less for a highly educated wife. Anne bore her husband two children, but the bitterness between them reached intolerable proportions, and it was this, plus Katherine Parr's early teaching, which led Anne to become a religious fanatic.

Meanwhile, on her return home, Anne might have had some back-handed consolation for the way in which she had been treated from the fact that on 3 October 1536 her father, going about his business as a commissioner to collect the King's taxes, was seized by an angry mob and brought before a crowd of twenty thousand people outside Caister in the north of Lincolnshire, where they had assembled to demand a redress of their grievances.

It was the signal for the start of an uprising, to become known as the Pilgrimage of Grace, which spread throughout the North of England, and for supporting which Katherine Parr and Lord Latimer came within an inch of losing their lives.

6 The Pilgrimage of Grace

By the execution of Anne Boleyn and her brother, the dismissal of her father, the Earl of Wiltshire, the damping down of Cranmer's religious reforms, and the promotion of the then neutral Seymour family, Henry had brought an end to the party of hawks which he had created among the Humanists. Their purpose had been served: the breach with Rome had been completed without incurring a European crusade against him, the control of the Church in England by the State had been accomplished, and Henry's own position as Supreme Head of both Church and State had been irrefutably established by Act of Parliament, the will of the people. Now was the time to bring on the doves again, to become once more the benevolent Father of his People and reassure a fearful nation that he was as true and good a Christian as any Bishop of Rome. However, he had to go through with the dissolution of the monasteries. Even allowing for the often biased evidence of Cromwell's visitors, Doctors Layton, Leigh, and London, there was no doubt that a very large number of monasteries were corrupt and took from the people far more than they gave. The seizure of their wealth was also a temptation which Henry could not resist.

Nevertheless, when the dissolution got under way during the first half of 1536, there was a general amazement at the sheer numbers of people involved. Chapuys reported to the Emperor's secretary on 8 July:

> It is lamentable to see a legion of monks and nuns, who have been chased from their monasteries, wandering miserably hither and thither seeking means to live, and several honest men have told me that what with monks, nuns, and persons dependent on the monasteries suppressed, there were over 20,000 who knew not how to live. I doubt not that God will one day hear their complaints and avenge them.

In addition to the monks and nuns, there were the beggars and vagrants who had been accustomed to shelter in the monasteries and who now became a charge on the local parishes who had neither the means nor the staff to deal with them. The people, who in any case had been only partially appeased by the slowing down of religious reforms, became increasingly alarmed. Chapuys' reference to the vengeance of God was a very real possibility to their superstitious minds, and there was a rumbling of fear and discontent.

The situation was not helped by the activities of the Court of Augmentations, a new institution which was set up by Act of Parliament early in 1536 to handle the disposal of monastic property. Officially, all property of the dissolved monasteries became the property of the Crown, and the first function of the Court of Augmentations was to record and receive this property in the King's name. A further section of the Act, however, also made the Court responsible for the subsequent disposal of the property to other people, by grants or sales, as authorised by the King. In practice, applications for grants or for the purchase of monastic property had to be made through Cromwell; if approved, the application then had to be processed through the Court of Augmentations. The man appointed to be Chancellor of the new Court was Sir Richard Riche, one of Cromwell's close associates, and equally unscrupulous.

The Humanists, who had fully approved of the dissolution, at least of those monasteries which had been shown to be corrupt, had believed that this redistribution of Church property would be for the benefit of the poor and for the foundation of new schools and colleges, and they had assumed that the Court of Augmentations was to be the means for achieving these ends. They were quickly disillusioned. Within a few months, under Sir Richard Riche's guidance, the Court became instead an instrument for speculations in property, and opened the door to simony and greed on a scale which had seldom been seen before. Sir Richard Riche, in present-day idiom, was a smooth operator, glib of tongue, easy and assured in manner, well-versed in the law, and with no qualms about making as much as he could out of his new appointment. By ensuring that the needs of the King, and of Cromwell, were always satisfied, he made his position secure and proceeded to exploit it to the full. Those who could gain his favour, by whatever means, became wealthy citizens overnight; everyone else suffered interminable delays and exorbitant legal fees in pressing their claims, and often went away empty-handed.

The first real sign that the discontent might erupt into violence came on 28 September, when Cromwell's Commissioners for the dissolution of the monasteries in the North reported that the monks and people of Hexham in Northumberland had taken up arms against them and had thrown them out of the town.

The Privy Council had barely digested this most disturbing news when, on 3 October, they received a panic report from Thomas, Lord Borough of Gainsborough (the eldest son of Katherine Parr's first husband), that some twenty thousand people had risen in Lincolnshire and had seized the King's commissioners for collecting taxes – Sir William Askew, Sir Robert Tyrwhitt, Sir Thomas Misselden, and others.

Under duress, Askew wrote to the King:

> This 3rd October, your commission for levying the second payment of your subsidy, were assembled at Caister. There were, at our coming within a mile of the town, 20,000 of your true and faithful subjects assembled because the report went that all jewels and goods of the churches were to be taken away to your Grace's Council, and the people put to new charges. They swore us to be true to your Grace and to take their parts, and then conveyed us from Caister to Louth, 12 miles distant, where we remain till they know further of your gracious pleasure.

The letter went on to beg the King to issue a general pardon to the rebels, 'or else we be in such danger that we be never like to see your Grace nor our own houses,' and concluded, 'Your said subjects desired us to write that they are at your command for the defence of your person or your realm.'

This was hardly the language of revolutionaries determined to unseat the throne, and Henry's alarm subsided. But three days later Lord Darcy sent an urgent report from his castle at Pontefract that the people of Yorkshire had risen and were marching south, and Christopher Askew, Sir William's cousin, wrote to Cromwell telling him that the Lincolnshire rebels now numbered thirty thousand men. On the next day, 7 October, the Lord Admiral, Sir William Fitzwilliam, reported from Hampshire that there was widespread support for the Lincolnshire rebels.

At this stage, the King and his Council had only a confused picture of what was happening. Messengers were arriving almost hourly, but Henry had not yet appreciated the fact that the most serious trouble was in Yorkshire, and he was far from pleased to receive advice from Lord Darcy at Pontefract that he should proceed with caution and use persuasion rather than force in dealing with the rebels.

From the point of view of Katherine Parr and Lord Latimer, the trouble began, probably on 7 or 8 October, when a crowd of several thousand – the son of Lord Lumley reckoned between eight and ten thousand – assembled outside Snape Hall, demanding to speak with Lord Latimer. They told him that the whole of Richmondshire had risen, but that they lacked commanders to lead them. They begged him to take up their cause and lead them south to join the people from the other Ridings. They explained their grievances: the suppression of the monasteries which dishonoured God and left the poor unrelieved; the Act of Uses, a new law which sought to control bequests made in wills; the new taxes on sheep and cattle which would impoverish them. So far, neither Lord Latimer nor Katherine Parr could afford to be more than mildly sympathetic, but then the people's spokesmen put forward a point which got their full attention. They had written on a paper which they showed Latimer: 'The King takes of his Council, and has about him, persons of low birth and small reputation, who have procured these things [the dissolution of the monasteries and the new taxes] for their own advantage, whom we suspect to be Lord Cromwell and Sir Richard Riche, Chancellor of Augmentations.'

A final article complained about the new bishops appointed in Anne Boleyn's time whom they considered had subverted the true faith of Christ.

Having shown him their grievances, they went on to explain that they understood that a gentleman – they stressed the title *gentleman* – called Robert Aske had summoned a meeting at Skipwith Moor of all who sympathised with these grievances.

Katherine Parr and her family depended wholly on the King; Lord Latimer had been born and bred in the tradition of absolute loyalty to the Crown. They wavered, undecided as to what they should do. The insurgents had made it clear that it was Cromwell and Riche whom they sought to depose; it was they whom they saw as the cause of all their troubles, not the King, to whom they swore full allegiance and whom they thought had been misled by the evil men of low birth around him. While Katherine and her husband debated the situation, undoubtedly attracted by the plan to get rid of Cromwell and Riche, the crowd began to get impatient. They might not have used the same words that they used a week later to the citizens of the City of York, but the threat will have been the same: 'If you will not come with us, we will fight against you and all who stop us.'

Although Lord Latimer claimed later that it was only this threat to his wife and family that made him decide to join the rebels, it seems clear from his subsequent actions as one of their principal leaders that he was also much swayed by the idea, typical of Katherine Parr's political philosophy, that by joining them he might be able to moderate their violence and their plans. His decision was greeted by cheers, and their spokesman swore him in with the following oath:

> Ye shall not enter to this our Pilgrimage of Grace for the commonwealth, but only for the maintenance of God's faith and Church militant, preservation of the King's person and issue, and purifying the nobility of all villein's blood and evil counsellors; to the restitution of Christ's Church and suppression of heretics' opinions, by the holy contents of this Book.

Once having made up his mind to join the Pilgrimage of Grace, Lord Latimer acted fast. He organised the insurgents into a reasonable semblance of a military force, and sent word to Lord Scrope at Bolton and to Lord Lumley, telling them to join him – or else their estates would be destroyed. He failed to persuade either his cousin, the Earl of Westmorland, or the Earl of Cumberland to join him, but everyone else came in, and they set off south to join Robert Aske.

By 9 October, the situation became somewhat clearer to the King and his Council, who were now, for the safety of the King's person, ensconced in Windsor Castle. The Lincolnshire rebels were on their way to Stamford where Katherine Parr's uncle, Sir William Parr, was ready to resist them. The Pilgrimage of Grace insurgents were mustering on Skipwith Moor and from there would march on to York and Pontefract. In the event, the Lincolnshire rising rapidly collapsed.

But meanwhile, events had taken a major turn for the worse in Yorkshire. Unlike the Lincolnshire rebels, who were badly led and uncoordinated, the Pilgrimage of Grace was armed and organised as a disciplined military force. They adopted the banner of St Cuthbert, the patron saint of the North of England, as their symbol, and white uniforms bearing the five red wounds of Christ were provided, as from nowhere, at least for the ten thousand men of the vanguard, and probably for many more of the army which now numbered twenty-eight thousand men on foot and twelve thousand on horse. Robert Aske, a lawyer who had some experience as a military commander, was appointed Captain of the whole army, and Lord Latimer, with his near neighbours, Lord Lumley and Lord Danby, were in command of the vanguard.

By 19 October, the rebels had reached Pontefract Castle, and had found little difficulty in persuading Lord Darcy, who was responsible for its defence, to surrender it to them. Then in his seventieth year, 'Old Tom', as Lord Darcy liked to call himself, was a convinced loyalist, but like the other aristocratic leaders of the Pilgrimage, he too detested the new régime which Cromwell, he was convinced, alone had instigated. Some months later, he told Cromwell to his face:

> Cromwell, it is thou that art the very original and chief causer of all this rebellion and mischief, and art likewise causer of the apprehension of us that be noble men and dost earnestly travail to bring us to our end and strike off our heads, and I trust that before thou die, though thou wouldst procure all noblemen's heads within the realm to be stricken off, yet shall there one head remain that shall strike off thy head.

With Lord Darcy's support added to their already substantial forces, and in control of Pontefract which commanded the main routes north and south, the rebels were in an impregnable position. They outnumbered the King's forces by three to one; they were better armed, better paid, and better led; above all, they were convinced of the justice of their cause. A herald, whom Henry sent to Pontefract on about 20 October, was treated with contempt and forbidden to read the proclamation he had brought. Instead, he had to listen to a harangue by Robert Aske and was forced to accept a signed statement of their grievances to be taken back to the King.

In this situation, the Duke of Norfolk, commanding the Government troops, believed that he had no choice but to try to negotiate with the rebels. On 25 October, he received Henry's permission to treat, and informed Henry that he was now riding in advance of his troops to join the Earl of Shrewsbury at Doncaster. He might, he added, make false promises to the rebels to induce them to disperse.

Norfolk's plan was successful in that it prevented the rebels from launching an attack on Shrewsbury's army, but in carrying it out he was forced to agree in principle to all their major demands – the restoration of the abbeys, a Parliament to be held immediately at York, and the redress of their other main grievances. Robert Aske and Lord Latimer were the chief spokesmen for the rebels, but it was Lord Latimer who arranged the one vital requirement from Henry's point of view at that moment, namely, the dispersal of the rebel army. This was agreed on condition that Norfolk first disbanded the King's army, and that two emissaries would be accepted at Court to arrange a full conference within a month to confirm the settlement made with Norfolk. On 28 October both armies withdrew.

The taste of defeat was bitter to Henry. He refused to accept that Norfolk could not have struck a better bargain, and he was incensed that he should have disbanded the army without his permission. Norfolk defended himself by blaming Shrewsbury for advancing too far north, where the plague, the cold, and the lack of food made it impossible to fight, and by impugning Lord Darcy whom he called 'a most arrant traitor'. Henry was not satisfied, and in a second letter, written a month later, Norfolk told the Council that it was their fault for putting him, Norfolk, in charge. He was, he said, 'an old, forgetful fool, more meet to sit in a chair by the fire than to mayne [meddle] in such great affairs'. With the Duke of Suffolk engaged in preserving the peace in Lincolnshire, however, there was nobody else that the Northerners would trust, and the Duke of Norfolk remained in command.

During the month that elapsed between the dispersal of the armies at Pontefract and the conferences planned to be held at Doncaster, however, there was time for the husbands to go home and consult with their families and friends. In the case of the Latimers at Snape, it may be presumed that Katherine Parr received news from her contacts at Court. In one sense the news would have been good. As a result of her uncle's actions at Stamford, the only successful military stand made by the King's forces, Katherine Parr's family stood higher than ever in the King's esteem. Against this had to be set the fact that Lord Latimer had played a leading rôle on the side of the Pilgrimage of Grace. The key political factor was whether Cromwell could be brought down or not. If he did fall, then all would be well; if not, his notorious thirst for vengeance would put the lives of all who had opposed him in jeopardy.

On this point the news was bad. Henry had taken the rebellion as a direct challenge to his authority, and if he were to sacrifice Cromwell at this stage, he would be surrendering a part of that authority. Whatever the justice of the charges against him, therefore, Cromwell was, if anything, more secure than ever before. The alternative possibility of bringing down the King himself was unthinkable. His popularity, and the deep respect, almost awe, in which he was held from the highest to the lowest in the land would have doomed any such attempt from the start.

It was a delicate position for Katherine Parr and her husband. On the one hand, Lord Latimer was already under some suspicion from the more militant members of the Pilgrimage of Grace for making the settlement by which their army had been disbanded. By now they could have been in London, holding Cromwell and the Council by the throat. On the other hand, it was by no means certain that Henry had appreciated what Latimer had done on his behalf. This, however, was where Katherine Parr could, and surely did, help her husband, through her brother and sister who were both with the King at Court. The evidence of her success is in the instructions which Henry issued for the meeting at Doncaster and in which he specifically names Lord Latimer as being the man on the rebel's side most likely to help the King's cause.

Meanwhile, preparations for the meeting at Doncaster had been proceeding on both sides. On behalf of the King, accusations were made that the rebels had not fully disbanded, and the Duke of Norfolk was ordered to threaten Lord Darcy that unless he succeeded in tricking Robert Aske to surrender himself, he, Lord Darcy, would be accused of treason. Darcy hotly denied the accusations against him, and refused as a matter of honour to have any part in an underhand plot against Aske. On the rebel side, there seems little doubt that some of the militants had kept a few bands of troops intact, but the main action was an internal meeting at York to elect their spokesmen and decide on their policy. At this meeting, the pro-Papal clergy played a much bigger part than hitherto. In addition to the restoration of the monasteries, they demanded the abolition of heresy laws against Roman Catholics, the restoration of Papal supremacy, the legitimisation of the Princess Mary, and death by burning for anti-Catholic heretics, including the newly created bishops (Cranmer, Hugh Latimer and Shaxton). The rebels agreed to the addition of these demands, but excluded the clergy from acting as spokesmen. They chose instead Lord Latimer, Lord Scrope, Lord Lumley and Lord Darcy, to be supported by Robert Aske in the background. The King's delegation was headed by the Duke of Norfolk, supported by the Earl of Shrewsbury, the Earl of Rutland, Sir William Fitzwilliam (Lord Admiral), Sir John (later Lord) Russell and four others. The date of the meeting was fixed for 4 December 1536.

On 2 December, Henry issued his final instructions to the delegation. Norfolk and Fitzwilliam were to be the principal spokesmen. After a suitable delay, Henry told them, in which they would pretend to be soliciting him on the rebels' behalf, they could grant a general pardon. If strongly pressed, and after a yet longer delay for a pretended consultation with the King, they could agree to a special Parliament to be held in September the following year at a place which would be chosen by the King. Nothing else was to be granted without the King's written and explicit consent. Sir John Russell, who brought these instructions as the King's personal messenger, also held the pardons already signed and sealed, but he was instructed not to deliver them unless all the above conditions were fulfilled.

Overnight, the venue of the meeting appears to have been changed to Pontefract Castle, some fourteen miles from Doncaster, and on 4 December the meeting began with the case for the Pilgrimage of Grace. It consisted mainly of a lengthy accusation against Cromwell for the way in which he had controlled the election of members for the Parliament which had passed the laws to which they now objected. The rebels claimed that this Parliament had not been representative, and they demanded a new Parliament which would fairly, and without interference, put forward their views. They also accused Cromwell of molesting people for his own private gain. This was followed by the presentation of the exceptionally long list of their grievances which now began with the demands formulated by the clergy.

Norfolk and the rest of the King's delegates appear to have been nonplussed by the scope and force of the rebels' arguments, and hastily sent to the King for further instructions. Henry replied on 8 December. He told them to reject the rebels' demands, and he chided them for being so weak and down-hearted as not to pursue their two main aims, namely to except from the pardon some persons to be punished as an example to the rest and retain control over the suppression of the monasteries. He insisted that the information which was reaching him from all parts of the country was that the people wanted peace, and that he did not for one minute believe that the rebels were as firm as they seemed to be. He insisted further that they must be brought to obedience without conditions, otherwise he would put them down by force.

Henry's reading of the situation was correct. The majority of the rebels did not want another confrontation, which, now that the King had had ample time to muster his forces properly, they might well lose. There is some evidence that Lord Latimer stepped in and cut out the militant clergy who were the main stumbling block to reaching an agreement. Lord Latimer's brother, Marmaduke Neville, who was in Lord Latimer's retinue at the meeting, later stated that there were strong suspicions about the King's good faith, and that 'evil disposed persons' had put about the rumour that any pardon would except certain people. They said that they should 'all die on a day rather than to lose the worst upon the field [i.e., no obtain their demands] and that if they called us traitors, we could call them heretics'. Neville also stated that it was all the gentlemen could do to restrain them. 'We thought we should be fain [forced] to divide, calling all them that were disposed to take the King's most gracious pardon to come to a side.'

Reason prevailed, and on 9 December, the rebels humbly sought the King's forgiveness.

A fortnight later, Cromwell wrote to the Bishop of Winchester (Stephen Gardiner) who was then in France:

> As to the making of conditions, it is true that conditions were demanded by the rebels, but in the end they submitted entirely to the King's pleasure with the greatest repentance. Their chief article next their pardon was for a Parliament to confirm it, but they remitted the appointment of the same wholly to the King. My Lord of Norfolk is now going thither [to York], as the King's Lieutenant [of the North], and will have a Council as the Duke of Richmond had.

Henry graciously granted a general pardon, with no exceptions, for all offences committed before 9 December, and commanded Robert Aske to come and see him immediately after Christmas. He trusted that Aske would discuss the whole affair frankly and plainly with him, and he assured Aske that he need have no fear since he would be under full protection of the general pardon. Lord Latimer was also sent for, or obtained permission, to wait on Henry at Court at the end of December.

In spite of all the show of peace and goodwill, there were still many men in the North of England who were dissatisfied. Their greatest disappointment was that Cromwell had survived. As long as he was alive there would be no trust in the Government, and there was a widespread belief that the general pardon was not worth the paper it was written on. On 26 December, less than three weeks after the meeting at Pontefract, the Mayor of Newcastle wrote to a friend: 'There are yet very liberal sayings in Richmondshire and Yorkshire.' A week later, the Earl of Westmorland was warned of a new rising at Auckland, in the Bishopric of Durham.

The news reached London two days later, on 4 January. Fearing that this new rising might be the signal for another general uprising, Robert Aske received Henry's permission to break off their discussions and hurried north to stop it. He had been delighted, one might say charmed, using the word in its literal sense, by his meetings with the King. Henry had treated him almost as an equal. They had sat down alone together, and man to man had thrashed out the truth behind the Pilgrimage of Grace and its causes. According to Aske, the King had shown himself a man of rare wisdom and tolerance, sympathetic to the problems of the North, and had promised to remedy their grievances. On arrival in Yorkshire, Aske circulated a statement to all his former colleagues:

> Loving neighbours, the King by mouth has declared to me that the pardon granted at Doncaster shall extend to all, and that your reasonable petitions shall be ordered by Parliament. His Grace, for the love he bears to this country, intends to keep Parliament at York and to have the Queen crowned there. His Grace esteems the commonwealth of the realm and the love of his subjects more than any other earthly riches and will send down the Duke of Norfolk to minister justice till his coming.

Aske's words had some success in restraining the people of Beverley, one of the centres of the new revolt, but on 9 January, the Earl of Shrewsbury reported to Henry that more people were rising again, and he suggested that he should postpone the collection of taxes which was just about to begin.

On the 12th, Aske reported the causes of the new revolt to the King. Certain ships had arrived at Hull with stores for Lent, but the rumour spread that the ships had brought materials to fortify Hull and Scarborough which were to be used to support the Duke of Norfolk who was said to be marching northwards with twenty thousand men. The people had further believed that the King did not intend to honour the general pardon nor to settle their grievances, but Aske thought that he had now put a stop to the rumours and he hoped there would be no more trouble.

Aske, however, was over-optimistic. Four days after he had written to Henry, one John Hallam, urged on by Sir Francis Bigod, an intellectual from Lord Latimer's district in Richmondshire, made an attempt to seize Hull. He was betrayed and the mayor had him seized as he entered the city. Hallam's attempt, however, added fuel to the rumours, and within two days bands of men were gathering together, this time not only in Yorkshire and Durham, but throughout the Northern counties. Newcastle refused to pay its taxes, and Aske appealed to the King to send the Duke of Norfolk to the North as soon as possible. He pointed out that he had not yet received any written confirmation of what the King had told him, and that without any such letter he was having great difficulty in persuading the people to believe him.

Lord Latimer, like many other noblemen from the North, was still in London, showing his loyalty to the King and trying to appease Cromwell, but on receipt of the news from Yorkshire, on 18 January, the King told him to go back home and restore order. On his way, and uncertain as to how successful he had been with Cromwell, Lord Latimer wrote to a friend at Court:

> Recommend me to my Lord Privy Seal [Cromwell], showing him I was sorry the people spake otherwise than became them of him. For though he be in favour of the King, it letteth not [does not prevent] his Grace to grant what he pleases to the people, and I think his lordship [Cromwell] would not be a hinderer of such of their desires as reasonable. Though I durst not much contrary them, I did my best to reduce them to conformity to the King's pleasure. My being among them was a very painful and dangerous time to me; I pray God I may never see such again.
>
> from Royston [Hertfordshire], returning homewards
>
> by the King's command.

The principal ringleader of the new revolt was the man who had urged Hallam to attack Hull, Sir Francis Bigod. A scholar and very much a man of the New Learning, Sir Francis Bigod was a close acquaintance of Katherine Parr and her husband, with whom he had been in the process of making an agreement for the marriage of his son to Lord Latimer's daughter, Margaret Neville. His taking up of the cause of the new revolt seemed out of character and was totally unexpected. Nor, in his case, was there any question of being forced into it. In a letter which he wrote to Sir Robert Constable, one of the big landowners in Yorkshire, on 18 January 1537, he explained that the people had in fact been highly suspicious of him because of his 'learning and conversation' and because of his association with those whom the people judged to be the enemies of Christ's Church and the commonwealth. He appears indeed

96

to have been motivated not by any religious beliefs, but by the liberal Humanist teaching that a man's first duty was to his fellow-men. He was convinced that the people had been tricked by the King, and he was their self-appointed leader to save them. His letter to Sir Robert Constable continues:

They [the people] have now the greatest confidence in me. Now messengers come from the Bishopric [Durham], Richmondshire, and the West, for me to go forward with the commons, especially to bring John Hallam, whom the Mayor of Hull has imprisoned, to their great offence. I have sworn to go with the commons having good reason to doubt the Duke of Norfolk is coming rather to bring them to captivity like those of Lincolnshire than to fulfil our petitions.

But Bigod found himself rejected by the rest of the Northern nobility.

The people, however, had no intention of letting the matter drop. On about the same day as Sir Francis Bigod was writing to Sir Robert Constable, Katherine Parr, alone with her husband's children in Snape Hall, found herself surrounded by an angry mob demanding to know what Lord Latimer was doing in London. Why had he deserted them? What new trickery was afoot? Terrified, she tried to reason with them, but they would not listen and demanded to be let into the house or else they would burn it to the ground. Katherine had no option but to surrender, and she stood by while the men roamed through the rooms, taking an inventory of their contents. They did little damage, and Katherine and the children were unmolested, but the threat was effective, and Katherine got a message through to her husband to make all haste to come and rescue them.

Katherine's message reached Lord Latimer on 20 January at Stamford in Lincolnshire. His reactions were complex. He did not wish to find himself once more forced to join the rebels, who were now, according to a handbill which had been posted up the day before in the town of Richmond, more ready than ever to resort to violence. The handbill stated 'that the commons in every township should rise on pain of death and make all lords and gentlemen swear on the mass book' to a number of articles:

1 To maintain the profit of the Holy Church, which was the upholding of the Christian faith.
2 That no Lord nor gentleman take anything of their tenants but their rents.

3   To put down the Lord Cromwell, that heretic, and all his sect, the which made the King put down praying and fasting.

4   That no Lord nor gentleman go to London.

'If any Lord or gentleman,' the handbill continued, 'refuse this oath, to put him to death and put the next of his blood in his place, and if he deny it, to put him to death likewise, and so on.'

He had an excuse for keeping clear in that he had been instructed to assist the Duke of Norfolk in restoring order in the North, but on the other hand he could not leave Katherine and his children at the mercy of the rebels. He wrote to another friend at Court, Sir William Fitzwilliam, the Lord Admiral, for advice. After explaining how he came to be at Stamford, Lord Latimer continued:

> Now, at Stamford, I learn that the commons of Richmondshire, grieved at my coming up [to London], have entered my house at Snape and will destroy it if I come not home shortly. If I do not please them, I know not what they will do with my body and goods, wife and children. I beg to know the King's pleasure and shall follow the same whatsoever come of it, likewise as I adventured my coming up [to London] now.

Somewhat pathetically, and clearly wishing to be rid of the whole dangerous business, Lord Latimer ended his letter:

> If it were the King's pleasure that I might live on such small lands as I have in the South [Wyke Hall, in Worcestershire], I would little care for my lands in the North.

from Stamford, 20th of January, 1537. John Lord Latimer

There is no record of any reply to Lord Latimer's letter, but it can be inferred from a number of other reports that he did go to Snape and managed to rescue Katherine and the children while his brother, William Neville, and their neighbours, Gregory Conyers and Roger Middlewood, created a diversion by a direct attack on Sir Francis Bigod. The attack was unsuccessful, but Katherine Parr and the children were brought to safety to another of Lord Latimer's houses near Malton, some seventeen miles from York.

The worst aspect of Sir Francis Bigod's rising was that it gave Cromwell (and, one must suppose, the King) the opportunity to revoke the general pardon for the Pilgrimage of Grace. Even though the leaders of the Pilgrimage had proved themselves innocent of any complicity in the new rising, the majority had in any case been in London when it started and all had tried to stop it, all had had some contact with the rebels, and this could be construed as a new treason committed after 9 December, the limiting date of the general pardon. Whether or not Sir Francis Bigod's original fears concerning the Duke of Norfolk's mission to the North could be justified, therefore, his actions made those fears come true.

The Duke arrived at Doncaster on 2 February. He travelled with a train of some two hundred staff and servants, and he was accompanied by Katherine Parr's brother, William Parr. Lord Latimer went to Doncaster to meet them. At this stage, Katherine Parr's whole attention would have been riveted on protecting her husband, and it was clear that whatever their neighbours might think of them, Lord Latimer had to do all in his power to help the King's Lieutenant, the Duke of Norfolk, if he was to overcome not only the stigma of his part in the Pilgrimage of Grace, but also, now, that of the disloyalty of his tenants at Snape. The presence of William Parr in close attendance on the Duke seems part of the plan and is not likely to have been accidental; he had some excuse for being there on account of his interest in his Westmorland property, but the main impression is of the Parr family rallying solidly to the help of Katherine and her husband.

In a report which he sent to the Earl of Sussex on 4 February, the Duke of Norfolk showed that he had been much impressed by Lord Latimer's waiting upon him at Doncaster. He pointed out that Lord Latimer had not been bound to do so until he, the Duke, reached York, and it enabled the Duke to write back that he thought no man was ever more welcome to the gentlemen of Yorkshire than himself. Lord Latimer appears to have made excuses for his neighbours, for the Duke went on to say that Lord Conyers and others from Richmondshire had been prevented by the rebels from coming to him, but that he, the Duke, had sent 'such sharp messages' to Middleham and Richmond that he thought the rebels would be afraid to hold the meeting they had planned.

Cromwell was not impressed. His comment on the Duke's report has not been preserved, but from the Duke's letter to him, written from York on 9 February, Cromwell must have warned him against associating too closely with Papists. The Duke of Norfolk indignantly replied that all the gentlemen and substantial yeomen of the shire would bear him witness that he was neither a Papist nor a favourer of traitors. Cromwell, however, seems to have feared that the Duke might prove too weak a tool for the vicious revenge he had planned for his enemies, and, from the safety of London, he continued to snipe at the Duke. On 11 February, the Duke happily reported that Sir Francis Bigod had been captured at Carlisle, but instead of the praise he expected, he received another taunt from Cromwell. The Duke waxed hot and told Cromwell that 'dreadful execution' had been begun at York. Eight ringleaders had been convicted and were to be hanged in chains at various places in the city. Four days later, on 16 February, the Duke arrived at Richmond and the rebels there dispersed. He was still smarting under Cromwell's jibes, and on the same day he reported that he had sent a force out under Sir Thomas Wharton, the captain of Carlisle Castle, utterly to destroy the rebels and their property in Westmorland. 'Now shall appear,' he wrote to Cromwell, 'whether for favour of these countrymen I forbore to fight with them at Doncaster, as the King showed me had been said.'

The Duke's efforts were successful, and within a week he was able to report that seven hundred rebels had been killed, many more had been captured, and he was now trying the captives under martial law at Carlisle. In a report written on 21 February, he added his opinion that Westmorland had been very badly handled in the past by excessive taxes, enclosures and oppressions 'which, as I and all others here think, was the only cause of this rebellion'. On the following day, before he could have received this last report, the King wrote personally to the Duke. He thanked him for his services thus far, and he told him he was now assured of his determination to put down Papists. He instructed the Duke to apply civil, not martial law, and ordered him to 'cause such dreadful execution upon a good number of inhabitants, hanging them on trees, quartering them, and setting their heads and quarters in every town, as shall be a fearful warning, whereby shall ensue the preservation of a great multitude'.

The main ringleaders, including Sir Francis Bigod, were to be sent to London.

Two days later, on 24 February, the Duke of Norfolk reported that seventy-four rebels from Westmorland, Cumberland and Cockermouth, were being executed. He thought this was more than had ever been done at one time before, and he stated that more than six thousand people had been involved in the rebellion. It is not known whether or not it was the Duke who also sent another document, thought to be of the same date, from Carlisle, but it is highly probable. It stated that Sir Francis Bigod, in his confession, accused Cromwell of having arranged the conviction of Lord Thomas Howard, the Duke of Norfolk's brother, so that he, Cromwell, might himself marry the King's niece, Margaret Douglas. Sending such a document up to London was a nice touch, calculated to make Cromwell pause before he threw any more darts at the Duke.

While the Duke of Norfolk was subduing Bigod's rebellion in the North, the Duke of Suffolk and Katherine Parr's uncle, Sir William Parr of Horton, were busy settling affairs in Lincolnshire. Here, too, the minor leaders were taken into custody, and in a succession of trials presided over by Sir William Parr from the middle of February to the first week in March, thirty-four men were condemned to death. One prisoner, Sir William reported, pleaded his case so well that if the King's solicitor and sergeant-at-law had not argued even more cleverly against him, Sir William might have been obliged to acquit all the prisoners. He now intended, so he informed the King, to be personally present at the executions.

The noblemen who had led the Pilgrimage of Grace, challenging Henry's authority and charging Cromwell with corruption, were, however, still at large. Given sufficiently convincing proof of their repentance and future co-operation, Henry might, just conceivably, have been content to let things be, but Cromwell never let an insult or an injury go unavenged. Legally the general pardon had covered their activities, but only up to 9 December. For Cromwell, therefore, it was simply a matter of procuring evidence of offences committed after this date. He tried to compel the Duke of Norfolk to help him, but all the Duke would do was to persuade Robert Aske to go up to London. In letters which Katherine Parr's brother, William Parr, brought to the Court for him, the Duke told Cromwell that he had strong suspicions about Lord Darcy and Sir Robert Constable, but could find no proof. He added that the bearer of his letters, young William Parr, 'has handled himself wisely in this business'.

Undeterred, Cromwell went into action. By the beginning of April, Robert Aske, Lord Darcy, Lord Husey, Sir Robert Constable, Sir Thomas Percy (brother of the Earl of Northumberland), Sir John Bulmer and Margaret Cheyney (Sir John Bulmer's wife 'by untrue matrimony'), and

George Lumley, a neighbour of the Latimers, were all in the Tower. The Duke of Norfolk had intervened to save Gregory Conyers, another neighbour of the Latimers, on the grounds that he had been instrumental in the capture of Sir Francis Bigod.

Lord Darcy and Lord Husey were tried and found guilty by their peers on 15 May, and the rest were tried and found guilty by a jury of which young William Parr was a member. Most were executed during the last week of May, the men being hanged and quartered, the one woman, Margaret Cheyney, being burnt, but Lord Darcy was left to contemplate his sins until 30 June, when he was beheaded at the Tower, and Lord Husey, Aske, and Sir Robert Constable were sent to York or Hull to be executed there as an example to the people.

So far Katherine Parr and her husband had avoided Cromwell's attentions, but in the course of Cromwell's search for evidence against the nobles, Lord Latimer's name came up on a number of occasions. His brother, Marmaduke Neville, had been arrested in January by the Earl of Oxford for boasting that the leaders of the Pilgrimage of Grace knew the King's orders to the Duke of Norfolk even before the Duke had received them. Katherine Parr, unlike the Countess of Westmorland, had failed to stop the rebels at Snape and had let them into the house. One of Lord Latimer's servants had been in contact with Bigod. George Lumley, one of those executed, had given evidence of how Lord Latimer had forced his father, Lord Lumley, to join the Pilgrimage. One of Lord Latimer's bailiffs had been a ringleader of the rebels in Lancashire. Another witness said that if Lord Latimer had not gone to London after Christmas there would have been no rebellion. There was also the proposed marriage between Lord Latimer's daughter and Bigod's son.

Compared with the evidence against some of those who had been brought to trial and convicted, this was more than enough to justify action against Lord Latimer, and sometime before the end of May, Cromwell informed the Duke of Norfolk of his suspicions. The Duke replied on 2 June. He thanked Cromwell for telling him that 'the King' did not much favour Lord Latimer, and asked what he was meant to do about it.

The Duke took two weeks to make up his mind. The Parrs were no ordinary family. Katherine's uncle, brother and sister, stood very high indeed in the King's favour; Katherine herself always received a warm welcome when she attended at Court. The Duke might well one day require their help. In the end, he compromised. On 16 June, he wrote to Cromwell that he had contrived, 'with Mr Pollard's help', to persuade Lord Latimer to go to London 'as a suitor on his own affairs'. He added, however, that he had not been able to find any evidence that Lord Latimer had done anything wrong except under the threat of violence. 'No man,' the Duke wrote, 'was in more danger of his life.'

The Latimers arrived in London towards the end of June. Katherine's brother and sister were both at Court, and they welcomed Katherine with the news that it had just been confirmed that Queen Jane Seymour was three months pregnant. This, they explained to Katherine, had put the King in an exceptionally cheerful mood, not only because it was excellent news in itself, but also because it gave him a much-wanted excuse for putting off his proposed visit to York. There was no more talk of trials or executions, and the time could hardly be better for Katherine to approach Henry personally on behalf of herself and her husband. In confirmation of the Duke of Norfolk's findings, she could give the King a vivid eye-witness account of the extreme pressures to which she and Lord Latimer had been subjected. Their only alternative would have been death, which might have been more honourable, but then Lord Latimer would not have been able to have done all that he had done to further the King's cause within the rebel camp. They had no quarrel with Cromwell, indeed they had gone out of their way to make it very clear that they strongly disapproved of the rebel complaints against him, and Cromwell was mistaken if he thought that they had acted from any other motives than those they had explained. It was a plain statement of facts, and Katherine should simply ask Henry to judge her and her husband on those facts.

Henry knew Katherine well. He doubted her expressions of goodwill towards Cromwell, but the formal words of respect were correct, and he was sure that the rest of her story was true. Moreover, the loyalty of the Parr family as a whole was beyond question, and Henry did not wish to weaken or alienate that loyalty by throwing Katherine and her husband to the wolves. To Cromwell's intense chagrin, he cancelled the order for their arrest, and agreed only that Lord Latimer's name should be struck off the list of proposed members of the new Council of the North.

Katherine's relief was beyond words. To her, the whole affair had been a political nightmare from which she and Lord Latimer had been lucky to escape with their lives. Yet, her success in handling Henry and outmanœuvring Cromwell had been no small achievement, and though her nerves were frayed to breaking point, there was a secret thrill of pleasure at her triumph. It gave her a new sense of confidence in her understanding of men and politics, and when, towards the end of July, she and Lord Latimer gratefully headed west to the haven of Wyke Hall in Worcestershire, she felt there was no crisis she could not overcome.

7 The Fall of Cromwell

On 12 October 1537 Queen Jane gave birth to the son for whom Henry had been waiting for so long. There was at last no doubt as to the child's legitimacy. Whether Henry's previous marriages had been legal or not, both his former wives were dead before his marriage with Jane Seymour, nor was there any question of consanguinity. Bonfires were lit throughout England, free wine and beer were provided for the citizens of London for a week, and on 15 October, amid scenes of wildly rejoicing crowds, the infant was christened Prince Edward. The ceremony took place at Hampton Court, but, because of fear of the plague, there was a severe restriction on the numbers allowed to attend, and of the Parr family, only Anne was present.

Nine days later, at noon on 24 October, to Henry's intense grief Queen Jane died, either from pneumonia or puerperal fever. But apart from Henry, few showed any signs of sorrow. The position of Queen of England was vacant once more, and everyone's first thoughts were about who was to fill it. At home, the vacancy offered possibilities of a repetition of the same sort of bid for power which the Boleyns, and to a lesser extent the Seymours, had exploited; abroad, it opened up new approaches for diplomatic alliances. Temporarily bemused by Jane Seymour's death, Henry left everything to Cromwell.

Cromwell moved fast. Since he had only two months before married his son, Gregory, to Jane Seymour's sister, Elizabeth,[1] the only woman in England he might have trusted in the position of Queen, he summoned an immediate meeting of the Council and, forestalling any hopes any of them might have had, obliged them to agree to use the situation for diplomatic moves in Europe. With the Pope urging all and sundry to mount a crusade against England, and with the ever-present fear of an alliance between Spain and France, none could deny the force of Cromwell's arguments, and private ambitions were suppressed in favour of the national interest. The dissolution of the monasteries was rapidly making Henry the richest monarch in Europe, and an alliance with him, through marriage, was a bait which could be dangled with great effect before both the Spanish Emperor, Charles v, and the French King, Francis 1, preventing, or at least postponing, the joint attack they were thought to be planning against England. Sir John Dudley, a new star at Court, who had begun to make a name for himself as a result of outstanding service in the King's navy, was sent to join Sir Thomas Wyatt to open negotiations with Charles v, and Gardiner, the Bishop of Winchester, already resident at the French Court, was instructed to sound out Francis.

In a letter to Gardiner, Cromwell explained the situation as far as France was concerned. He told him to tell Francis that:

The Queen, by the neglect of those about her who suffered her to take cold and eat such things as her fancy in sickness called for, is dead. The King, though he takes this chance reasonably, is little disposed to marry again, but some of his Council have thought it meet for us to urge him to it for the sake of his realm, and he has framed his mind both to be indifferent [impartial] to the thing and to the election of any person from any part that with deliberation shall be thought meet. Two persons in France might be thought on, namely the French King's daughter (said to be not the meetest) and Madame de Longueville [Mary of Guise], of whose qualities you are to inquire, and also on what terms the King of Scots stands with either of them. Lord William[2] must not return without ascertaining this, but the inquiry must be kept secret.

On the Emperor's side, the bait consisted not only of a wife for Henry, but also of a husband for Princess Mary. The young widowed Duchess of Milan, the Emperor's niece, was a possibility for Henry, and the Infant of Portugal was suggested for Princess Mary. As the Duchess of Milan was on her way to stay with the Emperor's sister, Regent of the Low Countries, Henry's ambassador in Brussels, John Hutton, was brought into the picture as well and was asked to report on the Duchess and any other possibilities in Flanders. All these letters and instructions were sent off by Cromwell within a few days of Jane Seymour's death and more than a week before her funeral, which took place with elaborate ceremonial on 12 November.

Replies started coming in early in December. John Hutton was one of the first to report. He offered Henry, who was then in his forty-sixth year, the following possibilities from the Court in Brussels:

There is in the Court waiting upon the Queen [Mary, the Emperor's sister] the daughter of the Lord of Brederode, 14 years old and of a goodly stature, virtuous, sad [serious], and womanly. Her mother, who is dead, was daughter to the Cardinal of Liege's sister, and the Cardinal would give her a good dote [dowry]. There is the widow of the late Earl of Egmond, who repairs often to Court. She is over 40, but does not look it. There is the Duchess of Milan who is reported a goodly personage and of excellent beauty. The Duke of Cleves has a daughter, but there is no great praise either of her personage or her beauty.

Hutton ended his report by apologising for his lack of knowledge of ladies, but said that he had written the truth as best he could. Five days later, he followed his report up with a more detailed description of Christina, the widowed Duchess of Milan. 'She is 16 years old,' he wrote, 'very tall, taller than the Regent, of competent beauty, soft of speech, and gentle in countenance.' She normally spoke French, but she could also speak Italian and High German. In a postscript, he added: 'She is not so pure white as the late Queen, whose soul God pardon, but she hath a singular good countenance, and when she chanceth to smile there appeareth two pits in her cheeks and one in her chin, the which becometh her right excellently well.'

It had been suggested that the King should marry the Duchess, and that Princess Mary should marry the son and heir of the Duke of Cleves.

The news from France was less encouraging. The French King said that Henry could have any lady in France for a wife except the one he wanted, Mary of Guise, as she had already been promised to the King of Scotland. Apart from the fact that it was a continuing part of English policy to try to disrupt alliances between France and Scotland, the refusal was enough to rouse Henry's interest. He instructed the Bishop of Winchester to urge Francis to break off the negotiations with Scotland, claiming that the marriage contract had not yet been ratified and that Francis was under no obligation to fulfil it. Francis hesitated. Henry's reported wealth was a matter for serious thought, and Francis instructed Castillon, his ambassador in London, to play for time. On 30 December, Castillon reported back that Henry was on fire for Mary of Guise and would not take no for an answer. He was big in person, he had told Castillon, and had need of a big wife. The next day Castillon wrote again to the French Court and warned them that they were playing too dangerous a game with Henry. Unless they were prepared to break the alliance with Scotland, they must squash Henry's hopes at once and make it clear that Mary of Guise was not available, 'for the King of England would have given half his kingdom for her'. With many regrets,

Francis took his ambassador's advice and politely but firmly told Henry that he could not, and would not, break the agreement with Scotland.

(It is one of the more fascinating hypothetical questions of history to consider what might have happened if Henry's suit for Mary of Guise had been accepted. The mother of Mary Queen of Scots was possibly the most formidable woman of her times, but it was to be her misfortune to be cast in a rôle where her exceptional talents and strength of character were to be half lost in the murk of Scottish politics. Had she married Henry, the situation would have been very different, and the imagination gasps at the probable effect of the combination of two such overwhelming personalities. The marriage might not have lasted long, but, while it was in force, the whole of Europe would have trembled.)

Against the setback in France, Sir John Dudley's mission to Charles v was highly successful. The Emperor declared himself delighted at the prospect of Henry's marriage to his niece. There was a slight difficulty in that she had of course been related to his aunt, the late Catharine of Aragon, but the Emperor felt sure that a dispensation to allow the marriage could be readily obtained.

The main effect of Cromwell's diplomatic activities, however, was to shake Henry out of the lethargy into which he had fallen ever since Jane Seymour's death. This had been so marked that the country was alive with rumours that in fact the King was dead, but at the beginning of 1538 he bounced back into the political arena with all his former energy. His particular skill in the art of government was to juggle with three or four different, and preferably conflicting, policies at the same time. It was the method he used for confusing his enemies – and bewildering his friends – while he either waited for new developments or made up his mind as to the best course of action. He now proceeded to exercise this skill as brilliantly as ever before. At home, Cranmer was encouraged and allowed to step up the reformation of the Church by ordering an English translation of the Bible to be placed in every church and by abolishing the countless holy relics and trick images with which the old style of priests had preyed on the minds of a superstitious people. At the same time, pro-Catholics like the Bishop of Winchester and the Duke of Norfolk suddenly found themselves back in favour. Abroad, the German Protestants were invited to send a delegation to England to negotiate England's possible membership of their League and to discuss matters of religion, while at the same time English missions on the Continent pursued alliances, separately, with Spain and France. Within a matter of months, Henry had everybody guessing, even Cromwell, as to what his real intentions were.

Meanwhile, in spite of all this activity, Cromwell had not forgotten Katherine Parr and her husband. Katherine's success in avoiding arrest had pricked his pride, and while the Latimers were recuperating in the peace of their Worcestershire home, he had cast around for some way to make them pay for his humiliation at their hands. His first move was to commandeer Lord Latimer's house in the Charterhouse for a friend. It was a petty act of revenge which he knew the Latimers would not dare to resist, and the following letter, in which Lord Latimer replied to Cromwell's demand, gave Cromwell the pleasure of knowing that he had drawn blood:

To the Right Honourable and very especial good Lord, my Lord Privy Seal.
After my most hearty recommendations to your good Lordship.
Whereas your Lordship doth desire for one of your friends my house within Charterhouse Churchyard beside London, I assure your Lordship the getting of a lease of it cost me 100 marks, besides other pleasures [improvements] that I did to the house, for it was much my desire to have it, because it stands in good air out of the press of the city. And I do always lie there when I come to London, and I have no other house to lie at. And also I have granted it to farm to Mr Newdigate, son and heir of Sergeant Newdigate, to lie in the said house in my absence, and he to void [leave] whensoever I come up to London. Nevertheless, I am contented, if it can do your Lordship any pleasure for your friend, that he lie there forthwith. I seek my lodgings at this Michaelmas Term myself.
And as touching my lease, I assure your Lordship it is not here, but I shall bring it right to your Lordship at my coming up at this said term, and then and always I shall be at your Lordship's commandment, as knows Our Lord, who preserve your Lordship in much honour to his pleasure.
from Wyke in Worcestershire, the last day of September [1537].
Your Lordship's assuredly to command,
John Latimer

The grovelling tone of the letter was deliberately phrased to keep Cromwell quiet, but at this point, one of Katherine's uncles, Sir George Throgmorton, who, it will be remembered, had once twitted the King about his relationships with the Boleyn women (see note 1 on p. 23), came into Cromwell's orbit. Sir George Throgmorton owned land which bordered on some of Cromwell's property in Northamptonshire. There was a boundary dispute, but Throgmorton refused to be cowed into a settlement in Cromwell's favour and threatened to take Cromwell to court. Infuriated by this further example of the effrontery of Katherine's family, Cromwell ordered his spies to investigate Throgmorton's background. They came up with some evidence that Throgmorton had been a Roman Catholic, and might still be one. It was enough for Cromwell, and on 15 October 1537, the day on which Prince Edward was christened, Sir George Throgmorton was arrested and sent to the Tower on charges of being a Papist.

It was a nice move. Guilt by association did not exist in law, but the Latimers had already been under suspicion for their adherence to the old forms of religion at Snape, and if Katherine now intervened, as Cromwell hoped she would, there was a good chance that she could be implicated in the same charges as were brought against her uncle. Moreover, if Throgmorton was found guilty, Cromwell could confidently expect to be awarded his victim's estates.

The evidence of Papist sympathies was based mainly on Sir George Throgmorton's support for Catharine of Aragon's case against the divorce, but there was also some other evidence that Throgmorton had disapproved of Cranmer's reforms. On the first point, Throgmorton claimed that what he had said to the King had been under privilege of his rights as a Member of Parliament, and in any case was no more than a jovial comment intended to impress bystanders with his familiarity with the Court. On the second point, he admitted that the evidence was correct, but he said that he had expressed these opinions some seven years ago. Since then, he had read *The Bishops' Book*[3] and the New Testament in English, and he was now a reformed man. Cromwell scornfully rejected this defence, and Throgmorton was remanded to the Tower to await the King's 'pleasure' as to what should be done with him.

Lady Throgmorton thereupon wrote to Katherine's brother, William Parr, and begged him to intercede with the King on her husband's behalf. But William could do nothing. Jane Seymour was then on her death-bed, and Henry was unapproachable. Everything was referred back to Cromwell, who doubtless told William to keep out of the affair unless he too wished to join his uncle in the Tower.

Warned by her brother, Katherine persuaded Lord Latimer to postpone the visit which, as he had written to Cromwell, they had planned to make to London in the autumn. Her uncle was in no immediate danger, and there was no point in putting her head in a noose at a time when she could expect no help from the King.

The Latimers waited until January 1538, when they were invited to be the principal guests at the weddings of Katherine's sister and her two young friends, Joan Champernown and Joan Guildford, who were all due to be married in February. It was a perfect excuse for going up to London, and Katherine put out delicate feelers at Court concerning Sir George Throgmorton. It seemed that little could be done to help him. There was some sympathy for him, since he had made a full recantation of his former beliefs, but nobody was prepared to oppose Cromwell. The King was back in active life, but he was in the middle of his political juggling act and his reactions were too unpredictable for Katherine to risk an appeal to him. The only possibility, so her friends advised her, was to play on Cromwell's susceptibility to bribes. Both the price and the method would have to be right, and Katherine would be wise to include Cromwell's principal colleague, Sir Richard Riche, the Chancellor of Augmentations, who might otherwise make things difficult for her, but given all this, her uncle might be saved.

This was a new field for Katherine, but fortunately Lord Latimer was well versed in this aspect of Court life, and he took the matter in hand. It was cleverly arranged. Lord Latimer sold some of his Buckinghamshire property to Cromwell for £280, about a fifth of its real value, and at the same time, he bought the abbey and lands of Nonnemonkton in Yorkshire through Sir Richard Riche for £1,678 17s 6d, which was about three times the true value, thus netting Cromwell about £1,000 (worth today about £25,000) and putting about half that sum into Riche's pocket – though in the latter case, the payment was spread over eight years. For this, Cromwell agreed only to postpone Throgmorton's trial indefinitely and to allow him certain privileges in the Tower. In the event, Katherine was to get a lot more for the money paid to Sir Richard Riche, but at the time she could not have foreseen this, and she considered the payment to him to be no more than a form of insurance that Cromwell would keep his word.

Katherine had hoped to have achieved more than she had done, but at least her uncle's life had been spared for the time being, and she and her husband could now enjoy the weddings for which they had ostensibly come up to London.

The first wedding was that of Katherine's sister, Anne Parr, to William Herbert, an Esquire of the King's Body. It was possibly not a match that Katherine would herself have recommended. William Herbert was a 'mad, fighting fellow', a rough and almost illiterate soldier who, on the surface, would hardly have seemed a suitable mate for a girl who had been as gently brought up and as highly educated as Anne Parr. His father, however, had been the illegitimate son of the Earl of Pembroke (of the first creation), and he himself had won a high reputation in France with the French king, as well as in England, for both his courage and his competence. Nor would Henry have kept him as close to his side as he did if he had been ignorant or stupid. He was essentially a man of action, with a cool head in moments of crisis, and admirably fulfilled his rôle of personal bodyguard to the King (at the time of his marriage to Katherine's sister, he had been in the King's service for ten years).

From Anne Parr's point of view, William Herbert must have seemed to her as good a match as she was likely to make. She could not expect to inherit the Parr fortune and, without wealth, she had little chance of obtaining an offer from any of the gay, ambitious courtiers she might have preferred. Henry himself appears to have promoted the marriage, for shortly afterwards, and for the next few years, Anne and her husband received a succession of royal grants which included the magnificent abbey of Wilton in Wiltshire, together with its parks and lands in other parts of the West Country, which gave them the means to keep up with their friends in the upper strata of society. The marriage also enabled Anne to remain at Court which, now that there was no Queen, would otherwise have been difficult. Katherine Parr, therefore, had far more reason to be pleased than alarmed at her sister's fate, and her opinion of the rough-and-ready soldier who was now her brother-in-law was drastically changed by so much evidence of the King's goodwill towards him and her sister.

The bridegroom in Joan Champernown's wedding was Anthony Denny. Possibly no man, other than the Duke of Suffolk, enjoyed the King's confidence more than Anthony Denny. A Gentleman of the Privy Chamber, he was the King's intellectual sparring partner, the touchstone for new ideas, and also the King's confidential agent for all his private affairs. The second son of a Chief Baron of the Exchequer, Anthony Denny was born in 1501 and attended St Paul's School under William Lily, the great Humanist teacher. From St Paul's, he went on to St John's College, Cambridge, where he made his mark as an outstanding Humanist scholar and attracted the King's attention. Henry then invited him to Court where he began his career as a Groom of the Stole. His promotion to Gentleman of the Privy Chamber was rapid, and by the time of his marriage he had been established in his favoured position next to the King for some nine or ten years. His education and close association with Cambridge, which he maintained throughout his life, made him a strong supporter of the Humanist cause, but, like Cranmer, he tempered his zeal according to Henry's directives. His political sense was much more highly developed than Cranmer's, and his quiet unbiased appraisal of people and events was of great value to Henry. He was in a unique position to influence Henry's decisions, but until Katherine Parr became Queen he took no part in the power-game, knowing that his place at Court depended as much on his neutrality as on his discretion. Even more than his strong-arm colleague, William Herbert, he was to benefit enormously from the King's favour, receiving Waltham Abbey in Essex for his home and the great abbey at St Albans plus several thousand acres of land in Hertfordshire for his income.

His marriage to Joan Champernown was also almost certainly promoted by Henry. It was a good match, for Joan had grown up from being a pretty girl with brains into a beautiful and talented woman with no trace of vanity. She still retained her fervour for religious reform which had been inspired by Anne Boleyn, but her husband taught her how to be discreet, and she learnt to share his enthusiasm for the New Learning and the Humanist cause without making a public demonstration of their interests or feelings. For her, as for Anne Parr, marriage was to be a means of remaining at Court, and the two women and their husbands became the cornerstones of Henry's domestic establishment, taking it in turns to be on duty, except on special occasions when all four would be present, and ensuring with quiet efficiency the smooth running of the King's household.

The third wedding, between Joan Guildford and Sir John Dudley, was more the natural result of the fact that Dudley had been brought up from childhood in the Guildford family than from anything else, but here again Henry probably spurred on the event. At that stage of his career, Sir John Dudley was a senior commander in the King's navy, with the open-hearted direct approach of a sailor combined, paradoxically, with a remarkable flair for diplomacy. His dash and brilliance had endeared him to the King and, when he was not at sea, he was a welcome favourite at Court. Joan Guildford, on the other hand, was a home-loving woman who saw her intelligence and education as a means for creating a firm secure base for her husband, a port, as it were, where he could shelter from storms and where he could plan, with her help, future operations. It was exactly what Sir John Dudley needed, and through all the vicissitudes of his colourful life, the one constant factor was the happiness of his marriage.

Indeed, all three marriages were exceptionally stable, and in spite of the easy-going morals of the Court, there was never any hint of infidelity on the part of any of the women or of any of the men. Henry, in his rôle as match-maker, had done his work well. One other significant fact was that, contrary to the custom of many intellectual women, all three brides discarded their maiden names, and henceforth Anne Parr became known as Mrs (later Lady) Herbert, Joan Champernown became Mrs (later Lady) Denny, and Joan Guildford became Lady Dudley. (In order to distinguish herself from Sir John Dudley's step-mother, Honor Lady Lisle, Lady Dudley continued to be known as Lady Dudley even after her husband's promotion to the title of Viscount Lisle.)

After the weddings, Katherine Parr and Lord Latimer were obliged to return to Yorkshire where the latter had to see to his estates and to fulfil his judicial functions at the York assizes. In April 1538, he paid a further fee of £40 to Cromwell, presumably being the legal costs of the transactions at the beginning of the year but possibly as an additional inducement to keep him quiet. In the same month, Lord Latimer also had the gruesome task of witnessing the execution at York of three people, including one woman, who had been found guilty of treason, but for the rest of 1538 he and Katherine Parr were left in peace at Snape.

In January 1539, however, Cromwell made another attempt to attack the Parr family. His grounds this time evolved from the economic state of the country. The symptoms, familiar enough in our own age, were then a novelty. In general terms, they consisted of widespread poverty in the midst of booming trading conditions, coupled with inflation. Part of the cause was attributed to the rapacity of large landowners and the enclosing of common land, and Cromwell sent one of his main agents, Dr John London, 'the filthy prebendary of Windsor' who was one of the chief investigators of the state of the monasteries, to Northamptonshire to see if he could find anything against the Parrs. He reported as follows:

I see in Northampton notable decay: first, of the houses, whereof part belonged to the religious houses lately suppressed, which were evil repairers of their lands, and part to gentlemen of the country, who extort as much rent as they can, and leave all repairs to the tenants, who now let their housing fall in ruin, to the great deformity of the town. The fee farm is very big, so that the bailiffs, though they make great exactions, are themselves put in charge. They have to maintain the town hall, prison, walls, highways, and bridges; yet at every entrance there is a franchise, and the tollings and pollings make men loth to resort thither. It is a pity such franchises should incommode so great a town for the benefit of one private person.

Enclosures likewise in this shire have laid down houses and villages which used to repair to the market and fairs here. There used to be much clothing here, but now is very little, and many are out of work; the artificers decrease, and the tipplers and ale houses increase daily, as they do in most other great towns in this realm. The worshipful inhabitants beg your succour to have the candle rents which pertained to the abbeys ... By your help, these men would set up cloth-making, spinning, weaving, fulling and dyeing ...

Dr London was to be convicted four years later for falsifying some of his reports, but this one was probably correct in the general picture of decay which it gives. Its emotional appeal, however, fell on stony ground. Henry and his merchant-banker advisers, whose grasp of economics compares favourably with that of today's experts, knew that the real cause of the trouble was something much more complex than extortionate landowners, and they had already put in hand a wide variety of controls by which they hoped at least to contain the situation, even if they could not cure it. Nor was Henry prepared to tolerate any more sniping by Cromwell at the Parrs, and three months later, in March 1539, he elevated Katherine's brother to the peerage, giving him the rank of a Baron.

At first William Parr intended to take the title of Lord Fitzhugh after his grandmother's family, but on second thoughts he maintained a Parr family tradition and assumed the title of Lord Parr of Kendal instead. It was a high honour for so young a man – he was then but twenty-three years old – but the only comment at Court noted in the records was some surprise that it had not been awarded earlier. Like Katherine, he had been brought up as a member of the King's family; he had also lately taken possession of his vast inheritance; and it was probably the combination of these two facts, as well as the need to snub Cromwell, that led Henry to make the creation at this time.

Katherine Parr did not attend the ceremony of installing her brother as a peer. There was a threat of a joint invasion of England by France and Spain, and Lord Latimer had been ordered to muster his men and remain on guard in the North in case the Scots took advantage of the situation to attack the Borders. The threat was averted by a surge of solidarity behind Henry which enabled him to put on an impressive display of strength, and by skilful diplomacy by Gardiner in Paris and by Sir Thomas Wyatt in Madrid, who persuaded Francis I and Charles V respectively, that they had nothing to gain and much to lose from obeying the Pope, who was urging them on. Nevertheless, Henry did not relax his defence in the North, and the Latimers were to remain at Snape until well into 1540.

Another notable absentee from London during this period was the Duchess of Suffolk. Her husband was in constant attendance upon the King, but she remained in their new home at Tattershall in Lincolnshire with her two sons. The result was that neither Katherine Parr nor the Duchess of Suffolk played any part in the major developments which occurred in 1539, and the reversal of which was to be their principal objective when Katherine eventually became Queen.

The main development was in the field of religion. The movement for reform, begun in the days of Anne Boleyn, had released passions which were as unexpected as they were virulent, and although Henry had been able to hold the country together by exploiting the threat of foreign invasion, the division of religious opinions had reached a point where, unless something was done soon, there would be a serious risk of civil war beside which the Pilgrimage of Grace would pale into insignificance. This situation had arisen primarily because of the insistence of the Humanists that the Christian religion was meaningless unless the people could be educated to understand the inner meanings of its spiritual doctrines. They deplored the old form of captive audiences forced by fear and superstition to listen to the mumbo-jumbo of dog-Latin recited by ignorant priests. Knowledge, they insisted, was as important as faith, and both were essential for the spreading of the good life. This was the main motive for translating the Bible into English and for the so-called 'paraphrases' which Erasmus and others wrote to explain the more difficult concepts of the New Testament to the lay public.

But it is a curious fact about Christianity that although superficially its teachings seem clear enough, a detailed examination of the Gospels and the writings of the early Christian Fathers reveals a complex assortment of statements which are often contradictory, and the meanings of which are far from clear. Since the days of St Paul, intellectuals have found an extraordinary fascination in trying to reconcile the discrepancies and in building up a variety of sets of religious beliefs and ceremonies from these early writings. It is another fact about Christianity that these intellectual exercises engendered (and still engender) high passions on the part of the proponents and opponents of any particular set of beliefs. So long as these passions were confined to the upper orders of the priesthood little harm was done, and throughout the angry controversies which raged from the days of the Council of Nicaea in 325 AD to the birth of Humanism towards the end of the fifteenth century, ordinary worshippers were, except in a few cases, unaffected by the emotions of the intellectuals.

What the Humanists had not appreciated was that education would enable the ordinary man and woman to experience the same intellectual fascination as the scholars had done, and with the same heated passions. Now, however, it was to be on a much wider scale, on a lower level of intelligence, and without the restraints of good manners or delicate feelings. One Joan Butcher, for example, a lively woman of the people, proclaimed to the world at large in the tavern where she held court, that in her opinion the Holy Water used in baptism was 'no more holy than the parson's piss'. She was arrested, but she was subsequently released on pleading that she did not understand what she had said.

In bringing religion to the market-place, therefore, the Humanists, far from encouraging and promoting the good life, unleashed violent emotions which caused riots in the taverns and disorder in the streets. Husbands and wives were set at each other's throats, the authority of parents over their children was undermined, and the Church and its laws were brought into contempt. In general terms, the reformers would tolerate only those beliefs and ceremonies for which a clear statement could be found in the Bible, while the opponents to reform, mostly Roman Catholics, maintained that it was damnable heresy to question the findings and teachings of the learned men of the Church who had been studying these matters for centuries, and who had been directly inspired by God.

Of the many points over which conflict raged, three in particular separated the believers in the New Faith from those of the Old. The first concerned the Sacrament of the Altar in which consecrated bread and wine is consumed by priest and congregation as an act of communion with Christ and His Church. The Old Faith maintained that the bread and wine, after being consecrated by the priest, became the Real Presence, the actual flesh and blood of Jesus Christ. Those of the New Faith maintained that this was not the case: the bread and wine were but symbols of Christ's presence in spirit, and the sacrament was but a simple re-enactment of the Last Supper in which the congregation reaffirmed their faith in Christ and their membership of His Church.

The second point concerned the celibacy of the priesthood. Adherents of the New Faith maintained that celibacy was not called for in Christ's teaching. It was in any case better for a priest to be married than, as so many did, to live in sin. The Old Faith maintained that celibacy was an essential prerequisite for the priesthood, an act of denial of earthly pleasures as required by the teachings of the early Christian fathers.

The third point was auricular confession, the act of confessing one's sins on regular occasions by voice to a priest and receiving penance and absolution afterwards. Those of the New Faith claimed that any confession should be made in silent prayer direct to God, and they denied the authority of the priest to give absolution.

Until the end of 1538, Henry had for the most part given more support to the New Faith, whose principal leaders were Cromwell and Cranmer, than to the Old, but the Pilgrimage of Grace and, possibly more important, the need to avoid stirring up religious passions on the part of England's enemies on the Continent, caused him to reconsider his position, and he began to listen much more to men like Gardiner and the Duke of Norfolk, who, apart from being supporters of the Old Faith, were bitterly opposed to Cromwell's régime.

The first indication of Henry's drift away from Cromwell and Cranmer came in the trial of a man called Lambert (or Nicholson in some accounts) who had written a short treatise in favour of the New Faith with particular reference to the Sacrament of the Altar. Henry attended Lambert's trial in person, clothed all in white. He was accompanied by Cranmer and a number of bishops, each of whom had been selected by Henry to debate one of the ten reasons which Lambert had given for denying that the bread and wine became the real flesh and blood of Christ. Henry took the first point himself; Cranmer, who at that time was genuinely undecided on this particular issue, took the next; and the rest of the bishops the remaining points in turn. The trial lasted for five hours throughout which Lambert was compelled to stand. Although he began well, he was overawed by Henry, and towards the end he could no longer give any effective answers. The case against him – and against the New Faith – was considered proven and, as Lambert refused to recant, he was condemned to death and burnt at Smithfield.

Immediately after the trial, which took place in November 1538, a proclamation established a censorship of English books and declared that no man, other than divinity scholars, should argue about the sacraments. A man was hanged in London for eating meat on a Friday, and Henry himself set an example of Catholic piety by creeping to the Cross in public and by his devout observance of the Mass. Gardiner and the Duke of Norfolk took new heart, and foreign ambassadors reported a gleeful anticipation that Cromwell would fall when Parliament assembled at the end of April (1539).

Cromwell, however, was too astute a politician to be caught by the new situation, and, regardless of his private opinions, he set about promoting the King's wishes as faithfully as ever. Cranmer tried to stem the tide of reaction at the Convocation of Bishops which was held at the same time as Parliament, but the situation was a mirror image of the one that had preceded the secession from Rome. Now it was Cranmer who won the support of the bishops, and Gardiner who appealed to Henry for help. Once again Parliament stepped in and, directed by Cromwell at the King's command, swung the debate in favour of reaction. The result was the Act of Six Articles, called by some the most vicious piece of legislation ever passed by an English Parliament, and hailed by others as a return at last to the path of sanity and salvation.

The Six Articles were:

1 that in the Sacrament of the Altar, the bread and wine became 'the natural body and blood of our Saviour Jesus Christ';
2 that communion in both kinds, i.e. both bread *and* wine, was not necessary for all persons;
3 that priests must not be married;
4 that vows of chastity or widowhood must be observed, e.g. monks and nuns who reverted to secular life as a result of the dissolution of their monasteries were still not allowed to marry;
5 that private masses were necessary and should be continued;

119

6   that auricular confession was mandatory for all subjects of the King at the times 'commonly accustomed within this realm and Church of England'.

But what earned the Act the epithet of 'vicious' were the punishments: first offenders who refused the first article and any who preached against the articles as a whole were to be burnt as heretics; first offenders against any of the other five articles were to be treated as felons, second offenders were to be burnt. Moreover, only two witnesses were required for a person to be condemned under the Act, which made the Act as much a potential weapon of private revenge as of religious uniformity.

Cranmer, having again obediently submitted to the King's arguments, retained his position as Archbishop of Canterbury, but he took the precaution of immediately sending his wife back to Germany. Two of Cranmer's friends, however, Hugh Latimer, the Bishop of Worcester, and Nicholas Shaxton, the Bishop of Salisbury, refused to submit to the new Act, and both resigned from their bishoprics. Due to their long personal association with the King, no drastic measures were taken against them, and they were committed only to perpetual house arrest in the homes of friends.

Cromwell, on the other hand, commands one's unwilling respect. He had been obliged to bow before the forces arraigned against him by Gardiner and Norfolk, but he had seen to it, first, that all arrangements for prosecutions under the Act of Six Articles were left in his hands, and secondly, that, in exchange as it were for the Six Articles, Parliament had granted the final dissolution of all remaining monasteries. These measures enabled him to retain control of the Government and the main source of the King's wealth. Early in July 1539, and only two weeks after the prorogation of Parliament, he followed this up with a plan to turn the tables against Gardiner and Norfolk by securing a Protestant alliance through marrying Henry to Anne, the sister of the Duke of Cleves. He obtained Henry's acquiescence to his plan on the grounds that the alliance had nothing to do with religion, but was needed as an essential safeguard against the renewed threat of invasion from France and Spain. Furthermore, since the Protestants in Cleves and Germany would be deeply disturbed if any action was taken to enforce the Six Articles, he also obtained Henry's permission to suspend for the time being all prosecutions under the new Act.

Cromwell's plan was foolproof save in one respect, and that was the nature of the woman he had chosen to be Henry's fourth bride. Anne of Cleves fell far short of the English ideal of womanhood. Nicholas Wotton, Cromwell's emissary to Cleves to make the marriage arrangements, reported:

> She can read and write her own tongue, but French, Latin, or other language, she hath none, nor yet she cannot sing nor play upon any instrument, for they take it here in Germany for a rebuke and an occasion of lightness that great ladies should be learned or have any knowledge of music. Her wit is good, and she will no doubt learn English soon when she puts her mind to it ...

There was also a difficulty in that her father, who was now dead, had once promised that Anne should marry the son of the Duke of Lorraine. The Council of Cleves, however, were prepared to waive this engagement and to declare publicly that Anne was free to marry anyone she liked.

Cromwell was not deterred, and the marriage negotiations were successfully concluded early in October 1539, but when Henry first met her, secretly, on New Year's Day in an inn at Rochester, he could not conceal his disappointment. 'How like you this woman?' he asked Lord Russell on their way back to Greenwich where the wedding was to take place. 'Do you think her so fair and of such beauty as report hath been made unto me of her? I pray you tell me truth.' Lord Russell replied that he did not think she was fair, but rather of a brown complexion. Whereupon the King exclaimed: 'Alas! whom should men trust? I promise you, I see no such thing in her as hath been showed me of her, and am ashamed that men have so praised her as they have done, and I like her not.'

There was some confusion at Greenwich for it was found that the delegates from Cleves had forgotten to bring the declaration that Anne's pre-contract with the Duke of Lorraine was null and void. Cromwell, however, persuaded Henry that the marriage was an urgent political necessity, and he had no difficulty in securing a new declaration. When he returned to tell the King that all was in order, Henry begged him: 'Then is there no remedy but to put my head in the yoke?' Cromwell tried to comfort him by pointing out that in spite of her looks, she had a 'queenly manner withal'. 'That is truth,' said Henry a little more cheerfully. But on the morning after the wedding night, when Cromwell asked him if he liked Anne any better, Henry replied: 'Nay, my Lord,

121

much worse, for by her breasts and her belly she should be no maid, which, when I felt them, strake me so to heart that I had neither will nor courage to prove the rest.'

Neither Katherine Parr, nor Lord Latimer, nor, indeed, any of the Northern nobles, were invited to the wedding since Cromwell presumably argued that their presence, as supporters of the Old Faith, would upset the Protestants, but Katherine's brother was in the King's private circle, and her sister and Lady Denny had been appointed Anne's Ladies-in-Waiting. The Duchess of Suffolk had had the task of escorting Anne from Dover to Greenwich, and she, too, was nominated to a senior post in the new Queen's household, but his was an honorary rather than a permanent appointment. Katherine, however, was not to be denied any opportunity to meet the new Queen, and at about Easter time, probably early in April 1540, she came up to London, for the first time without her husband. The reason for Lord Latimer's absence is not known, but he did not attend Parliament that year, and he may well have been ill. Normally, Katherine would not have left him, but she had not seen her family for nearly two years, and it was as important to Lord Latimer as it was to her to keep in touch with the Court. There is no record of where she stayed in London, but on this occasion it is more likely to have been with the Duchess of Suffolk at the Duke's house in Southwark rather than with her sister at Court, for events were moving to a crisis in which she was deeply interested, but about which she had to be exceptionally discreet.

The situation was that Gardiner and Norfolk were once more in the ascendant, and they and their faction were making concerted moves which it was hoped would finally bring Cromwell down. They had been quick to realise that Cromwell's present position depended almost entirely on the need to maintain the Protestant alliance on the Continent. If a wedge could be driven between France and Spain, that alliance would no longer be necessary. Henry could then get rid of Anne of Cleves, which he obviously wished to do as soon as possible, and they could then get rid of Cromwell as having been the author of the King's latest misfortunes. Cromwell had been privy to their plans, but he had not been able to stop a diplomatic ploy which was so obviously to Henry's advantage, and early in February the Duke of Norfolk had been sent to Paris to see what he could do.

Norfolk's diplomacy was doubly successful. Working through the

Queen of Navarre and Madame d'Estampes, the French King's sister and mistress respectively, he persuaded Francis I to maintain his demand that Charles V should concede Milan to France, and this in turn caused the Emperor to fear that the French would break their truce with him. The result was that within two months of Norfolk's visit Henry had both Francis I and Charles V suing for his friendship, and he could safely thumb his nose at Cleves and the Germans.

Gardiner and Norfolk then engaged Henry's interest in one of Norfolk's nieces, Catherine Howard, and Gardiner played host to clandestine meetings between her and the King at his London house which, by a coincidence, happened to be within a stone's throw of the Duchess of Suffolk's house in Southwark. The combination of plots succeeded, and early in May Henry sent for Cromwell and told him to prepare the legal case for divorcing Anne of Cleves.

Katherine Parr's interest was twofold. First, the situation offered a hope that she might be able to secure the release of her uncle, Sir George Throgmorton, from the Tower, and secondly, the dismissal of Cromwell would remove the continuing threat of arrest under which she and Lord Latimer had been living for the past two years. On the other hand, she did not wish to ally herself with Gardiner and Norfolk whose morals and attitude to women disgusted her, and whose reactionary interests could be as much a danger to her sister and friends at Court as Cromwell had been to her and her husband. Nor could she seek or expect help from the Duchess of Suffolk or her sister and their friends at Court. In spite of all the wrong that Cromwell had done, he had remained throughout his career an unshakeable supporter of the Humanists, and none of Katherine's circle of women, not even Princess Mary, was prepared to support any move against him. Katherine, therefore, had to play almost a lone hand – almost, for the King had sent for the one man who might be able to help her, her childhood guardian, Cuthbert Tunstall. Henry needed him as the one moderate and experienced man in the kingdom on whom he could rely now that the power-game was reaching fever-pitch within the Council, and his presence was as much a comfort to the King as it was to Katherine. For the moment, however, Katherine made no move. Prudence dictated that the less she could be directly involved the better it would be for her, and it looked almost certain that Cromwell would fall without any intervention from her.

But Cromwell was by no means beaten. One of the most flexible politicians of all time, he contrived to remain in control by simply bowing to the prevailing trend of events. Parliament assembled on 12 April, and he once more showed his exceptional skill in manipulating it. One of his first moves was to take the wind out of Gardiner's sails by pushing through a resolution which set up a large number of judicial commissions for enforcing the Act of Six Articles. He followed this up by securing for the King the unprecedented grant of £3,000,000 (worth today about £75,000,000) in taxes and, on 18 April, the King rewarded him with the title of the Earl of Essex, which had become vacant in March as a result of the death of the previous Earl, Lord Parr's father-in-law, in a riding accident.

Then came Gardiner's and Norfolk's trump card: Henry's request for a divorce from Anne of Cleves. Cromwell did not turn a hair. It was a probability, he said, which he had always foreseen. Anne's pre-contract of marriage with the Duke of Lorraine and the non-consummation of her marriage to Henry were grounds enough for divorce. Why else had he chosen such a woman rather than any of the other German princesses to be Henry's bride? He cheerfully accepted the King's directive, and together with one of his principal secretaries, Sir Thomas Wriothesley, set about preparing the papers for Henry's case.

By the end of May, it was clear that Gardiner and Norfolk had been out-manoeuvred. Cromwell's position seemed as secure as ever, and they could see no way of toppling him. His earldom had been followed on St George's Day by his election as Knight of the Garter, and Henry was not a man to sully his highest order of chivalry by promoting to it a man who did not have his utmost confidence.

At this point, Katherine Parr probably consulted Cuthbert Tunstall and, assured of his support, decided that she must after all intervene. Neither she, nor her family, nor any of the North, would ever be safe so long as Cromwell remained in office. But it would be folly to attack him directly, and the ostensible cause she gave for seeking an interview with the King was the plight of her uncle, Sir George Throgmorton. In a curious rhyming history of the Throgmorton family, Sir George's son writes:

> Oh, lucky looks that fawned on Katherine Parr!
> A woman rare like her but seldom seen,
> To Borough first, and then to Latimer,
> She widow was, and then became a Queen;

My mother prayed her niece with watery eyes,
To rid both her and hers from endless cries.

She, willing of herself to do us good,
Sought out the means her uncle's life to save;
And when the King was in his pleasing mood
She humbly then her suit began to crave;
With wooing times denials disagree,
She spake and sped – my father was set free.

As Strickland points out, the poet mixed up his dates, for the event took place some three years before Katherine became Queen, but a more prosaic document, also in the Throgmorton family papers, authenticates the incident with the bare statement 'that Sir George was released through the influence of his kinswoman, the Lady Katherine Parr, and advised with by the King, at her suggestion, about Cromwell, immediately before the arrest of that minister'.

With Tunstall's help, Katherine's interview with Henry was kept secret from Cromwell. For the same reason, she could not prepare the ground, as she would have preferred to have done, by organising the witnesses who would doubtless be called, and she had to rely in the first instance on her own unsupported statements. She began by explaining to Henry that she sought only a fair hearing for her uncle who had now been kept in the Tower for two years without trial. She went on to point out the flimsiness of the religious charges against him. Sir George Throgmorton had never been a Papist; his only so-called crime had been his adherence to those parts of the Catholic doctrine which the King himself had embodied in the Six Articles, and the real cause of his arrest was his refusal to be brow-beaten by Cromwell over the boundary dispute concerning their lands. As for Cromwell, his lack of sincerity was proved by his acceptance of the bribes with Lord Latimer had paid him and Sir Richard Riche, the Chancellor of Augmentations, in an attempt to secure her uncle's release. She also informed Henry of the state of affairs in the North, which was still very unsettled, and where the feeling against Cromwell was so strong that it could cause a new uprising. People did not believe that he would uphold the King's policy of a middle course in religious beliefs, and they suspected, though she herself was sure it could not be true, that even now he was plotting a Lutheran reversal of that policy.

At first, Henry listened with little more than the amiable attention he always paid 'his' ladies, but as Katherine developed her theme, his interest deepened. He trusted all the Parr children – his nickname for Katherine's brother was 'My Integrity' – and he believed those parts of her story of which she had first-hand knowledge. But there were other matters on which she was quoting hearsay evidence, and here she could be acting as someone's unwitting tool. Her case for her uncle's release was strong, and he was disposed to grant it, but her case against Cromwell on those matters which were not directly connected with her uncle was less specific, and he was not prepared to act without further investigation. From Henry's point of view, Cromwell had been the best minister, Wolsey not excluded, that he had ever had. It would be impossible to replace him, and the only grounds Henry could accept for even considering dismissing him would be if, like Wolsey, he had over-reached himself and now sought to be the King's master rather than his servant.

After Katherine had gone, Henry sent for Sir Richard Riche and questioned him closely. Riche was terrified. He did not know what could or could not be proved against him, and he threw all the blame on Cromwell, quoting other cases where Cromwell had enriched himself by the improper use of his office. Sir George Throgmorton was then summoned from the Tower and confirmed Katherine's account of his case. Either he or Riche then added the statement, which was later published as one of the main reasons for Cromwell's disgrace, that Cromwell had told them that 'if the King and all the realm varied from his opinions, he would withstand them, and that he hoped in another year or two to bring things to that frame that the King could not resist it'. This was more than enough for Henry, and on 10 June, without warning any of the Council, he sent his Captain of the Guard into the Council chamber and arrested Cromwell.

Two days later, Cromwell wrote to Henry, begging for mercy. He denied emphatically the accusations that had been made against him:

Never spoke with the Chancellor of Augmentations and Throgmorton together at a time, but if I did, I never spoke of any such matter. Your Grace knows what manner of man Throgmorton has ever been towards you and your proceedings. What Master Chancellor has been to me, God and he know best; what I have been to him your Majesty knows. If I had obeyed your often most gracious counsels it would not have been with me as now it is. But I have committed my soul to God, my body and goods to your pleasure. As for the Commonwealth, I have done my best, and no one can justly accuse me of having done wrong wilfully. If I heard of any combinations or offenders against the laws, I have for the most part (though not as I should have done) revealed and caused them to be punished. But I have meddled in so many matters, I cannot answer all . . .

On 19 June, Cromwell was found guilty by the same legal procedure in the House of Lords by which so many of his victims had suffered, that is, without being allowed to appear in his own defence. Since his evidence was needed for the divorce case against Anne of Cleves, however, his execution was deferred.

Katherine's sister and her friends managed to avoid being involved in the divorce, and it was the Ladies Rutland, Rochford (the widow of Anne Boleyn's brother), and Edgecombe, who were called upon to testify that the marriage had never been consummated. They gave evidence of how they had teased Anne shortly before Midsummer, telling her that they thought she was still a virgin even after six months of being married to the King.

'How can I be a maid,' Anne had replied, 'and sleep every night with the King?'

The ladies had pressed for details

'Why,' Anne had said, 'when he comes to bed, he kisses me, and taketh me by the hand, and biddeth me "Good night, sweetheart": and in the morning, he kisses me, and biddeth me "Farewell, darling." Is this not enough?'
'Madame, there must be more than this,' Lady Rutland had commented, 'or it will be long before we have a Duke of York, which all this realm most desireth.'
'Nay,' Anne had maintained, 'is not this enough? I am contented with this, for I know no more.'

Cranmer presided over a Convocation which had been called to hear the case, and Henry confirmed that there had been no carnal copulation. Gardiner then proved that the pre-contract with the Duke of Lorraine was valid; Cromwell testified on both of the main grounds for the divorce; and on 9 July 1540, Convocation solemnly informed Henry that his marriage with Anne was illegal and must be annulled.

On learning that she could remain in England and that Henry had said he would treat her as if she were his sister, Anne raised no objections. In return, Henry gave her the wealthy manors of Richmond and Bletchingley in Surrey, £4,000 (worth today about £100,000) a year for life, and a substantial retinue of servants to maintain her status. It is hardly surprising that a month later the French Ambassador reported: 'As for her who is now called Madame de Cleves, far from pretending to be married, she is as joyous as ever, and wears new dresses every day; which argues either prudent dissimulation or stupid forgetfulness of what should so closely touch her heart. Be that as it may, it has thrown the poor ambassador of Cleves into a fever . . .'

From the point of view of both parties, it was a most satisfactory arrangement, and she and Henry developed a gay friendship with lasted for the rest of Henry's life.

Cromwell was beheaded on 29 July 1540. Nobody except those directly involved knew of the part Katherine Parr had played in his downfall. Unlike Anne Boleyn, whose gloating at the fall of Wolsey had aroused the fears of the Court, Katherine Parr kept her own counsel. Serene and quietly elegant, she slipped away through the galleries of Westminster Palace and returned almost unnoticed to Yorkshire. Only Henry might have watched her leave with thoughtful interest. This was a very different person from the frightened young woman of the Pilgrimage of Grace. Cool and confident, she had handled the affair with exceptional skill, and he admired the prudence with which she had concealed her success. However he would miss Cromwell, and he might well have wondered how much even he, the King, had been manipulated by this remarkable woman.

NOTES

1 Lady Ughtred, the widow of Sir Anthony Ughtred, a captain employed on the Scottish borders.
2 Lord William Howard, one of the Duke of Norfolk's brothers, who had been sent to join Winchester to acquire diplomatic experience.
3 *The Institution of a Christian Man*, prepared by Cranmer and his colleagues as a guide to the New Faith. It was drastically amended some years later by Henry himself, and then became known as *The King's Book*.

8   Catherine Howard

Katherine Parr and her circle were only involved in minor matters during the reign of Catherine Howard. The development of domestic and foreign affairs during this period, however, had a direct impact on Katherine Parr's reign, and an account of the main events has therefore been included here.

Two days after the execution of Thomas Cromwell, Henry demonstrated his own peculiar interpretation of the policy of 'invincible moderation', which was advocated by Cuthbert Tunstall who was for the moment his principal adviser, by sending Dr Barnes and two other so-called heretics to the stake for denying that the sacramental bread and wine was the body and blood of Christ and, on the same day, by hanging three priests who had spoken in favour of the Pope. The French Ambassador reported thus:

> It was wonderful to see adherents of the two opposing parties dying at the same time, and it gave offence to both. And it was no less strange to hear than horrible to see for ... the perversion of justice of which both parties complained, in that they had never been called to judgement, nor knew why they were condemned, and that the condition of Christians in this age of grace was worse than that of the Jews under the rigour of the Law, by which a man was to be heard and convicted before he was judged ... This and the affirmations of the others so moved the people that if they had had a leader there might have been a great tumult; to obviate which, commissioners have been suddenly appointed to inquire touching those who approve or speak of what the doctors said at their execution, which is fresh matter for a greater butchery than ever, because it is difficult to have a people entirely opposed to new errors which does not hold with the ancient authority of the Church and the Holy See, or, on the other hand, hating the Pope, which does not share some of the opinions of the Germans. Yet the Government will not have either the one or the other, but insists on their keeping what is commanded, which is so often altered that it is difficult to understand what it is.

A week later on 8 August 1540, almost as if he were celebrating this new wave of butchery, Henry married Catherine Howard, the daughter of the Duke of Norfolk's brother, Lord Edmund Howard.

Catherine Howard was then nineteen years old, 'rather graceful than beautiful', according to Marillac, 'and of short stature'. A gay and frivolous girl, she had been brought up by her indulgent grandmother, the Dowager Duchess of Norfolk, who had encouraged her from an early age to enjoy a life of pleasure with little, if any, restraints. Evidence was later produced that she had happily surrendered her virginity when she was barely in her teens, and she had already had a number of love affairs before she met Henry. Surprisingly, however, Henry seems to have been unaware of her reputation, and he entered into the marriage with unfeigned enthusiasm.

Henry was now forty-nine years old. Until his early forties, constant exercise and an occasional moderation of his diet had kept his large, square frame firm and muscular, but during the past four or five years he had begun to let himself go. The muscle had turned to fat, and the fatter he had become, the more he drank and ate. He was not yet as gross as he was to become, and well-cut clothes concealed his drooping paunch, but only flatterers could pretend that he was still the 'bluff King Hal' of his youth. He was determined to keep up with his frolicsome young bride, however, and towards the end of the year he instituted a new daily routine – 'to rise between 5 and 6 a.m., hear Mass at 7 a.m., and then ride until dinner which is at 10 a.m.' This, he declared, and the fresh country air of Windsor Park, to which he had moved because of a new outbreak of the plague in London, had made a new man of him, and for a time he was able to put on a convincing act of unflagging attention at the endless banquets and balls with which Catherine Howard now filled the time of the Court.

Catherine herself was in her element. She revelled in the task, as she saw it, of being Queen, and she was delighted by the way in which everyone at Court jumped to serve her slightest whim. Henry showered presents on her, caressing her in public and making so much fuss over her that she soon got the impression that there was no limit to what she could do, or to her pursuit of pleasure. Her frivolity and waywardness, however, made her useless as a political tool, and it was probably these elements in her character that caused Henry to connive at the obvious plot by Norfolk and Gardiner to make her his Queen in order to promote their interests. Of all his Queens thus far, she was the least likely, so Henry must have thought, to be able to have any effective influence on public affairs. Her early activities seemed to prove him right, for almost from the beginning of her reign she showed a total disregard, or just plain ignorance, of the interests of the faction led by Norfolk and Gardiner, first by snubbing Princess Mary, an act which much upset the Catholics, and then, two days after the New Year, by holding an extraordinary reception for Anne of Cleves, which made matters worse.

She [Anne of Cleves] was received by the Duchess of Suffolk, the Countess of Hertford, and other ladies, who conducted her to her lodgings and then to the Queen's apartments. (She was graciously received by the Queen, whom she insisted on addressing on her knees, and who showed her the utmost kindess.) The King then entered and, after a low bow to Lady Anne, embraced and kissed her. She occupied a seat near the bottom of the table at supper, but after the King had retired, the Queen and Lady Anne danced together, and next day all three dined together. At this time the King sent his Queen a present of a ring and two small dogs, which she passed over to Lady Anne, and that day the Lady Anne returned to Richmond.

Norfolk and Gardiner must have been greatly angered when they heard of the incident; neither was there at the time, and there was nothing they could do. Now that Catherine was Queen she was beyond their control, and they could not risk the ignominy which their faction would suffer if they unseated her.

In spite of the continuous round of pleasure, the King neither then, nor at any time after the fall of Cromwell, neglected his duty to govern and protect his realm. His main motive in marrying Catherine Howard was to reassure the old nobility of his support, but at the same time he was not prepared to abandon the new man he had brought to the fore or the exceptionally efficient government they had created. As a result, his new Privy Council was made up of a balance of opposing forces which ensured that never again would it be dominated by any single man as it had been by Cromwell and by Wolsey, and the King, by favouring first one side and then the other, was able to create situations in which he was always in control, and by which he hoped to avert any further outbreak of rebellion by either one faction or the other.

Apart from Cranmer, whose lack of political sense made him a pawn rather than a principal in the power-game, the opposition to the Duke of Norfolk and Gardiner centred round Edward Seymour, Jane Seymour's elder brother. He was now (1540–1) about thirty-four years old. A strangely sensitive man, who was nevertheless capable in wartime of brutal acts of violence, he was in some respects an early example of the ideal of soldier/statesman/intellectual which was later to be immortalised in the character of Sir Philip Sidney in the reign of Elizabeth I. Educated at both Oxford and Cambridge, he had at first followed the same military career as his father, Sir John Seymour, who had given notable service to both Henry VII and Henry VIII. From the outset, he had shown himself to be a brilliantly quick tactician, cool under fire, a competent leader of his troops, and an excellent administrator. The Duke of Suffolk had knighted him on the field in France in 1523, when he was possibly not yet eighteen years old, and in the following year, the King had taken him into his service at Court.

Partly because of his youth, partly perhaps because Henry considered him to be primarily a soldier, Sir Edward Seymour's progress at Court was slow until the early 1530s when he took as his second wife Anne Stanhope, the daughter of Sir Edward Stanhope of Sudbury in Suffolk. Anne never allowed anyone to forget that she was descended through her maternal great-grandmother from Thomas Woodstock, the youngest son of King Edward III, and she considered herself therefore to be of royal blood. Her snobbery and pride were often intolerable, even to those she was bound to consider her superiors, but at the same time she was a highly intelligent woman, determined to regain the position in society to which she believed she was entitled, and though fate had given her a mere knight for a husband, she saw in him a potential of brains and ability which, with good management, could take him – and her – to the top. There are a few references in the records from which one can deduce the early manoeuvring by which Anne pushed her husband forward, and which led eventually to the King's choice of Edward Seymour's sister, Jane, as the successor to Anne Boleyn, but by the middle of 1535 it is clear that Anne and her husband already stood high in the King's favour. A few days after the King's marriage to Jane Seymour, Sir Edward was created Viscount Beauchamp, and early in the following year, 1537, he was made a member of the Privy Council. This was followed in October of the same year, a week or so after the birth of Prince Edward, by his creation as the Earl of Hertford, and Anne, as the Countess of Hertford, had reached her first major objective.

The most important of all Edward Seymour's honours, however, was his appointment to the Privy Council, for this brought him directly into the top level of government and into the front line of the power-game. His early success can be judged from the fact that the death of his sister, which could have meant the end of his political career, made no difference to his position, and he remained one of Henry's inner circle of advisers. Regarded by most of the Council as a military staff officer, and by the Duke of Norfolk as an upstart, his sympathies inclined towards Cromwell and Cranmer, both of whom were more appreciative of his intellectual and administrative qualities; but, doubtless guided by his wife, he managed to avoid any direct confrontation with Cromwell's enemies, and within a year or two of his joining the Privy Council he had gained the reputation of being 'a wise young man' to whom the majority of the Council were prepared to listen.

After the fall of Cromwell, the line-up in the Privy Council left the Earl of Hertford with the effective support of only one man, the Duke of Suffolk, for Cromwell's former allies had either retreated into nervous silence or, like Lord Russell, had crossed over to the Gardiner/Norfolk faction. But the Duke of Suffolk, reluctant though he was to play politics, was a powerful friend, and it is significant that from the end of 1540 the records show an almost constant attendance at Court, not only of the Duke, but also of the Duchess of Suffolk.

Outside the Privy Council, in the Court at large, the Earl of Hertford had much more support. His younger brother, Sir Thomas Seymour, one of the few eligible bachelors, was a forceful, if somewhat erratic ally. Sir John Dudley, whose naval and diplomatic service had won the King's admiration, was becoming a good friend and, though they were obliged to stay discreetly in the background, Anthony Denny and William Herbert, Katherine Parr's brother-in-law, could also be counted on for help when required. And in addition to the men, there were their wives, all highly educated women who were devoted to the Humanist cause, and who were beginning to appreciate their political strength.

But for the moment Henry firmly squashed any attempts to play the power-game inside his council. There was trouble in Ireland, where some of the local Council were accused of treason; the alliance between France and Scotland, now firmly cemented by the marriage between James v and Mary of Guise, was showing its teeth in the form of a big increase in Border raids; in France itself a major dispute had arisen about the frontier between the Pale of Calais and the surrounding French territory; and there was a threatened breakdown of the trading agreements with the Low Countries and Spain.

With Cuthbert Tunstall and the Duke of Suffolk at his side, Henry took control with all his usual skill and energy. Norfolk was sent north to check the Border defences; Hertford was sent to Calais to sort things out there; Gardiner was appointed as special ambassador to deal first with the Queen Regent in Brussels and then with the Emperor who was en route to Germany to quell the Protestants; and various plans were put in hand to trick the suspects in Ireland and others in Europe to come to England where they could be arrested and tried. At the same time, there was no abatement of the domestic actions against heretics and Papists alike, and commissioners were appointed in almost every county to enforce the new laws.

So much work, combined with his strenuous efforts to please his new Queen, took its toll on Henry, and towards the end of February 1541 he suffered a severe recurrence of a former complaint in one of his legs. The illness also affected his spirits and brought about a rare disillusion with himself and his subjects. Marillac reported the event:

> This [the King's proposed visit to Dover] was prevented by an illness which happened to him at Hampton Court in the form of a slight tertian fever, which should rather have profited than hurt him, for he is very stout, but one of his legs, formerly opened and kept open to maintain his health, suddenly closed, to his great alarm, for, five or six years ago, in like case, he thought to have died. This time prompt remedy was applied, and he is now well and the fever gone. Besides the body malady, he had a mal d'esprit which is to be considered, namely, that, hearing that his subjects in divers places murmured at the charges which, contrary to their ancient liberties, are imposed upon them, and at their ill treatment for religious opinions, and having conceived a sinister opinion of some of his chief men, he said in his illness that he had an unhappy people to govern whom he would shortly make so poor that they would not have the boldness nor the power to oppose him, and that most of his Privy Council, under pretence of serving him, were only temporising for their own profit, but he knew the good servants from the flatterers, and if God lent him health, he would take care that their projects would not succeed. He spent Shrove-tide without recreation, even of music, in which he used to take as much pleasure as any Prince in Christendom, and stayed in Hampton Court with so little company that his Court resembled more a private family than a King's train.

Henry's gloom about the mood of his subjects had more foundation in fact than he might have realised. In the North of England particularly, the gentry and common people alike were exacerbated rather than appeased by the ruthless enforcement of the King's middle-of-the-road policy and, although they had been excused part of the taxes which had been imposed on the rest of the country (as an inducement to win their support against the Scots), rebellion was once more in the air. This time, since there was no Cromwell to take the blame, the anger of the people was aimed directly at the King, and in the middle of April 1541, a group of Yorkshire conspirators, which included Lord Latimer's cousin, Sir John Neville, set out for Pontefract with the intention of killing the Bishop of Llandaff, who was acting as the King's principal representative in the North while Cuthbert Tunstall was in London. Having killed the Bishop, the conspirators then intended publicly to denounce the King's tyranny and to raise the country in open revolt against the Government. The Bishop, however, was warned of the plot (perhaps by Katherine Parr), and the conspirators, who numbered forty or fifty people, were seized before they had been able to strike a single blow. The majority were executed in London, but Sir John Neville was sent back to York, where he was hanged, drawn, and quartered as an example to any more would-be rebels.

The incident roused Henry's ever latent spirit of defiance, and he decided that the time had now come when he must finally confront his rebellious Northern subjects in person. Preparations were therefore put in hand for a Progress to York which was to be greater and more magnificent than any previous Progress of the King's reign. Chapuys wrote:

> ... of the King's determination, on hearing of this conspiracy, to go North in person. Having lately heard that the affair threatened to grow worse, he has now issued orders for stores of provisions and intends going thither in pomp, followed by at least 5,000 horse. Several Lords and gentlemen have been summoned. His object in going with so large a train seems to be to gain a reputation in parts of his kingdom that he has never yet visited, and that the money spent may remain in the country, as the people of the North complain that the King has seized the rentals not only of the abbeys, but also of the principal Lords, like Northumberland; so that the money which formerly circulated in the North now comes up to London.

A month before his departure, the King decided to clear up outstanding treason cases in London, and on 27 May, the eighty-year-old Countess of Salisbury, the mother of Cardinal Pole, was executed, having been imprisoned in the Tower for two years. No reason was given to the shocked Londoners, but she was one of the last of the Plantagenets, the daughter and sole heir of the brother of Edward IV, and thus a possible claimant to the throne. However, her age ruled out her possible succession to Henry, and one can but suppose that she was executed to remove any rallying point, however improbable, for incipient rebels. This was followed by the execution of Lord Leonard Grey, the brother of the late Marquis of Dorset, for his share in the treasonable activities that had been unearthed in Ireland, and thereafter Henry gave orders for the Tower to be cleared of all prisoners, either by execution or pardon, presumably in order to make way for those he might send back from the North.

At last, on 30 June 1541, the King and his huge retinue – for each of the five thousand horsemen and the members of the Court were accompanied by a train of servants, so that the total number must have been well in excess of ten thousand people – set off on what was to be the most spectacular Progress of his reign. Like a swarm of locusts, devouring everything in their path, they lumbered slowly north, seldom covering more than fifteen miles in a day, and at the end of each stage stopping for a day or two, sometimes longer, to hunt and to be feasted and entertained by the local nobility. Before entering any sizeable town, the King, Queen, and principal members of the Court would change from their travelling clothes into glittering ceremonial dress and ride in procession through the town, stopping to be addressed by, and to make a suitable reply to, the mayor and chief citizens.

Their route took them through Enfield, St Albans, and Dunstable, to the King's own castle at Ampthill in Bedfordshire where they rested for four days. The weather was exceptionally wet, and the carts and wagons had much difficulty in getting through the flooded roads, so much so that it was said the King might have turned back had it not been for the great preparations which the Duke of Suffolk had made for his reception at the Duke's house at Grimsthorpe in Lincolnshire to which he had recently moved from Tattershall. During the last week of July the Progress passed through Northamptonshire, arriving at Grimsthorpe on 5 August, exactly on schedule in spite of the heavy rains.

After a short stop at Lincoln, the King eventually reached Pontefract Castle, where he set up his Court, to which the nobles and gentlemen of Yorkshire were invited to come and make their submissions. Marillac wrote:

The King has entered Yorkshire and been received in divers places by the gentlemen of the country, coming in bailiwicks and stewardships, to the number of 5,000 or 6,000 horse. Those who in the rebellion remained faithful were ranked apart and graciously welcomed by the King and praised for their fidelity. The others who were of the conspiracy, among whom appeared the Archbishop of York, were a little further off on their knees; and one of them, speaking for all, made a long harangue confessing their treason in marching against their Sovereign and his Council, thanking him for pardoning so great an offence and begging that if any relics of indignation remained he would dismiss them. They then delivered several bulky submissions in writing. Receiving a benign answer, they arose and accompanied the King to his lodging; and after staying a day or two about the Court, were commanded to return home. No Lord or gentleman dares to come to Court unless summoned, or to follow it beyond the limits of the bailiwick or stewardship through which it is passing; so that all of those between York and Berwick not one is in this company, lest, in the absence of the governors, the frontier should be unfurnished, or else to avoid great assemblies of this barbarous and mutinous people, for the King distrusts such assemblies, especially of these Northern men, who, in truth, look like men of great execution [capability] than the rest of his subjects.

There is no record of the names of the ex-rebels who made their submissions to Henry, and thus it is not known whether Katherine Parr and her husband, Lord Latimer, were there or not. Since both Katherine's brother and sister were in the King's train, however, it seems highly probable that the Latimers obtained the King's permission to attend the meeting at Pontefract. It was also at Pontefract that the King showed his continuing favour for the Parr family by granting Katherine's brother, William Lord Parr, various offices and lands at Rayleigh, Rochford and several other places in Essex which had formerly belonged to the Boleyn family.

After staying for the best part of a fortnight at Pontefract, the King went east to Hull where he carefully inspected the harbour and its defences, giving orders for extensive repairs to be carried out. Finally, on 17 September, he entered York. It was the climax of the Progress. Marillac reported that more than twelve hundred men had been working night and day to convert an old abbey into 'a great lodging', and that Henry had had sent on from London 'his richest tapestry, plate, and dress, both for himself and his archers, pages and gentlemen, with marvellous provisions of victuals from all parts. This seems to betoken some extraordinary triumph, like an interview of Kings or a coronation of his Queen . . .' Both possibilities had, as Marillac knew, been provided for, but in fact neither took place.

Throughout the Progress, the Privy Council was divided into two parts: the first, consisting of a Secretary and a few of Henry's closest advisers, travelled with the King, while the other, consisting mostly of those with executive responsibilities, remained in London. King's Messengers, who were capable of covering upwards of a hundred and fifty miles a day by a carefully organised 'post' system of fresh horses every fifteen or twenty miles, kept the two Councils in close touch with each other so that, in spite of the daily round of hunts and banquets, the government of the country continued without serious interruption. (It took only two days for an urgent despatch to reach London from Berwick-on-Tweed on the Scottish border.)

The main political events during the Progress had all been concerned with foreign affairs. First, and the most important in Henry's eyes, was the attempt to achieve a satisfactory peace agreement with Scotland. For this purpose, much of the time in Council was spent on devising plans to persuade the King of Scotland, James v, to venture into England for a meeting with Henry – hence Marillac's comments. James v had played hot and cold with the project, but in the end, while declaring his deepest friendship and respect for Henry, had stated that he did not dare leave his country in its present unruly state.

The second set of negotiations, which were being conducted with the highest degree of secrecy, was with the Emperor, Charles v. The official purpose was a new trade agreement covering the Low Countries and Spain, but the private objective, on both sides, was a military alliance directed against France. From Henry's point of view, the alliance was aimed mainly at preventing the French from giving help to the Scots should the situation between England and Scotland erupt into open warfare. From the Emperor's point of view, the alliance was to obtain a big diversion on France's western front while he regained lands he had lost in the North and East.

The third set, which was typical of Henry's policy of backing every horse in the race, was to arrange a marriage between the Princess Mary and the Duke of Orleans as a prelude to a new peace treaty with France. This was the reason why the French Ambassador, Marillac, had been invited to accompany Henry on the Progress. It kept him out of London while the Council there carried on negotiations with the Emperor's ambassador, Chapuys, and, as a result of being summoned at least once a week to discussions with the Council with the King, led him to believe that the agreement with France was foremost in their minds.

Marillac, however, does not appear to have been allowed to make direct contact with Princess Mary, and he had to make strenuous efforts during the Progress to find someone who could give him a reliable report on her character to send back to France. Eventually, three months after the Progress had started, and when it was passing through Lincolnshire on its way back to London, he found a chamberwoman in the Princess' household who was married to a Frenchman and who was prepared to talk. Her description, which Marillac may have touched up a little, shows a very different person from the bigoted hypochondriac which the unfortunate Princess was said to be:

> She [Princess Mary] is of middle stature, and is in face like her father, especially about the mouth, but has a voice more man-like for a woman than he has for a man. To judge by portraits, her neck is like her mother's. With a fresh complexion, she looks not past 18 or 20, although she is 24. Her beauty is mediocre, and it may be said that she is one of the belles of the Court. [Presumably a comment on how ugly the others were.] She is active, and apparently not delicate, loving morning exercise and walking often two or three miles. She speaks and writes French well. She understands Latin and enjoys books of Humanist studies, which were her solace in sleepless nights at the time she was molested. She delights in music and plays the spinet singularly well. In conversation, together with sweetness and benignity, she is prudent and reserved. The chamberwoman says that when her mother was first repudiated, she was sick with ennui, but, on being visited and comforted by the King, soon recovered and has had no such illness since. Her physicians and apothecary are Spaniards, and to enquire of them would arouse suspicion; but the apothecary once said that he never gave her anything but light things, conserves and similar medicines, which she took more often because it was her father's command than because she needed them. The chamberwoman thinks her of a disposition to have children soon, if married. Have tried to get a portrait of her, but no painter dare attempt it without the King's command.

The King's homeward journey was faster than the outward one had been. He left York, after a ten-day stay, on 27 September, and arrived back at Windsor on 26 October. It had been a much more exhausting Progress than usual, and in recognition of this fact the King gave the Privy Council and the Court leave to go to their homes for the best part of a week. Henry moved to Hampton Court on 29 October, and sometime during the following week, probably on 4 November, an exceedingly nervous Cranmer, having spent two or three days plucking up his courage, slipped a note into the King's hand during Mass telling him of the infidelity of his Queen.

The first account of Catherine Howard's misbehaviour had been given to Cranmer early in October by John Lassels, a gentleman of the Court, who had been told about it by his sister, Mary Lassels, who had waited on Catherine Howard while she was in her grandmother's household. Mary Lassels said that Catherine had been seduced at the age of thirteen by one Francis Dereham, that since then she had continued her affair with him, and had also slept with a spinet-player called Mannox, and possibly with her cousin, Thomas Culpeper, a Gentleman of the King's Privy Chamber. Mary Lassels went on to say that this had all happened before Catherine's marriage with Henry, and that she had been so ashamed that the King should marry such a woman that she had then refused to continue in Catherine's service.

Cranmer appears to have hesitated before taking any action. These events, if true, had all taken place before Catherine's marriage with the King, and Cranmer's immediate reaction might well have been to let sleeping dogs lie. However, his second thoughts were to reveal the matter to the Chancellor, Lord Thomas Audeley, and the Earl of Hertford, who shared with him the principal duties of the Council in London while the King was on Progress. Hertford will almost certainly have seen in the case a magnificent opportunity to discredit the Duke of Norfolk and the Howard family, and possibly also Gardiner who had encouraged the King to make the match, but he agreed with the others to proceed with the utmost caution, and it was decided not to say anything until Henry returned from the North.

Originally, Henry seems to have been disposed to take the matter lightly. He instructed Cranmer to charge the Queen with the story, to test her reactions, and if nothing more was proved, to promise her his pardon.

Cranmer reported back to Henry on 6 November. He stated that the Queen was in such a pitiable condition that 'for fear she would enter into a frenzy' he had departed from his instructions and had first told her of the King's offer of mercy. She was so relieved that she had promptly confessed everything – everything, that is, that had happened before her marriage with the King. A little while later she modified her story, saying that Dereham had taken her by force.

Henry kept his word about his promise of mercy, and Catherine was sent off to the monastery at Syon. She was deprived of her jewels and her finer clothes, but otherwise no great harm seems to have been intended for her.

There were, however, two other points in the story which needed further investigation. The first was that she had taken Francis Dereham into her service after she had become Queen, which did not accord with her story that there had been nothing more between them since she had reached the age of eighteen, and the second concerned her contacts with her cousin, Thomas Culpeper. A highly suspicious note in Catherine's handwriting, and obviously written while she was on the recent Progress, had been found among Culpeper's belongings. After stating that the writer had thought Culpeper was sick, the note continued:

> It makes my heart die to think I cannot be always in your company. Come when my Lady Rochford is here, for then I shall be best at leisure to be at your commandment . . . I would you were with me now that you might see what pain I take in writing to you.
>
> Yours as long as life endures,
> Katherine

Culpeper and Lady Rochford were again interviewed and, possibly under torture, the whole dismal affair was disclosed. There was no doubt that, at every major stopping place on the Progress, Catherine Howard and Culpeper had spent night after night together, and there was also a strong suspicion that, on the rare occasions when Culpeper had not been available, Francis Dereham had taken his place.

There was also little doubt that Lady Rochford had given Catherine every encouragement to pursue her extra-marital love life. Her motives are difficult to assess, and, according to Chapuys, she was indeed thought to be half mad at her trial. By contributing to the evidence which had brought down Anne Boleyn and Viscount Rochford, Lady Rochford had retained the King's favour, and she had been allowed to continue as a Lady-in-Waiting at Court ever since. In the days of Jane Seymour she is recorded as having been at Court, but little else. Then, during the reign of Anne of Cleves, she emerges once more from obscurity, and is one of the three ladies who testify that Anne was still a virgin after six months of marriage, probably laughing up her sleeve at the veiled implication that Henry was impotent. Finally, in the case of Catherine Howard, she plays the leading rôle of *agent provocateur,* but one suspects that it was not Catherine, but Henry who was her target. Either from remorse about her part in her husband's death, or from a mind unhinged by malice, she used a woman's weapons to attack Henry in his most sensitive spot, his pride as a man. Catherine Howard's youthful indiscretions might have been overlooked, but Lady Rochford, by encouraging Catherine's flagrant adultery after her marriage to Henry, made a cuckold of the King and demonstrated to the world at large Henry's inability to satisfy his wife. It was the first and only time that Henry's masculinity was publicly challenged,[1] and he exploded with rage and frustration.

Marillac reported what he had heard at Court:

> This King has changed his love for the Queen into hatred, and taken such grief at being deceived that of late it was thought he had gone mad, for he called for a sword to slay her whom he had loved so much. Sitting in Council he suddenly called for horses without saying where he would go. Sometimes he said irrelevantly that that wicked woman had never such delight in her incontinency as she should have torture in death. And finally he took to tears regretting his ill-luck in meeting with such ill-conditioned wives, and blaming his Council for this last mischief. The ministers have done their best to make him forget his grief, and he has gone 25 miles from here with no company but musicians and ministers of pastime.

Parliament was summoned for the Trial, and on 25 January, the House of Lords found the Queen and Lady Rochford guilty of high treason. Chapuys, reporting the verdict, added: 'She [the Queen] is still at Syon, making good cheer, fatter and more beautiful than ever, taking great care to be well apparelled and more imperious and troublesome to serve than even when she was with the King, although she believes she will be put to death, and confesses she has deserved it.'

But Catherine's outward appearance of calm did not last long, and the violence of her emotions made everyone reluctant to undertake the task of bringing her to the Tower. Eventually, on 10 February, the unfortunate Duke of Suffolk, whose renowned way with women caused Henry always to select him for dealing with difficult females,[2] braved her screams and weeping, and brought her down the river Thames in a barge. She was given two days to compose herself, and on 13 February she and Lady Rochford were executed on the same spot as Anne Boleyn.

On 25 February, Chapuys, reporting details of the event, informed Charles v that Henry was in much better spirits after the execution:

> During the last three days before Lent, there has been much feasting. Sunday was given up to the Lords of his Council and Court; Monday to the men of Law, and Tuesday to the ladies, who all slept at Court. He himself in the morning did nothing but go from room to room to order lodgings to be prepared for these

ladies, and he made them great and hearty cheer, without showing particular affection to anyone. Indeed, unless Parliament prays him to take another wife, he will not, I think, be in a hurry to marry.

Chapuys added drily that he doubted whether any woman would now aspire to such an honour since Parliament had just passed a new law which made it a crime, punishable by death, for any lady whom the King might wish to marry to conceal any charges of misconduct which could be brought against her.

Most of the Parr family were now at Court. Anne Herbert, Katherine Parr's sister, had been entrusted with the Queen's jewels when the Queen was taken away from Hampton Court but, fortunately, does not seem to have had any other part in the affair. Lord Latimer had attended Parliament and, as usual, Katherine Parr accompanied him to London. William Parr had also been in his usual place next to the King, and was probably one of those 'ministers of pastime' who had accompanied the King to his retreat in the country while the Council were completing their investigations into Catherine Howard. There had in fact been an obscure reference to Lord Parr in Culpeper's statement: Catherine Howard had told Culpeper that she would use him as 'Lady Bray used my Lord Parr'. But who or what was Lady Bray has not come to light. Sometime in 1541, however, Lord Parr's wife, Anne Bourchier, had left him and had gone to live with another man. Lord Parr's marriage had not been successful, but the separation seems to have been without bitterness, and he and his wife had been able to reach an amicable settlement about the disposal of the estates which Anne had inherited (each took an equal share), though two years later Lord Parr was to be obliged to take steps to prevent his wealth being inherited by the children that Anne bore her lover.

Of the rest of Katherine Parr's circle, the Duchess of Suffolk had been in close attendance on the late Queen at the beginning of her reign, supporting her husband and the Earl of Hertford against the Bishop of Winchester and the Duke of Norfolk, but before the Progress had started, she had returned to her new home at Grimsthorpe to prepare for the King's visit. And Grimsthorpe seems to have been one of the very few places on the route of the Progress where Catherine Howard had not misbehaved herself. Princess Mary had kept herself to herself, as she usually did, but of the King's nieces, Margaret Douglas was once more in trouble because of the Howards, this time on account of Lord Charles

Howard, the Duke's nephew. Cranmer was sent to warn her that there should not be 'a third time', and she was put for the time being, and somewhat surprisingly, in the charge of the Duchess of Richmond at the Duke of Norfolk's home at Kenninghall. Anthony Denny had had to give evidence that, at one of the places on the Progress, he had been sent one night with a message from the King to the Queen, but that he had got no reply when he had knocked at the Queen's locked door. His wife, Joan, however, had not been involved. The Countess of Hertford had remained behind in London with her husband, and Lady Dudley had also managed to avoid all contact with the Queen.

With the exception of Margaret Douglas, there was nothing, therefore, to connect any of them with the scandal, and it was this circle of women, together with Katherine Parr and her sister, that the King had made so much fuss of at the Mardi Gras banquet mentioned by Chapuys. They brought back for him the bright intellectual atmosphere of former years, and the wit and laughter was a wonderful relief from the vanity and silliness of Catherine Howard's circle, or the bourgeois dullness of Anne of Cleves. Chapuys was right: with such female company on call, and no political aim to be achieved by marriage, the King was in no hurry to marry again. He installed Princess Mary as the First Lady at Court, and for at least the rest of 1542, he devoted all his time to affairs of State.

NOTES

1 In the case of Anne Boleyn, Henry considered that he had discarded her, and not *vice versa.*
2 It was the Duke of Suffolk who had had to escort Catharine of Aragon to Kimbolton; he who had brought Anne Boleyn to the Tower; and it was he who carried out the negotiations with Anne of Cleves.

9 The Rise of the Parrs

At the beginning of 1542, the hopes of the Parr family centred round Katherine's brother, William, Lord Parr, for her uncle, Sir William Parr of Horton, had now reached the age of semi-retirement. Never a major figure in politics, Sir William had nevertheless served his King and his family well. He had made no pretence of being an intellectual, and his value to the King had been that of the practical field commander, reacting quickly to a crisis, and doing the right thing more by instinct and training than by logical thought. He was often in trouble with his tenants, partly over boundary disputes, partly because of his high-handed disregard of their rights, but he never evaded their attempts to bring him to court, and if he lost the case, as he often did, he always accepted the verdict with no more than an irritable curse. It was probably for this reason that, in spite of his actions, his tenants were intensely loyal to him, and he never had difficulty in raising two or three hundred men to follow him to the wars or to restore order in times of revolt.

To many, Sir William was little more than a prosperous country squire, more at home with his hawks and greyhounds than in the learned company of the King's Council, but this would be to underrate his grasp of public affairs, and it was on men like him that the King depended for controlling the country. He was an efficient, if harsh, administrator, and as one of the King's Chief Commissioners for the Peace he showed a nicer understanding of the law, possibly because of his frequent court cases with his tenants, than his fellow Commissioners, though this did not stop him from carrying out the rough justice called for in suppressing rebellion or sedition. He was also a shrewd man of business and, as a joint executor of his brother's will, he had taken good care of his nephew's inheritance, personally visiting and checking the stewards of the widespread estates in Kendal, Yorkshire, Lincolnshire, Buckinghamshire, and in his own Northamptonshire, to ensure that they were doing their work well and as honestly as could be expected.

It was also to his uncle that young William Parr, during the years he spent with the King's illegitimate son, the Duke of Richmond, owed his training in field sports and military duties – much to the annoyance of his tutors who grudged any time the boys spent away from their books. In Henry's England, however, there was no place for delicate men, whatever their intellect, and even poets – the Earl of Surrey and Sir Thomas Wyatt were notable examples – were expected to be able to fight for their King and to take part in the jousts and other military tournaments which served to build up the courage and discipline needed in war.

Young William Parr's first taste of quasi-military and political service had come in 1537, when he was twenty-one, and had accompanied the Duke of Norfolk to the North of England for the suppression of Bigod's rebellion. This was followed by some months spent with Sir William Parr in the settling of affairs in Lincolnshire. He was praised on all sides for the way in which he had conducted himself, and in 1538 there were already rumours that he was to be elevated to the peerage. As has already been noted, he was in fact created Lord Parr of Kendal in March 1539, a mark more of the King's great hopes for him in the future than of past service, which, though obviously praiseworthy, had hardly been of sufficient extent to justify such a big promotion. In 1540, he took part in the trial of Thomas Cromwell, and he may have helped his sister behind the scenes in promoting Cromwell's fall. His other and more important 'uncle', Cuthbert Tunstall, was then summoned to the King's Privy Council, and his already favoured position in Henry's inner circle was further strengthened. During that and the following year, 1541, he received several grants of lands and offices, and by the beginning of 1542 there is little doubt that, in spite of his youth, his influence at Court had risen to the point where it was becoming a significant factor in the power-game.

There is no record of the time or occasion on which Henry first gave William Parr the nickname of 'My Integrity', but one can guess that it was probably during his rise to favour in 1538–9, when Henry was suspicious of both the rival factions on his Council. Lord Parr, like Cuthbert Tunstall, belonged to neither faction at that time, nor did he have any obvious axe to grind. Good-natured and efficient, he shared the King's love of music and learning, and acquitted himself well in debate, not afraid to argue a point, but instinctively knowing when to defer to Henry's opinion. At the same time, he was able to give a good account of himself in jousting tournaments, and he was as tireless in the chase as Henry once had been. During his boyhood and teens, Henry had treated him almost as if he had been his own son, but now that he had taken over the responsibilities of a great landowner and was settling down to his duties as a peer, Henry's interest in him changed from that of an indulgent guardian to that of a King testing a promising young nobleman for higher office, and it only remained for a suitable opportunity for young Lord Parr to prove himself. That opportunity came at the end of 1542 after a sequence of events which played into Lord Parr's hands and which was to place the Parr family in the position that the Boleyns and Seymours had previously held.

The significant events as far as the Parrs were concerned were all related to the North Country and the Scottish Borders. They arose out of a complex diplomatic situation in which the French had broken their truce with the Emperor and formed an alliance with the Turks against him. Henry decided to throw in his lot with the Emperor against the French and, as a result, the French poured money and troops into Scotland, encouraging James v to harass Henry's Northern frontiers. Informed by spies of what was going on, Henry thereupon started to strengthen the Northern defences, and sent the Earl of Rutland as Lord Warden of the Scottish Marches with headquarters at Berwick. At the same time, Katherine Parr's ambitions for her husband were finally realised, and Lord Latimer was appointed a member of the Council of the North, to join Rutland at Berwick.

These moves, however, were too little and too late. On 19 August 1542, ten thousand Scots began an advance against the Borders. The alarm was sounded, but only three thousand men could be raised under Sir Robert Bowes to meet the Scots, and when the attack took place, at Haddon Rig on 24 August, the English force was roundly defeated with the loss of about four hundred prisoners.

An infuriated Henry immediately ordered the Duke of Norfolk to raise as big an army as possible and, despite the late season of the year, told him to make a punitive expedition into Scotland. With chaotic disorganisation, which has seldom been equalled in English military history and for which the Duke of Norfolk was largely to blame, the expedition, consisting of forty thousand men, eventually crossed the Scottish border on 24 October. After five days in Scotland, during which a few villages were burnt, but with little else to show for all the expense and effort, Norfolk and his army returned to England.

On the day they got back to Berwick, the Earl of Hertford, who had been sent at the last minute to help Norfolk, wrote a letter to Henry which was to prove of vital importance to the Parrs, though it was not written with that thought in mind. Hertford begged Henry to be relieved of his command under Norfolk on the grounds that he was a stranger 'among these noblemen of the North', who, he said, resented his taking command of their men. Henry granted his request, but asked him to remain at Berwick as Lord Warden in the place of Rutland until the end of November, when he would send John Dudley, now the Viscount Lisle, to take his place as a temporary measure.

Then, on 21 November, spies reported that James v was advancing in person with a large army against the western end of the Borders. Sir Thomas Wharton, in charge at Carlisle and already frustrated by the Duke of Norfolk's inept handling of the October operation, sent out an urgent summons to the tough Border families – the Musgraves, Curwens, Prestons, Lowthers, Stricklands, and Layburnes – to muster with their men outside Carlisle. He would show the soft Southerners how to deal with the Scots, and with an army of less than two thousand men, he set out at midnight on 23–24 November to find the King of Scots. The sortie was brilliantly successful. Although the Scots numbered seventeen thousand men, Wharton trapped them at dawn on the 24th in a swamp known as Solway Moss, with the flooded river Esk before them. The Scots did not know whether to advance or retire. Panic ensued, and what should have been an orderly retreat to a stronger position turned into a rout. Hundreds were drowned in the river, and Wharton's small force took twelve hundred prisoners, including 'two Earls, five Barons, and 500 lairds and gentlemen'. James v, who had been watching the battle from a hill, retreated hastily towards Stirling, disgusted with his men and broken-hearted at the death of his favourite, Oliver Sinclair. Subsequently, he fell into a fever, and on 15 December, having been further disgusted by the news that on 2 December, his Queen, Mary of Guise, had given birth to a daughter, not a son, he turned his face to the wall and died.

The victory of Solway Moss, the death of James v, and particularly the capture of so many of the Scots nobility, more than made up for the disasters of the previous four months. Henry was overjoyed. He wrote an enthusiastic letter to Wharton, praising him and 'all who were with him'. Of the latter, the first whom Wharton had named in his report was the 'standard of Lord Parr under the rule of my cousin, Sir Walter Strickland', who, he wrote, had been with him throughout the action. It is not clear whether Lord Parr was present himself at Solway Moss, but the sight of his name, and in the foremost place of honour to which Wharton had assigned it, confirmed an idea which had been developing in Henry's mind ever since he had received Hertford's request to be relieved.

Although the reason which Hertford had given for his resignation was no more than a face-saving excuse, it made sense to Henry. The Pilgrimage of Grace, Bigod's rebellion, the abortive rising of 1541, had all shown that the North resented control by Southerners. While taking steps to deal with the immediate situation, Henry therefore began to look for a long-term solution to the problem of keeping the North loyal and obedient. It was a recurring problem, which, in the light of the Scottish threat, could become critical to the peace of the country.

In the past, the problem had been solved by vesting authority in the great feudal families of the North – the Percys, Nevilles, Marmions, and Fitzhughs – but those who were left after the collapse of feudalism were either incompetent or corrupt. Henry needed new blood to take their places, or at least a link with London which would satisfy Northerners that their interests were being cared for by their own kin. And the only Northern family which Henry was sure he could trust were the Parrs.

It seems certain that Henry was already thinking along these lines before the victory at Solway Moss, for early in November Lord Latimer was summoned from Berwick to come to London and to bring Katherine Parr with him. Early in December, however, shortly after arriving in London, Lord Latimer died,[1] and for the second time Katherine became a widow. Thus both brother and sister were at Henry's disposal just at the moment when Solway Moss confirmed Henry's judgment of the value and standing of the Parr family, and at the end of the victory celebrations which were combined with the Christmas and New Year festivities, Henry finally made up his mind.

As far as Lord Parr was concerned, Henry decided to give his young 'Integrity' the chance he had been waiting for, and he sent him to Newcastle to join the Duke of Suffolk whom he had appointed his Lieutenant of the North in place of the Duke of Norfolk. Lord Parr was to serve a period of three months as a principal member of the Council of the North, and thereafter he was to relieve Lord Lisle in the key position of Lord Warden of the Scottish Marches. The period of three months was to give him experience of the inner workings of the organisation and politics of the North before letting him loose with his own command. It was also, of course, a trial period, and doubtless Suffolk was ordered to watch him closely for any signs of incipient weakness or indecision, but Lord Parr was to come through the ordeal with flying colours and fully justify Henry's judgment of his character.

In Katherine's case, it is probable that Henry first considered marrying her off to some powerful nobleman of the North, but during the celebrations at Court, he began to have other ideas. Chapuys reports:

> These successes have rejoiced the King, who, since he learnt of the conduct of his last wife, has continually shown himself sad, and nothing has been said of banquet or of ladies; but now all is changed, and order is already taken that the Princess [Mary] shall go to Court at this feast, accompanied with a great number of ladies; and they work day and night at Hampton Court to finish her lodgings. It is possible that amid these festivities, the King might think of marrying, although there is yet no bruit of it.

Although it was to be some months before Henry's intentions became generally known, Chapuys had guessed right and there is little doubt that immediately after the New Year Henry made up his mind to marry Katherine himself.[2]

The main motive for all Henry's marriages so far had been political rather than personal. A king, as he had remarked to Cromwell when discussing Anne of Cleves, was the only man in the realm who was not free to marry whomsoever he chose. This is not to say that Henry did not have any affection for any of his wives – he patently adored Jane Seymour – but desire always followed, never preceded, the selection of the bride-to-be. In other words, Henry first chose the woman whom he believed, or had been persuaded to believe, would be best suited, politically, to be his Queen, and then tried, with varying degrees of success, to work up a romantic relationship with her. The romance could be stifled, either through political necessity, as in the case of Anne Boleyn, or through the stupidity of the woman, as in the case of Catherine Howard, or it could die a natural death, as in the case of Catharine of Aragon, but the need for romance in marriage was a genuine, if adolescent, streak in Henry's nature, and he worked hard to achieve it. In spite of being physically repelled by Anne of Cleves, for example, it is clear from the divorce evidence that during the six months between

150

marriage and divorce, Henry had developed a sincere fondness for her.

In the case of Katherine Parr the political motives were, first, her strong connections, both through her own family and through her late husband's, with the nobility and common people in the North of England (the principal troublespot in the Kingdom), and, secondly, the fact that, like her brother, she was neither Protestant nor Papist, but a firm adherent of the original Humanist doctrines of Erasmus and Vives. As a Parr, therefore, Katherine offered Henry the means of securing loyalty and obedience in the North, and at the same time, in her own right, she offered the possibility of becoming a base for what Henry most needed at Court – a middle-of-the-road faction to maintain the balance between the Old and New Faiths.

Unlike his previous Queens, however, Katherine Parr was, in January 1543, virtually unsupported by any substantial 'party' at Court. She had friends enough, but there was no declared political or religious allegiance. Her prudence had dictated that she should avoid taking sides, and with her brother and Cuthbert Tunstall both being away in the North, she had to stand on her own feet. On the other hand, she had shown by the way in which she had extricated Lord Latimer and herself from the repercussions of the Northern rebellions, and by the way in which she had directed the dagger into Cromwell's back, that she had a flair for politics which Henry had not encountered in a woman since the days of Anne Boleyn. It was an interesting, albeit alarming, parallel, but at least it gave some assurance of her courage and of her ability to attract others to her side. In the event, Katherine Parr was to model herself, in public, on Catharine of Aragon, after whom she was probably named, and it was only in private that the steel of Anne Boleyn was to appear.

Katherine's personal qualities, therefore, probably played as big a part in Henry's choice of her as did his political motives. A further point was that Henry had known her ever since she was a babe in her mother's arms. He had watched her grow up with his daughter, Mary, and his nieces, had been informed of her progress with her tutors, had followed her development as a child bride, and had seen how she had behaved herself as a teenage widow and then as wife and step-mother in a great household. The Cromwell affair had revealed her hidden depths, and as far as any man could ever be sure of his judgment of a woman,

Henry would have been sure about Katherine. There would be no unpleasant surprises, no twists of character or temperament which he did not already know about. Her behaviour in any given situation seemed to him to be entirely predictable. It was a rare situation for any man to be in: for a King who considered that he had suffered nothing but disaster both political and personal, from his former marriages, it appeared that Heaven smiled on him at last.

There is a story, related by Leti and quoted by Strickland, that when Henry made his first tentative approach to Katherine Parr on the subject of marriage, Katherine was aghast. She would be anything, she pleaded, but his wife. Let him take her for his mistress, let him do with her whatever he wished, but let him not put her in the most dangerous position in England for a woman, that of being his Queen.

Nothing could be less likely to be true. Apart from the fact that Katherine Parr's virtue was her proudest asset, she had been brought up from birth to believe that she had been born to rule. The hands that had been 'ordained to touch crowns and sceptres' were not going to reject these symbols of sovereignty now that they were at last being proffered to her. Her own story is that she had set her heart on marrying Sir Thomas Seymour, the Earl of Hertford's brother, but that God intervened and 'made that possible which seemed to me most impossible: that was, made me renounce utterly mine own will, and to follow His will most willingly'. This statement was made four years after the event in a letter to Sir Thomas Seymour (see p. 230) written shortly after Henry's death.

Sir Thomas Seymour seems to have been the most sought-after bachelor in Henry's Court. The seventeenth-century historian, Hayward, describes him as 'fierce in courage, courtly in fashion, in personage stately, in voice magnificent, but somewhat empty in matter'. Like Lord Lisle, he had served his military apprenticeship at sea, but whereas Lisle had developed a sailor's direct practical approach to problems, Thomas Seymour possessed an elaborate mind which lost itself in a confusion of detail, with the result that he often failed to see the key point in a situation and his errors of judgment were notorious. The one outstanding chink in Katherine Parr's armour was her weakness for him, but her letter mentioned above makes it clear that she did not reveal her feelings when Thomas Seymour reappeared at Court in February 1543, after some eight months spent abroad as an 'observer' in the war against the Turks.

This is further proof that Henry had then already made his proposal to her, and her belief in her destiny – to her, it was God's will – prevented her from making any false move. Henry may have known of her weakness, or she may have put in a word herself, for barely two weeks after Sir Thomas Seymour's return, he was appointed special ambassador to the Queen Regent in Brussels, though he did not actually leave the country again until the end of April, but thereafter he was almost continuously abroad, or at sea with Lisle, until the last few months of Henry's reign.

Although Katherine Parr accepted Henry's proposal in principle at the time he made it, she insisted on a period of mourning for her late husband before she married again. Vives had warned her long ago that all men liked to think that they would be missed by their wives after they were dead, and that a man who might be thinking of marrying a widow would change his mind if he saw her treat her widowhood lightly, since he would suppose that she would do the same when his turn came to die. With a man as impatient as Henry, it might be thought that Katherine took some risk in insisting on delay, but she knew her Henry, possibly as well as he knew her, and Henry's weak spot was that resistance to his will always made him more determined than ever to have his own way. Chapuys, who was still not sure of the King's intentions, reported on 22 February: 'The King has shown the greatest possible affection and liberality to the Princess [Mary], and not a day passes but he goes to visit her in her chamber two or three times with the utmost cordiality.'

Henry was quite fond of his daughter, but this was an excessive display of affection and, since Katherine and Princess Mary were close friends, it seems much more likely that Henry was using the same method for meeting Katherine as he had used before for his secret meetings with Jane Seymour, whom he used to visit in the Court lodgings of her brother and sister-in-law. In short, already in February, Henry was following the familiar pattern of previous occasions and, having chosen Katherine Parr to be his next Queen, he was now building up the romantic atmosphere which was indispensable in his concept of marriage. There could, therefore, be no doubt in Katherine's mind that her future was assured, and that she could begin to prepare the ground for the day when she would be Queen.

Her first and main concern was the rôle she should play in the struggle between the Hertford and the Gardiner/Norfolk factions. The year 1543 had not begun well for the latter. The Emperor was still making difficulties about the treaty with Henry, the negotiation of which had been Gardiner's prime responsibility, and on 19 and 20 January, the Earl of Surrey, the Duke of Norfolk's eldest son, went on a drunken rampage in the streets of London with a party of friends, throwing stones at windows and smashing market stalls. They kept it up for two nights, but worse was to come, for in the investigation which followed, one of Surrey's maidservants, apparently repeating what she had heard in his house, said that Surrey was a 'Prince', and that 'if ought other than good should become of the King, he [Surrey] is like to be King'. The Duke of Norfolk seems to have been able to forestall any immediate action by the authorities, but the matter could not be concealed and, on 1 April, the Earl of Hertford saw to it that Surrey and his friends were brought before the Privy Council and sent to prison. The charge, however, was only for causing damage and creating a nuisance, and Hertford kept back the far more serious charge of treason, which was implicit in the maidservant's evidence, as a threat to be used later if need be.

On the religious front, matters had also gone badly for Gardiner for, in the middle of February, Cranmer succeeded in persuading Convocation to agree to, and received the King's permission for, an injunction that the name of the 'Bishop of Rome' (i.e. the Pope) and 'the names and memories of all saints which be not mentioned in the Scripture or authentical doctors should be abolished and put out of' all religious books and calendars. Cranmer rubbed his triumph home by also persuading Convocation to grant the King a subsidy of four shillings in the pound of the Church's income for the next three years.

On 11 February, however, Gardiner was finally able to report the successful conclusion of the treaty with the Emperor, and he was then free to return to religious affairs. In his capacity as Bishop of Winchester, he began his process of retaliation against Cranmer by a heresy hunt. Since his objective was to bring down the Hertford faction and to unseat Cranmer, whose position as Archbishop of Canterbury he had long coveted, he directed the search, with cold contempt for the possible consequences, into the Court itself. Using as his agent the notorious Dr London who had served Cromwell so faithfully in the dissolution of the monasteries, Gardiner pulled in some seven people who were

154

either at Court, which was then at Windsor, or had had close associations with the Court.

The most important captive was Dr Haynes, a famous preacher of the New Faith who had been closely acquainted with Cranmer and Hugh Latimer for many years, and who had been sent down to Exeter to keep him out of harm's way after the passing of the Act of Six Articles to which he had vehemently objected. He was brought before the Privy Council on 16 March and committed to the Fleet prison. The rest of the captives, three gentlemen of the Household and three musicians, were tried on the following three days, and all but two of the musicians were also sent to the Fleet.

One of the three gentlemen was Philip Hobby, a close friend of Katherine Parr's brother. A week later, on 24 March, he was released, the only one to be set free at that time. There is no evidence that Katherine intervened on his behalf, but whether she did or not this 'local' trial of heretics brought home to her the real malevolence of the Gardiner/Norfolk faction. It represented a danger not only to her friends, but also to herself, and it became clear to her then that she would have to take steps to neutralise their activities. Anne Boleyn's big mistake had been to make her support for the New Faith, and her opposition to the old Establishment, too vigorous and, above all, too public. If Katherine Parr was to survive, she would have to act more circumspectly and with a great deal more prudence, and it was then that the idea came to her of working with and through women rather than by attempting to sway the Council directly herself. However, until she became Queen and could once more fill the Court with Ladies-in-Waiting, there was little that she could do other than by her own personal influence with the King. Apart from Princess Mary's household, who were for the most part either apolitical or secret Papists, the only women then at Court on whom she could rely were her sister, Anne Herbert, and Joan Champernown, the wife of Anthony Denny, but they were too few to make an impression and their husbands, through whom they would have to act, were not yet prepared to risk any overt moves. Earlier historians believe that it was during this time, the period of Henry's courtship, that Katherine became 'converted' to the New Faith, but this does not in fact seem to have happened until a year or more later, and she was now far more concerned with survival than with religious salvation.

The quick success which he had achieved by his direct assault on the

Court, and Henry's apparent acquiescence therein, decided Gardiner to try at once for his main objective, the fall of Cranmer, and Dr London was directed to look into promising reports that had come in from Kent of Cranmer's handling of suspected heresies in his own diocese.

The evidence against Cranmer was not as clear as Gardiner had hoped for, in spite of some twisting of the facts which Dr London wrote into the depositions of the witnesses, but, on 25 April, a restricted meeting of the Privy Council, consisting of Gardiner, Norfolk, the Bishop of Westminster, and Wriothesley, agreed that at least a *prima facie* case could be made out against Cranmer, and they presented their findings to the King. Henry agreed that they had a case, and he gave them permission to charge Cranmer on the following day before the full Council.

Late that same night, however, Henry sent for Cranmer. Anthony Denny was the messenger, and at about midnight he brought Cranmer to the gallery at Whitehall where the King was waiting for them. Henry told Cranmer that he had agreed to let the Council arrest him and send him to the Tower, and he asked Cranmer for his comments. Cranmer's secretary, Morice, later recorded the conversation that followed. Cranmer, he wrote, most humbly thanked the King for his warning, but said he would be very well content to stand trial for his beliefs. He was sure, he added, that Henry would see to it that he received an impartial hearing. Morice continues:

'O Lord God!' quoth the King, 'what fond simplicity have you; so to permit yourself to be imprisoned, that every enemy of yours may take vantage against you. Do you not think that if they have you once in prison, three or four false knaves will be soon procured to witness against you and to condemn you, who (as long as you are at liberty) dare not once open their lips or appear before your face?

'No, not so, my Lord,' quoth the King, 'I have better regard unto you than to permit your enemies so to overthrow you.'

Henry then gave Cranmer his ring, and told him that when the Council arrested him next day, he should show the ring and demand to be heard by Henry in person.

Cranmer did as he had been told, and when he produced the King's ring before the Council on the following day, they were dumbfounded. Lord Russell, the Lord Privy Seal, exclaimed that he had always said that Henry would only allow them to send Cranmer to the Tower on a clear case of treason, and cast the blame on Gardiner and Norfolk for their

156

action. Cranmer then took the Councillors with him to see the King. The Duke of Norfolk asserted that they had only wished to charge Cranmer with heresy in order to give him the chance of clearing himself. Henry revelled in the situation. It gave him yet another opportunity to keep the Council divided against itself, and hence easier to control, and after upbraiding Gardiner and Norfolk for what they had done, he accepted their excuses. He then ordered them to shake hands, and told Cranmer to entertain the Councillors to dinner.

Only three days before these events, however, on 23 April, the Hertford faction, and the Parr family in particular, received a great boost to their standing in the country. On that day, having been summoned to London from their posts in the North, Lord Lisle and Lord Parr were both elected to the Order of the Garter. On the same day, Lord Parr's appointment as Lord Warden of the Scottish Marches in place of Lord Lisle was confirmed, and Lord Lisle was sworn in as a member of the Privy Council. On 27 April, Lord Parr was introduced to his stall as a Knight of the Garter at Windsor by the Earl of Hertford but, as affairs in Scotland were once more threatening the peace of the Borders, he had to forgo the subsequent celebrations, and that night he set off post haste for Berwick. Although it is possible that Lord Parr owed his promotion and the high honour of the Garter to the King's interest in his sister, it is more probable, in view of Lord Parr's high standing with the King, that it was the other way round; that it was he who helped his sister, not she who helped him.

Most of June was taken up with preparations for defence against both France and Scotland. Early in the month, Henry set off by sea, accompanied by Lisle, to review the Fleet at Harwich and to make a personal inspection of the East Coast harbour facilities. For the fortnight that the expedition lasted, he put aside the subtleties of statecraft and became absorbed with almost boyish enthusiasm in the practical problems of seamanship and naval tactics.

This sudden return to a youthful, buoyant outlook, which was reflected in the instructions which Henry sent back to the Council during his absence, was almost certainly also due to the fact that, before he left, Katherine Parr had at last agreed to let him name the day for their wedding. She had spent the previous two or three months quietly building up an image of the domestic happiness which Henry could enjoy with her by taking pains to win the friendship of the nine-year-old

Princess Elizabeth as well as strengthening the close bonds she already had with Princess Mary, and, from a letter which Lisle wrote to Lord Parr on Henry's return to Greenwich on 20 June, it was a pleasant family scene which greeted the exuberant King's arrival back home. 'Other news is none,' wrote Lisle, 'but that my Lady Latimer, your sister, and Mrs Herbert be both here in the Court with my Lady Mary's grace and my Lady Elizabeth.'

Henry's doubts about Katherine, if there ever had been any, were removed. He had first to deal with an embassy from Scotland and the creation of some Irish peers whom he hoped to bedazzle into serving his interests in Ireland, but finally, on 10 July, Cranmer issued the following document from his palace at Lambeth:

Licence of Thomas, Archbishop of Canterbury, Primate of England, authorised thereto by Parliament, to Henry VIII (who had deigned to take the Lady Katherine, late wife of Lord Latimer, deceased) to have the marriage solemnised in any church, chapel or oratory without the issue of banns. Lambeth, 10 July 1543, a°rr. 35 Hen. VIII., consec. 11.

Unlike the marriages with Anne Boleyn, Jane Seymour, and Catherine Howard, which had all been conducted in secret, Henry's marriage with Katherine Parr took place in a solemn and public ceremony which was officially recorded and properly attested:

Witnesseth that, on 12 July 1543, 35 Hen. VIII., in an upper oratory called the Queen's Privy Closet within the honour of Hampton Court, Westminster diocese, in presence of the noble and gentle persons named at the foot of this instrument and of me, Richard Watkins, the King's prothonotary, the King and Lady Katherine Latimer *alias* Parr being met there for the purpose of solemnising matrimony between them, Stephen Bishop of Winchester [Gardiner] proclaimed in English that they were met to join in marriage the said King and Lady Katherine, and if anyone knew any impediment thereto he should declare it.

The licence for the marriage without publication of banns, sealed by Thomas Archbishop of Canterbury [Cranmer] and dated 10 July 1543, being then brought in, and none opposing but all applauding the marriage, the said Bishop of Winchester put the questions to which the King replied, *hilari vultu*, 'Yea' and the Lady Katherine also replied that it was her wish.

And then the King, taking her right hand, repeated after the Bishop the words, 'I, Henry, take thee, Katherine, to my wedded wife, to have and to hold from this day forward, for better for worse, for richer for poorer, in sickness and in health, till death us do part, and thereto I plight thee my troth.'

Then, releasing and again clasping hands, the Lady Katherine likewise said, 'I,

Katherine, take thee, Henry, to my wedded husband, to have and to hold from this day forward, for better for worse, for richer for poorer, in sickness and in health, to be bonair and buxom in bed and at board, till death us do part, and thereto I plight thee my troth.'

The putting on of the wedding ring and proffer of gold and silver followed; and the Bishop, after prayer, pronounced a benediction. The King then commanded the prothonotary to make a public instrument of the premises.

Present: Lord Russell, KG, Keeper of the Privy Seal
>   Sir Anthony Browne, KG, Captain of the King's Pensioners
>   and
>   Thomas Henneage, Edward Seymour,[3] Henry Knyvett, Richard Long,
>   Thomas Darcy, Edward Baynton, and Thomas Speke, knights,
>   and
>   Anthony Denny and William Herbert, esquires,
>   also
>   the ladies Mary and Elizabeth, the King's children,
>   Margaret Douglas, his niece,
>   Katherine Duchess of Suffolk
>   Anne Countess of Hertford
>   Joan Lady Dudley [Viscountess Lisle]
>   and
>   Anne Herbert.

Notarial attestation by Richard Watkins, Ll.B., King's prothonotary.

The main interest in the simple but impressive ceremony lies in the list of persons present. None of the women, nor any of their husbands, belonged to the Gardiner/Norfolk faction; all but Princess Elizabeth and the Countess of Hertford had been Katherine Parr's contemporaries at the Court school in the days of Catharine of Aragon; and the last four named represented the cream of intellectual society. One important name among the female intellectuals was missing, that of Anthony Denny's wife, Joan, and it must be supposed that she was either in the final stages of pregnancy or ill. She joined Katherine Parr some weeks later and became, like the others, one of her 'permanent' Ladies-in-Waiting.

Of the men, only Lord Russell and Sir Anthony Browne, plus, of course, Gardiner, who conducted the ceremony, were overt members of the Gardiner/Norfolk party. Norfolk himself was not present, but then neither was the Duke of Suffolk, and it must be presumed that Norfolk, like Suffolk, was detained on military duties, as were Lord Parr and Lord Lisle who would otherwise certainly have been there. (Lord Lisle was at that moment at sea searching for the French Fleet which was reported to be off the North Foreland.) On the other hand, possibly through an oversight, though it may well have been deliberate, the prothonotary failed to give Edward Seymour his proper title (Earl of Hertford), nor his rightful position in the order of precedence. Both as a peer and by virtue of his recent promotion to the position of Great Chamberlain in the Privy Council, he should have headed the list of those present. The notary also omitted the fact that, like Russell and Browne, he was also a Knight of the Garter. One should not, perhaps, read too much into this apparent slight to Hertford, but it may have been inspired by Gardiner, who, being a lawyer himself, probably checked and corrected the notarial instrument.

The marriage had many people guessing as to which direction the power-game was now about to take. Katherine Parr did not evoke fear, since very few knew of the part she had already played in politics, nor did she have the support of any particular party at Court. Her women friends, it is true, were of the Hertford circle, but against this was the fact that those who may have been considered to be guiding her were first, Cuthbert Tunstall, and her brother, who were strictly middle-of-the-road, and secondly, her real uncle, Sir William Parr of Horton, who, if anything, was a conservative. As a result of this uncertainty, most played for safety, and one of the first to react was the Secretary to the Council Sir Thomas Wriothesley, a Gardiner man, but one who always liked to keep his options open. In a letter to the Duke of Suffolk, enclosing letters from the Duchess, he wrote:

I doubt not but Your Grace knoweth by the same [the enclosed letters] that the King's Majesty was married on Thursday last to my Lady Latimer, a woman in my judgment, for virtue, wisdom, and gentleness, most meet for his Highness; and sure I am His Majesty had never a wife more agreeable to his heart than she is. Our Lord send them long life and much joy together.
[Dated 16 July 1543.]

The reactions from abroad were also highly complimentary. Edmund Harvel, Henry's ambassador in Venice, for example, passed on the Signory's congratulations on Henry's marriage 'to so prudent, beautiful (sic), and virtuous a lady as is by universal fame reported'.

Not all the reactions in England were favourable, however, and Chapuys took a little malicious pleasure in reporting that he had:

heard in a good quarter that the said lady [Anne of Cleves] would like to be in

160

her shirt, so to speak, with her mother, having especially taken great grief and despair at the King's espousal of this last wife, who is not nearly so beautiful as she, besides that there is no hope of issue, seeing that she had none with her two former husbands.

The week following the wedding was taken up with preparations for the annual summer Progress which this year was to be a gentle tour from Surrey, through Buckinghamshire and Bedfordshire, returning to London via Hertfordshire. At the first stop, at Oatlands in Surrey, Katherine at last found time, on 20 July, to write to her brother. The full text of the letter is not available, but the summary given in *Letters & Papers* reads as follows:

> It having pleased God to incline the King to take her as his wife, which is the greatest joy and comfort that could happen to her, she informs her brother of it, as the person who has most cause to rejoice thereat; and requires him to let her sometimes hear of his health as friendly as if she had not been called to this honour.
> Given at my Lord's manor of Oatlands, 20 July 35 Henry VIII (1543).
> Addressed to my well-beloved brother, the Lord Parre, Lord Warden of the Marches.

In short, the Parr family had arrived at last. It remained to be seen how they would use the power that destiny had enabled them to grasp.

NOTES

1 These statements are based on the fact that the last note in the records concerning Lord Latimer is dated 1 October 1542. His will was proved in March 1543, which places his death as not likely to be later than December 1542. Although his will states his request to be buried in Wells, near Snape, an unpublished history of the Neville family, quoted by Strickland, states that he was in fact buried in St Paul's Churchyard in London. He must, therefore, have travelled south from Berwick, where the note referred to above places him in October, in time to be in London in December. Katherine was certainly in London in January, and it is a fair assumption that she accompanied her husband on his journey south.

2 A bill incurred in January 1543, by Katherine Parr under her name of Lady Latimer, and due to Mr Skutt, the Court tailor who made the clothes for all Henry's previous Queens, was paid by Sir Thomas Arundell, a Treasurer of the Household. The bill was endorsed 'for your daughter', referring presumably to Lord Latimer's daughter, Margaret Neville. Since it was paid by Henry's treasurer, it was a gift from the King and shows that he was then beginning to pay court to Katherine. The items of the bill were for various Italian, French, Dutch, and Venetian gowns and hoods. The total value was £8 9s 5d (worth about £210 today).

3 Earl of Hertford.

10 Katherine, the Queen, K.P.

Katherine Parr had had six months in which to prepare herself for her rôle as Queen, and she had thought out with painstaking care how she would conduct herself during the first few months of her reign. In politics or religion, her prudent course was to do nothing to indicate a preference for one side or the other. One week before her marriage to the King, however, Cranmer's old friend, Dr Haynes, who, it will be recalled, had been arrested some four months earlier for heresy, was released from prison. This was much more probably the result of Cranmer's intercession than Katherine Parr's, but it seems to have decided Gardiner to give an immediate demonstration of his power. If it was Katherine who had persuaded the King to set Haynes free, then he, Gardiner, would show her at once who was the real master of the Council and at the same time make clear his cold indifference to her authority. He still had three of the so-called Windsor heretics in prison; they had all been found guilty, and he demanded that they should die.

Henry agreed. At the time of his marriage to Catherine Howard, he himself had used the same device to demonstrate the neutrality of the Queen by sending to the stake three Protestants and three Papists. Moreover, for the better part of a year now, he had been lenient in enforcing the Act of Six Articles. Several people had been arrested but, during this period, none had suffered death. Uncharacteristically, he may have hoped that tolerance on his part might breed tolerance among the people, but in fact religious discord had increased rather than diminished, and he may have decided, quite apart from satisfying Gardiner, that an example must once more be made of those who refused to conform. Accordingly, on 28 July, the three men were burnt at Windsor, a bare ten miles from Oatlands where the King was enjoying the third week of his honeymoon.

The event was later reported in a letter from Richard Hilles, a scholar turned merchant who was now living in Strasbourg, to the Protestant leader, Henry Bullinger: 'No news but that our King has within these two days (as I wrote to John Burcher) burnt three godly men in one day. For in July he married the widow of a nobleman named Latimer; and he is always wont to celebrate his nuptials by some wickedness of this kind.'

On the political front, there were other, and potentially more serious, matters to disturb Katherine's first few months as Queen, for her brother had become involved in a heated, albeit professional, dispute with Sir Ralph Sadler, the King's 'ambassador' in Edinburgh. The dispute arose out of the totally opposed views which each man held concerning internal developments in Scotland. From Katherine's point of view, the dispute was dangerous because Lord Parr, in effect, was saying that Henry's policy of bribing the 'assured Scots' was wrong and could not hope to succeed. Sadler, on the other hand, had finally succeeded in getting a peace and marriage treaty ratified by the Earl of Arran, who was acting as governor during the infant Queen's minority, and he had sent back report after report which, though they did mention the internal quarrels among the Scots, were aimed at proving that Henry's policy had been right. It was always dangerous to contradict Henry, particularly where his political judgment was concerned, and Lord Parr was playing with fire. Less than a week after the Scots delegates had agreed to the terms of the treaty, which included the sending of the infant Queen of Scots to England when she should reach her tenth birthday, Katherine's brother reported that spies had told him that Arran's Council had stated that no Scot would ever agree to it.

Sadler insisted that Parr's spies were lying, and that only his, Sadler's, reports, being those of an Englishman on the spot, should be believed. Parr retorted on the same day that he believed his spies: the Scottish Cardinal Beaton and his party (rivals to Arran) had no intention whatsoever of keeping the peace other than as they saw fit, nor any intention of ever delivering the young Queen to England.

Henry wished with all his heart to believe Sadler and, at this stage, anyone other than Lord Parr would have been recalled, or at least told to keep quiet. Apart from being the Queen's brother, however, Lord Parr was Henry's own protégé, and Henry decided to await further developments. These were not long in coming. Early in August, a Scottish ship, laden with goods bound for Edinburgh merchants, was arrested at Rye in order to force both parties to ratify the treaty which Arran had signed. The arrest infuriated the citizens of Edinburgh who showed their anger by violent demonstrations outside Sadler's house. This, coupled with an open alliance between Arran and Cardinal Beaton (who promptly questioned the validity of the treaty), convinced Sadler that Parr had been right and that Henry's policy had failed.

These developments brought peace between Parr and Sadler, and in a private letter written on 11 September, Sadler told Parr that never had an ambassador been so badly treated as he had been: 'Never man had to do with so rude, so inconstant and beastly a nation as this is, for they neither esteem honour of their country nor their own honesty, nor yet (which they ought principally to do) their duty to God, and love and charity to their Christian brethren.'

War against Scotland was now inevitable, and on 30 September, Henry told Suffolk, Tunstall and Parr (the Council of the North) that he doubted the wisdom of making any pact with the Scots and that he intended to send a herald to proclaim that unless they would deliver hostages as a surety for keeping the treaty, he would destroy them 'with sword and fire'. It was too late in the year, however, to mount a full-scale attack, and Parr was told instead to carry out a succession of strong Border raids while preparations were put in hand for the invasion and destruction of Edinburgh in the early summer of the following year.

Meanwhile, by means which are far from clear, a love-match was fostered between the King's niece, Margaret Douglas, who was then in Katherine Parr's household, and Matthew Stewart, Earl of Lennox, who was one of the principal military supporters of the Cardinal's party in Scotland. Lennox became so inflamed with passion for Margaret Douglas, whom he had never met, that he deserted the Cardinal and joined her father, the Earl of Angus, and the rest of Henry's 'friends'. Margaret Douglas became equally enamoured with him, or rather with his reputation for wit and gallantry, and for the next eight or nine months their long-range courtship, conducted by letters and messengers, form an intriguing and romantic thread in the otherwise turgid diplomatic wrangling which followed the breakdown of the treaty signed by Arran.

Since, in the event of the death of the infant Queen, Lennox (as a cousin of the Scottish Royal family) had a substantial claim to the throne of Scotland, Henry did everything to encourage the romance, though he made a great show of not forcing Margaret Douglas to do anything against her will, and insisted that no marriage contract should be signed until they had actually seen and approved of each other. There are no records to show that Katherine Parr played any part in the affair, but from Katherine's point of view, the match would remove Margaret Douglas forever from the clutches of the Duke of Norfolk's family, from whom Katherine had much to fear, and the diplomatic advantages were obvious. One is tempted, therefore, to see her hand in it, though how she, or anyone else, succeeded in rousing the interest of the Earl of Lennox remains a mystery.

But, however the romance arose, it caused Lennox to throw himself body and soul into Henry's cause. He seized French weapons destined for the Cardinal, helped Angus to raise troops in an attempt – which, however, proved to be in vain – to defeat Arran and the Cardinal outside Glasgow, and swamped Henry with advice on how to mount the invasion of Scotland. In the end, he had to flee for his life to England, but by then the Scots were so divided among themselves that they had become incapable of organised defence.

During the period covered by most of these events in 1543, from July until the middle of the autumn, Katherine and Henry were making their leisurely way on the Progress. For the most part they did not disturb the local nobility, and they stayed quietly at the King's own manors and castles. From Oatlands, they went to Guildford, then to Sunninghill, and from there to Moor Park, near Rickmansworth. By the end of August they had reached Ampthill in Bedfordshire, where they stayed for a week. After a short visit to Grafton, they moved to Woodstock, where they arrived on 14 September, and where, because of an outbreak of plague in and around London, they remained until the middle of October.

For the third or fourth year in succession, it was an exceptionally wet summer, so much so that on 23 August, Henry sent the following instruction to Cranmer: 'Whereas there has been and still is much rain and unseasonable weather, whereby is like to ensue great hurt to the corn and fruits now ripe, the Archbishop and other prelates are to exhort the King's people, with repentant heart, to make prayers severally and together for seasonable and temperate weather.'

In spite of the weather, Katherine and Henry rode and hunted together, sending the usual presents of deer and other game to those who enjoyed the royal favour. One recipient was Cuthbert Tunstall who received 'six pasties of red deer' which took ten days to reach him in Darlington. In his letter of thanks, Tunstall said that the gift had made him feel ten years younger. He added: 'Where the hart is a beast of long life, the flesh of him killed with a King's hand and sent by his servants with his comfortable letters declaring that he remembreth his old servant, being so far from him, must needs engender in him to whom it is sent a renewing of old spirits.'

Henry's spirits, too, were being renewed. The days of his youth were gone and he was now a mountain of flesh, finding it more and more difficult to ride and move about, but Katherine showed him that there was still much to enjoy in life. Instead of the wild parties with which Catherine Howard had filled the Court, or the sessions of reckless gambling with which the Boleyns and Seymours had kept Henry up until the early hours of the morning, Katherine surrounded the King with a cheerful family atmosphere of quiet comfort and affectionate attendance to his wants. The feasting, drinking, and dancing continued, but on such a moderate scale that a scholar, whom Katherine patronised, said that every day at Court was like a Sunday, 'a thing hitherto unheard of, especially in a royal palace'.

The main key to Katherine's success, however, was her treatment of the King's children. Vives had taught her as a child, and she had proved his teaching by experience, that a man valued few things more in a second, or subsequent, wife than affection and care for his children by his former wife or wives. The harsh stepmother, as common in real life as she was in fiction, stored up nothing but trouble for herself. 'She shows herself,' taught Vives, 'to be an enemy, gathering up hate without cause, and wreaking it upon the weak and innocent.' On the other hand, 'a good woman,' he said, 'will wish to be to her husband's children that which she may often hear them call her, that is "Mother".'

With Princess Mary there were no difficulties. She and Katherine were almost contemporaries: they had shared the same tutors and had been brought up as children together, and down the years Mary had come to respect Katherine's superior intelligence and her integrity. She remembered her own mother's friendship for Katherine's mother and, although nothing was ever to obliterate the bitterness left by Henry's treatment of Catharine of Aragon, she associated Katherine Parr with those who sympathised with her. Moreover, ever since the days of Jane Seymour, Mary had been welcome at Court, and all that Katherine had to do was to make sure that that welcome would be even warmer than it had been.

In the case of Prince Edward, Katherine's task was again comparatively easy. Motherless from birth, the six-year-old boy had known only the care of nurses and governesses who, however fond of him they might have been were bound by his position to treat him with a deference which precluded a normal show of affection. As Queen, Katherine's relationship with the boy was the other way round, it was he who had to defer to her, and he quickly found in her a person he could love and honour as much as, or, because of the pent-up emotions of his infancy, perhaps even more than he would have loved his natural mother. Within a very short time after their first meeting, he indeed took to calling Katherine 'Mother', and for the rest of Katherine's life he always used this title for her, and in the most affectionate terms.

Princess Elizabeth, however, was a very different matter. Unusually precocious, even for a Tudor child, she was now in her tenth year and keenly aware that, in the eyes of the Court, she was little more than a poor relation. For most of her life, Henry had ignored her, except as a pawn in the diplomatic game. (He had even offered her as a bride to the Earl of Arran's idiot son in exchange for Arran's signature on the treaty with Scotland.) She was, therefore, highly suspicious of any overtures made to her. Added to this was the fact that Henry was also suspicious of anyone who singled her out for special attention: some three years before, Wriothesley had felt the need to cover up a visit to her under the guise of a visit to Princess Mary, who at that time happened to be in the same neighbourhood.

In spite of the suspicions of both father and daughter, Katherine Parr was not deterred. There was no longer any valid reason why Elizabeth should be ostracised and, knowing Henry's emotional nature, Katherine was certain that once he could be persuaded to accept Elizabeth as a full member of the family, he would delight in the opportunity to play the part of a doting father. The result would be of benefit to them all, but particularly to Katherine herself, who, with all the King's children gathered round and dependent on her, would be in a stronger position than any of Henry's previous wives had been. This may not have been her reasoning, and she may have acted instead simply on the grounds of kindness to a lonely girl, but if this was so, her kindness covered an instinctive sense for security.

167

Father and daughter were both won over some time before Katherine's marriage to the King, for Elizabeth was already installed at Court in June and took second place to Princess Mary among the ladies at the wedding. Even at that age, Elizabeth's political sense was highly developed, and as soon as she was assured of Katherine's goodwill, she did not resist the invitation to join the Queen's household. But Katherine wanted far more than mere obedience to her wishes; she wanted Elizabeth's love, not so much for herself, but for Henry, and it was to this end that she concentrated her efforts during the first few months of her marriage. In the event, she succeeded in winning Elizabeth's affection for herself – Elizabeth was later to admit that she could never forsake Katherine whatever Katherine did.

As well as their individual affection, Katherine also sought the collective support of Henry's children. She wanted all of them together in the royal household, for only then could she create the impression of a close-knit family circle, impervious to outsiders, which was an essential feature of her policy. There were, however, practical difficulties. Edward's uncertain health caused the King to take excessive precautions to protect him from possible infection. Visitors were strictly controlled, and the Prince's lodgings were frequently moved from one part of the country to another in an attempt to avoid extremes of heat or cold and particularly fog and mists which were considered especially harmful to him. Katherine, therefore, met with stronger resistance when she tried to bring Edward to Court, but an opportunity arose during the Progress. Their route to Ampthill took them close to Ashridge where the Prince was then staying, and Henry was persuaded to make the short detour. It was thus at Ashridge at the end of August 1543 that, for the first time, Katherine was able to collect all the family under one roof.

It was a notable success, so much so that foreign ambassadors considered it sufficiently important to include it in their dispatches. Subsequently, while the Court remained at Ampthill, Katherine sent Elizabeth to stay with her half-brother at Ashridge, and from then on there was a constant correspondence between the two children and with their grown-up sister. Family gatherings, with everybody present, continued to be rare, but the ice had been broken, and a somewhat bemused Henry found himself surrounded from time to time by children and nurses like any other father of a young family.

Katherine's treatment was altogether a new experience for Henry, and though he may have chafed at the lack of excitement, the Duchess of Suffolk and the rest of Katherine's circle helped her to keep him entertained with gay, lively, talk so that gradually he became reconciled to his physical handicaps. He learnt to make light of the pain from which he often suffered, and he made a Court joke of resting his heavily bandaged leg on Katherine's lap while he gave audience to his Councillors. As a result of the quiet routine, his health steadily improved, the fits of depression disappeared, and with the lifting of his spirits, there came a new confidence in himself and in his subjects.

Early in November 1543, this new confidence received a tremendous fillip from an unexpected English victory in the preliminary campaign in Flanders, where, as part of Henry's agreement with Charles V, an English contingent of ten thousand men formed the vanguard of the Emperor's forces against the French. Led by Sir John Wallop, the English contingent attacked and routed a French force outside Landrechies. Francis I, who was in command of the force, barely escaped with his life, and Henry roared with delight when he heard of the discomfiture of his old rival. He only regretted that he had not been there to see the incident for himself, and, already revitalised by Katherine's treatment, he determined that he would lead the main campaign, planned for the following summer, in person. He would show both Francis and the Emperor that he was no longer the invalid they thought him to be and, full of bustling exuberance, he set about planning the strategy and tactics for the summer campaign. It was still only December, but anything which he was going to undertake in person had to be worked out in the finest detail, with the minimum risk of failure.

Katherine had now been Queen for six months, but so far neither she nor any of her family had received any material benefit from her position. Henry's present cheerful mood, coupled with the approaching Christmas and New Year holidays, offered as good an opportunity as she was likely to find for making her 'humble' requests. Her success became known on 23 December when, in an impressive ceremony at Hampton Court, her brother was created Earl of Essex, the title of his late father-in-law whose lands he had inherited, and her long-suffering uncle was finally raised to the peerage as Lord Parr of Horton. At the same time, her sister, Anne Herbert, and her husband, received further large grants of land, converting the leasehold of Wilton Abbey into an outright gift. On the following day, the newly created Earl of Essex was among those who elected Sir John Wallop to the Order of the Garter, 'to the joy of all who were present.'

For herself, Katherine had to wait until Parliament assembled on 14 January 1544 to confirm the settlement the King had made upon her. She was not disappointed. In addition to a life interest in all the lands which had been previously assigned to Anne Boleyn and Catherine Howard, she received outright grants of numerous manors, castles, and boroughs, which had formerly belonged to the Earl of Warwick, Lord Hungerford, and the Earl of March. Together with the settlements that had previously been made upon her by her two former husbands, the grants made her probably the wealthiest woman in England. To administer her vast estates, she appointed, with Henry's approval, a Council of which the principal members were her uncle, Lord Parr of Horton, as Chamberlain, Sir Thomas Arundell as Chancellor, and Robert Tyrwhitt, an old friend of the Parr family, as Comptroller.

The most significant grant which the King made at this time, however, and for which Katherine Parr must take the credit as being the direct result of her work in uniting Henry with his family, was the restoring of Princess Mary and Princess Elizabeth to the right of succession to the Crown. The grant was embodied in an Act made by the same Parliament which confirmed Henry's settlement on Katherine. The Act stated that if Prince Edward should die without leaving any legitimate children, and if there were no children from the marriage of the King and 'his most dear and entirely beloved Queen Katherine,' then the Crown should descend first to Princess Mary, and if she died without legitimate children, then to Princess Elizabeth.

This was a major political triumph for Katherine, for, ever since each Princess had in turn been made illegitimate as the result of the divorce of their mothers (Anne Boleyn was divorced before she was executed), the King, in spite of every pressure at home and from abroad, had refused to establish their rights of succession on the grounds that this would mean that he did not consider that the divorces had been valid. The preamble to the Act indicates that Katherine's arguments were that, in view of the danger to Henry's life which would arise from leading his army in person in France, and in view of the delicate health of Prince Edward, there was a grave risk that England would be left without an heir to the Crown, which in the present circumstances would mean civil war. A line of succession must, therefore, be established, and who had a better right to succeed Prince Edward than his half-sisters? The question of the legitimacy of their births need not be raised; it would be enough if Parliament agreed to name them as the rightful heirs to the Crown. Henry, full of his new-found affection for both his daughters, and puffed with pride, perhaps, that Katherine thought he would actually be risking his life in France, could not refute her arguments, and Parliament, which had long been aware of the danger of a lack of rightful heirs, gratefully passed the necessary Act.

Katherine's achievement was doubly clever: first, because it favoured neither the Hertford nor the Gardiner/Norfolk factions, and kept them both guessing as to which side she was on; and secondly, because it brought women to the fore. There had never been a Salic Law in England, but it did no harm to emphasise the fact, and thereby Katherine confirmed her position as an upholder of women's rights. If there had been any waverers among the women at Court before, there were none now; discreetly, they began to form a solid phalanx behind the Queen. And finally, of course, it bound Mary and Elizabeth irrevocably to her side.

During the next few months, however there was neither occasion nor opportunity for feminine political activity. The country was seething with excitement at the prospect of the forthcoming wars against Scotland and France, and nobody had time for anything other than the preparations for them. War in those days was considered not the horror it is today; the casualties and the destruction were minor elements, far outweighed by the loot, either in the form of moveable goods, or as ransome money for prisoners, which individuals on the winning side stood to gain. It was also the best occasion for a man to seek honour, by his bravery or brilliance, and although there were the few who sought honour as a means to material reward from a grateful King, in that age of chivalry, for most men, honour was an end in itself. As Sir John Wallop had said, on being praised for his victory at Landrechies, he desired no other reward 'but only a merry look of his Highness when his pleasure shall be that I may repair unto his presence'. The excitement, therefore, was understandable, and not even the women raised any protest.

The main plan of campaign was to stagger the dates of the two operations so that the country would not be fighting on two fronts at the same time. The Earl of Hertford, with Lord Lisle, was first to take an

army by sea early in May, sack Edinburgh, and then march south over-
land to Berwick, destroying the strongholds of the Scottish border-
raiders on their way. Meanwhile, Lisle was to bring the Fleet back to
embark the army for France in June with the object of laying siege to
Boulogne towards the end of July. The army in France was to be led by
the Duke of Suffolk, with the Duke of Norfolk as his deputy, until the
King arrived to take command in person, which was planned for the
middle of July.

Katherine's part in the preparations was to help with the somewhat
feverish diplomatic activities which preceded both campaigns. On 18
February, she entertained the Emperor's special envoy, the Duke of
Najera, with whom the Council had been discussing plans for coordi-
nating the attacks of the two armies in France. A Spanish account of the
reception she held for him shows her willingness to be as gay, at times,
as she was usually serious:

> After half-an-hour, the Duke of Najera came forth [from a private audience
> with the King] and was accompanied to the Queen's Chamber, where were also
> the Princess Mary and many attendants, including a daughter of the Queen of
> Scotland [Margaret Douglas]. The Duke kissed the Queen's hand and was then
> conducted to another chamber to which the Queen and ladies followed, and there
> was music and dancing. The Queen danced first with her brother, very gracefully;
> and then the Princess Mary and the 'Princess' of Scotland danced with other
> gentlemen, and many other ladies also danced. A Venetian of the King's house-
> hold danced some galliards with extraordinary agility.
>
> After dancing had lasted several hours, the Queen returned to her chamber,
> first causing one of the noblemen who spoke Spanish to offer some presents to
> the Duke, who kissed her hand. He would likewise have kissed the Princess
> Mary's hand, but she offered her lips; and so he saluted her and all the other
> ladies. The King is said to be a man of great authority and beauty. The Queen
> has a lively and pleasing appearance and is praised as a virtuous woman. Princess
> Mary has a pleasing countenance and person, and knows how to conceal her
> accomplishments. She is adored throughout the Kingdom.

Chapuys' account of the same affair states that the Queen and Princess asked 'very curiously' for news of the Emperor to whom they made
'their humble recommendations'. He added that Katherine was a little
indisposed, but that nevertheless she wished to dance for the honour of
the company. From the several hours which the dancing lasted, one can
only suppose that the indisposition was a tactful gesture to enhance the
honour being done to the distinguished guest.

Katherine was not so openly involved with the diplomacy which preceded the Scottish operation, but as Lennox pressed his suit for Margaret Douglas in stronger and stronger terms, she continued her quiet encouragement to Margaret to accept him.

On 14 March, Sir Thomas Seymour, who had been recalled from Brussels and was now at Court helping with the organisation for the French operation, wrote to his brother, the Earl of Hertford. There was no great news to report. The Council had reckoned that the additional cost of the King going to France would be £7,000 (about £175,000 today). 'Our master and mistress,' he added, 'with my Lord Prince are merry, so is my Lady, my sister [-in-law], whom I will visit ere I sleep. And thus most heartily fare ye well, and send you a prosperous journey.'

Hertford and Lisle formed the most efficient team of military commanders in England, and in spite of a number of difficulties, including a shortfall of supplies for which Gardiner was responsible and which Hertford strongly hinted was due to Gardiner lining his own pockets, the army was safely embarked at Newcastle on 26 April. They arrived at Leith on 4 May, and were able to land the whole army without meeting any substantial resistance. As they marched on the town, Arran, Cardinal Beaton, and some other Scottish nobles with some six thousand men appeared, but after a short, sharp fight, they retreated and, in Hertford's words, 'tarried not in Edinburgh, but fled to Linlithgow'. The Provost and burgesses of Edinburgh then offered to surrender Edinburgh on condition that they were not molested. Hertford replied that he was not prepared to discuss terms; if they delivered the town, he would receive it and use it as he thought right, but if they resisted, he would put them to the fire and sword as Henry had commanded him to do.

Hertford moved forward to the gates of Edinburgh on 7 May, but 'the citizens raised fire and smoke and prepared to resist'. Hertford accordingly gave orders to attack and duly seized Edinburgh, destroying Holyroodhouse and setting fire to the town, but leaving the castle, which was considered impregnable. Hertford reckoned that some six hundred Scots had been killed for the loss of twenty-seven English. The Army continued sacking and burning the country round Edinburgh for a further week and then, on 15 May, turned south to Berwick.

A few days before the attack on Edinburgh, on 3 May, Lord Audeley, who had served quietly and efficiently as Lord Chancellor ever since the days of Sir Thomas More, died. Of the lawyers on the Council, clearly the best qualified to succeed him was Gardiner, the Bishop of Winchester, but Henry had made up his mind after the fall of Wolsey that this, the most senior legal position in the country, should never again be held by a churchman, and Gardiner was passed over in favour of Wriothesley who had been created a Baron earlier in the year. Lord Wriothesley was thus duly installed as Lord Chancellor, and his place as one of the two Principal Secretaries was given to a comparative newcomer, Sir William Petre. These changes shifted the balance of power on the Council slightly towards the Gardiner/Norfolk faction, but it was to be several months before the difference became noticeable.

Now that Scotland had been virtually disarmed, the Council was able to concentrate all its attention on the French campaign. There were two major problems. The first was money, and the second was the King's determination to lead his army in person. The King's agent in Antwerp, Stephen Vaughan, had reported difficulties in raising money to pay for the supplies which were to be bought in Flanders, and one of the main causes was the surprisingly modern phenomenon of a run on English currency. On 16 May, the following proclamation was issued:

Whereas in Flanders and France the valuation of money is so enhanced that coin is daily carried out of the realm notwithstanding the King's commands to the officers of the ports to enforce the statutes against this, so that the only remedy seems to be the enhancing of the value of gold and silver in this realm, the King, by advice of his Council, fixes the value of an ounce of fine gold of 24 carats at 48s and of the ounce of the finest sterling silver at 4s.

The King has caused a piece of gold to be newly made which shall be called the 'Sovereign' and shall be current for 20s of lawful money; and a half-sovereign for 10s. The Royal of gold 'being weight' shall henceforth be of the value of 12s, the Angel, 8s, half-Angel, 4s, and quarter-angel, 2s. His Highness has also caused to be newly made certain pieces of silver, viz., a testoon to be current for 12d, a groat with a whole face, current for 4d, a half-groat of the same stamp, 2d. Gold and silver brought to the Tower to be coined shall be paid for at the above prices, 48s and 4s the ounce. All groats, pence, half-pence and farthings not clipped nor fully broken shall be lawful tender even though cracked, and persons refusing them are to be imprisoned.[1]

On the second problem, Chapuys reported to the Emperor on 18 May that he believed the despatch of English forces to France would be delayed. He continued:

The cause of the delay will be the zeal [not to say obstinacy] which the King shows to go in person, for whose surety so many things have to be done that they will not be finished for some days. My own foolish opinion is that the King will not act prudently in attempting the journey, for, besides his age and weight, he has the worst legs in the world, such that those who have seen them are astonished that he does not stay continually in bed and judge that he will not be able to endure the very least exertion without danger to his life, yet no one dare tell him so. It is clear that his presence might be very useful if health permitted it. but as he now is it will be a danger. Wherefore and for other reasons which I have lately written, it would be a good work, for which every means should be sought, to rid the journey of his presence, though, for the furtherance of affairs, he might remain at Calais during the enterprise.

Henry seems to have been partially persuaded by Chapuys and others, and he agreed to remain in Calais if the Emperor would remain in Artois. Charles v, however, replied that since he was ten years younger than Henry, and since his presence was essential to lead an army of such mixed nationalities as he had,[2] he must remain with them in the field. He would nevertheless be quite content if Henry decided to stay in Calais. The implied insult was enough, and nothing now would shake Henry's determination to go all the way with his army.

Katherine took no part in the issue and contented herself with doing what she could to get the King as fit as possible for the venture. Nevertheless, there must have been some disturbance at Court which worried the Hertford faction, for at the beginning of June the Countess of Hertford, probably at the instigation of her husband, wrote to the Queen via Princess Mary, asking her to use her influence to persuade Henry to recall Hertford, who had been ordered to remain in Newcastle until he was assured that the Borders were secure.

Princess Mary replied:

I have been nothing well as yet these holy days [Whitsun]; wherefor I pray you hold me excused that I write not this to you with my hand. I have delivered your letters unto the Queen's Grace, who accepted the same very well. And thus, good madam, I bid you most heartily well to fare.

at St James, 3rd day of June.

Your assured friend to my power during life,

Mary

Katherine added a postscript to Mary's letter:

Madam,

My Lord your husband's coming hither is not altered, for he shall be home before the King's Majesty takes his journey over the seas, as it pleaseth His Majesty to declare to me of late. You may be right assured I would not have forgotten my promise to you in a matter of less effect than this, and so I pray you most heartily to think. And thus with my very hearty commendations to you, I end wishing you so well to fare as I would myself.

Your assured friend,
Katherine the Queen, K.P.

Katherine was as good as her word and, on 10 June, Henry recalled Hertford to London for consultations, appointing the Earl of Shrewsbury to take Hertford's place in Newcastle.

From the outcome of the consultations, it is clear that the promise which Katherine had made to Lady Hertford involved more than simply the recall of her husband. Apart from the many details concerning the campaign in France which still had to be settled, there was the all-important question of the arrangements to be made for the government of the country while the King was away. He was only expected to be gone for about two months, but the uncertainty of communications through Calais meant that there could be occasions when there would be no time to wait for the King's directives on urgent issues. It was therefore considered necessary to set up a proper regency with full powers to exercise the King's authority during his absence. The selection of the members of the regency was obviously the issue which worried the Hertfords, and which gave full rein once more to the power-game.

It is also clear from the decision which eventually emerged that the care and education of Prince Edward became closely associated with the question of the Regency. Edward was heir to the Throne, and Henry had to be sure that, in the unlikely event of his losing his life in France, the six-year-old boy, no less than the government of the country, would be in trustworthy hands. And the most trustworthy person, in Henry's eyes, was Katherine. She had convinced Henry beyond doubt of her love and solicitude for the young Prince. She had persuaded Henry to let her have Edward with her during the Christmas festivities at Hampton Court, and again during Easter at Westminster. She had also shown an exceptional and intelligent interest in his education.

On the matter of the Prince's education, however, Katherine had for the first time begun to show her hand. Edward's first tutor, whose appointment Cranmer recommended and Katherine probably arranged, was Dr Richard Cox, a cautious, but nevertheless firm, proponent of the New Faith. His teaching methods tended to be old-fashioned, but his gentle ways endeared him to the Prince, and he proved an excellent if uninspiring teacher of the basic elements of learning. His appointment, moreover, would not have worried the Gardiner faction, since on all contentious questions he had shown himself as ready to side with Gardiner as he did with Cranmer. But, with the regency question on the table, Katherine now sought an additional tutor for the Prince, a man who would provide the inspiration and enthusiasm of Humanism, and whose views were much more clearly defined than those of Dr Cox. Her choice was John Cheke, an outstanding Fellow and scholar of St John's College, Cambridge, and a man whose arguments with Gardiner (cloaked under the academic question of the correct way of pronouncing ancient Greek) had shown no doubts as to where he stood on the principles and objectives of modern education. Later, the royal school, which Katherine in effect was now founding, was to include a number of John Cheke's colleagues and pupils from St John's, the more notable among whom were Roger Ascham and William Grindall (responsible for Princess Elizabeth's education) and Anthony Cooke.

The recommendation of John Cheke was Katherine's first open move against Gardiner, and Henry's acceptance of her recommendation showed how much progress she had made in winning his confidence. It also coloured Henry's decision concerning the regency, and eventually, on 7 July, five days before the King's departure for France, a Council document set out the results of the manoeuvring that had fully occupied the Court for the previous two weeks.

First, touching the Queen's Highness and my Lord Prince:
The King has resolved that the Queen shall be Regent in his absence and that his process shall pass and bear *teste* in her name, as in like case heretofore; and that a commission for this be delivered to her before his departure. She shall use the advice and counsel of the Archbishop of Canterbury, Lord Chancellor Wriothesley, the Earl of Hertford, the Bishop of Westminster [Thirlby], and Sir William Petre, secretary.

Item, my Lord Prince shall on Wednesday next remove to Hampton Court, and the Lord Chancellor and Hertford shall repair thither on Thursday and discharge all the ladies and gentlemen out of the house, and admit and swear Sir Richard Page, chamberlain to my Lord Prince, Mr Sydney to be advanced to the office of Steward, Jasper Horsey to be chief gentleman of his privy chamber, and Mr Cox his almoner, and he that is now almoner to be Dean, and Mr Cheke as a supplement to Mr Cox, both for the better instruction of the Prince and the diligent teaching of such children as be appointed to attend upon him.

Item, for the number of His Majesty's Council and their order. His Majesty has appointed to be of his Privy Council in his absence the Archbishop of Canterbury, Lord Chancellor Wriothesley, the Earl of Hertford, the Bishop of Westminster, and Sir William Petre, secretary, and either the Chancellor or Hertford, or both, shall ever be resident at Court, and if neither of them can be there, the Archbishop and Petre to remain with the Queen, but when convenient all five shall attend her. The Lord Parr of Horton shall be used in Council with them for matters concerning the realm ...

The rest of the document set out various administrative matters which had to be settled before the King left.

It was not an outright win for the Hertford faction, since Wriothesley and Thirlby, Bishop of Westminster, inclined towards Gardiner, but Gardiner himself had not been named, and this was a distinct win for the Queen. The most important point, however, was Henry's clear and unequivocal appointment of Katherine as Queen Regent with all the powers she needed to exercise the King's authority. Henry had only done this once before, in the case of Catharine of Aragon in the early years of his reign, and it was a signal demonstration of his trust in her.

On 12 July, Henry set off for France, dining that night at Gravesend. His escort was commanded by the Earl of Essex, Katherine's brother, and William Herbert, her brother-in-law. Her uncle was an ex-officio member of the Council, and she herself now held the reigns of power in England.

NOTES

1 Five days later, a further proclamation fixed prices. Examples: beef, ⅜d per lb; mutton 1d; veal, 1d; best swan, 5s; best capon, 20d; boiling capon, 8d; eggs from Easter to March, 16d per 100, from March to Easter, 20d per 100; butter, sweet, 2d per lb in summer, 3d per lb in winter; best wild duck, 3d; best chickens, 18d per dozen.
2 'I speak Spanish to God,' said Charles v, 'Italian to women, French to men, and German to my horse.'

11   The Queen Regent

The situation when Katherine took control was that in Scotland matters were now comparatively quiet. The Earl of Lennox had arrived in London early in June, and had captivated both Margaret Douglas and the Court with his youth and charm. It had taken a little time to settle the terms of the marriage contract, but by 26 June everything was agreed, and on the 28th the handsome pair were duly married in a ceremony which Katherine and Henry attended in person. Their honeymoon was short, however, for Lennox had to leave within the week on a naval expedition, which he had proposed himself, to attempt the capture of Dumbarton Castle. At the same time, the Earl of Shrewsbury had been instructed to continue harassing the Scottish Borders in order to prevent any build-up of a counter-attack which the Scots might have been planning to revenge the sack of Edinburgh.

In France, the Duke of Norfolk had taken the first detachment of the army to Calais, also in June. His main task was to prepare supplies and transport for the main army, but within a few days he had created appalling confusion. The muddle continued until the Duke of Suffolk arrived on 4 July. He went to work with his usual drive and efficiency, and within a week order had been brought out of the chaos. Norfolk was then sent to lay siege to Montreuil as a preliminary move to the advance on Boulogne, but mainly, one suspects, to get him out of the way before Henry arrived.

Katherine's first act as Regent concerned a practical question which arose on the Scottish Borders. The Earl of Shrewsbury wrote to her on 18 July, requesting instructions as to what he should do with some one hundred Scottish prisoners who had been taken during recent Border raids. He asked if he could return them to Scotland, for 'the gaols were so full before that many die for lack of food, and the numbers being so much increased, the penury and famine must needs be the greater'.

Katherine replied through her Council that he was to keep in prison those who were able to pay for their food and those who were 'stout, busy or otherwise like to do any hurt' if they were set free. The latter, 'if extreme necessity shall so require', could have some small relief out of the King's funds. The rest of the prisoners – the majority – were to be released on bond. Katherine added a personal note to Sir Ralph Evers, who had been responsible for taking the prisoners and whom she knew well, telling him that she had been appointed Regent, and congratulating him on his victory.

The raid was followed by a request from the Scots for a truce but, in spite of the relative humanity she had shown in the case of the prisoners, Katherine rejected the Scottish request. Her reason was that a truce might interfere with Lennox's expedition to Dumbarton, but this was not told, of course, to the Scottish herald. She felt well justified in her action, for on the following day, 31 July, she wrote to Henry to tell him of the capture of a Scottish ship in which letters to the French King had been found. She wrote to Henry that she thought this was a matter of great importance, not only because of the contents of the letters, but also because it was 'ordained by God to show the crafty dealing and juggling of that nation [the Scots]'.

Katherine took care to keep Henry informed of everything she did and, in each letter which she signed, she reassured him of the continuing good health of the Prince and his two sisters, all of whom were with her at Hampton Court. Nor did she neglect her duty as a wife, and in the following remarkable letter, written before she moved to Hampton Court and only a few days after Henry's departure, she shows the mixture of affection, encouragement and piety with which she won and retained the King's extraordinary trust in her:

Although the discourse of time and account of days neither is long nor many of your Majesty's absence, yet the want of your presence, so much beloved and desired of me, maketh me that I cannot quietly pleasure in any thing until I hear from your Majesty. The time therefore seemeth to me very long with a great desire to know how your Highness hath done since your departing hence; whose prosperity and health I prefer and desire more than mine own. And whereas I know your Majesty's absence as never without great respect of things most convenient and necessary, yet love and affection compelleth me to desire your presence. And again, [on the other hand], the same zeal and love forceth me also to be best content with that which is your will and pleasure. And thus love maketh me in all things to set apart mine own commodity and pleasure, and to embrace most joyfully his will and pleasure whom I love. God, the knower of secrets, can judge these words not to be only written with ink, but most truly impressed in the heart. Much more I omit, lest I should seem to go about to praise myself or crave a thank. Which thing to do I mind nothing less, but a plain simple relation of my zeal and love towards your Majesty, proceeding from the abundance of the heart. Wherein I must needs confess I deserve no worthy commendation, having such just occasion to do the same.

I make like account with your Majesty as I do with God for His benefits and gifts heaped upon me daily: acknowledging myself always a great debtor unto Him in that I do omit my duty toward Him, not being able to recognise the least of His benefits. In which state I am certain and sure to die. But yet I hope in His gracious acceptance of my good will. And even such confidence I have in your Majesty's gentleness, knowing myself never to have done my duty as were requisite and meet to such a noble Prince, at whose hands I have received so much love and goodness that with words I cannot express it.

Lest I should be too tedious unto your Majesty, I finish this my scribbled letter, committing you into the governance of the Lord, with long life and prosperous felicity here, and after this life to enjoy the kingdom of His elect.

from Greenwich.

By your Majesty's humble, obedient, loving wife and servant,

Katherine the Queen, K.P.[1]

Henry's letters to Katherine, the majority of which were dictated, were for the most part straightforward accounts of the progress of the siege of Boulogne, interspersed with instructions for sending gunpowder and money to enable him to keep his army in the field. At first, he was optimistic about a quick end to the campaign:

The King commands them [the Council with the King] to write that he trusts, as he told her, to have this place within 20 days from his beginning to make battery. Yesterday the battery began, and the walls begin to tumble apace, so that, as they are short of men and munition, everyone hopes shortly to have it. Evidently the French King doubts it too, for he has sent a gentleman to make large proffers [of peace]. Between this and Montreuil, the King has taken Hardelot, Frencq [?], Hubercent and three or four other castles.

His Majesty's camp outside Boulogne, 5th August.

The Duke of Norfolk, however, had made no progress against Montreuil (which was more critical to the taking of Boulogne than had been realised), and on the same day he wrote to the Duke of Suffolk, complaining about the slanders against him in the King's camp:

I am sorry in my old days to be thus spoken of; but some men's doings are taken better than others. For the old love and acquaintance between us, I heartily desire you to procure the sending hither, on some errand, of some man whom the King trusts, to report to His Highness what I have done and what more I might have done. This will do me more pleasure than if you gave me £500.

181

Suffolk tried to help him, but the man sent was Sir Thomas Seymour and, judging from the King's subsequent anger against Norfolk, his report must have destroyed what little was left of the Duke of Norfolk's reputation. In the event, it became clear within a week that the sieges of both Boulogne and Montreuil were going to take very much longer than had been hoped, but the King was not unduly dismayed and, according to Chapuys who was with him, he was thoroughly enjoying the campaign.

Katherine's main task was to keep an eye on Scotland, and on 9 August she was happy to report that Lennox's expedition was going well. In another private letter to Henry, enclosing Lennox's report, she wrote:

> This day I received advertisements from my Lord of Lennox which, being first showed to your Council, I address to you; trusting God, who prospers your affairs in Scotland, to hear shortly of your better success in France, for which all loving subjects pray.
>
> My Lord Prince and the rest of your children are in good health.
>
> Hampton Court.
>
> P.S. The good speed which Lennox has had is due to his serving a master whom God aids. He might have served the French King, his old master, for many years without attaining such a victory.

At home, Katherine's only positive action was to exempt the University of Cambridge from the requirement to muster men to be sent to the wars. Her contact with the University, since she became Queen, probably dates from the beginning of 1544 when she must have started the negotiations to obtain John Cheke as tutor for Prince Edward and the Court school. It was an association which Katherine valued highly, and from which the University was later to receive substantial benefits (see p. 208). She was moved partly by her own love of learning, but more perhaps because it was an association in the best traditions of the two women she admired most, Margaret Beaufort and Catharine of Aragon. With due allowance for flattery, this letter from Roger Ascham, quoted from his *Epistles* (303), thanking Katherine for what she had so far done for the University, shows that the respect was mutual:

> Write to us oftener, most erudite Queen, and do not despise the term eru-

182

dition, most noble lady; it is the praise of your industry, and a greater one to your talents than all the ornaments of your fortune. We rejoice vehemently in your happiness, most happy Princess, because you are learning more amidst the occupations of your dignity than many with us do in all our leisure and quiet.

The most significant fact of Katherine's regency, however, was the development of her ideals for religious and social reform. Three weeks before Henry had left for France, he had instructed Cranmer to revive the Catholic custom of holding processions through villages and towns to pray for 'the miserable state of Christendom'. The King granted Cranmer one major concession: the litanies and prayers chanted during the processions should be 'in our native English tongue'. It was an acknowledgment of Henry's continued belief, despite Gardiner's arguments to the contrary, in the basic Humanist doctrine that religion was meaningless unless it was conducted in a language which ordinary worshippers could follow and understand. It was also taken by Cranmer as an invitation not only to translate the old Latin prayers, but also to add new simpler prayers which would be more in tune with the spirit of the times and the daily life of the people. His work aroused Katherine's interest, and one of the first new special prayers – to be said for the soldiers going to France – appeared under her name:

> Our cause being now just, and being enforced to enter into war and battle, we most humbly beseech Thee, O Lord God of Hosts, so to turn the hearts of our enemies to the desire of peace, that no Christian blood be spilt; or else grant, O Lord, that with small effusion of blood and to the little hurt and damage of innocents, we may to Thy glory obtain victory. And that the wars being soon ended, we may all with one heart and mind, knit together in concord and unity, laud and praise Thee.[2]

It is a prayer in the pure spirit of Humanism, and there is little doubt that Katherine wrote it, though Cranmer's guiding hand can be seen in the cadence and clarity of the style. For it was almost certainly Cranmer who was responsible for directing Katherine's studies at this time, and who may have inspired her to take a leading rôle in religious matters.

As the principal minister in the Regency Council, Cranmer was in attendance upon the Queen without interruption for the best part of three months. It must be supposed that after the conclusion of each day's business, which was seldom very heavy during that quiet summer,

Queen and Archbishop would discuss many things. In some ways, it was a repetition of the stirring days with Anne Boleyn at Durham Place, and Katherine's eagerness to learn and to question the principles of the New Faith will have evoked long-suppressed memories in Cranmer's mind. They were treading dangerous ground, but there was still much to talk about in considering the simple teaching of Christ without necessarily challenging the rights or wrongs of the Act of Six Articles, the one issue that both knew they must avoid at all costs. It was also probably during this period that Hugh Latimer, Nicholas Shaxton, and Nicholas Ridley were first invited to enliven the discussions with the Queen and her ladies. Indeed, most of the ladies were more advanced in the New Faith than Katherine was herself, and they would have been delighted at this great show of interest on Katherine's part.

The beliefs which she developed over the next few months were in the basic concepts of Christianity: faith in the power of Jesus Christ to redeem the world from sin; hope in the knowledge that all fears and troubles would be resolved in the life everlasting after death; charity in thought and deed to all mankind. She did not believe in purgatory, for this contradicted the concepts of Christ's infinite mercy and of His redemption of all sinners in heaven. She particularly eschewed all form of superstition, such as lighting candles to, or erecting images of, specific saints to gain some 'miraculous' favour. Above all, she denied absolutely the pretence of priests to be the means of mediating with God on behalf of sinners. She believed instead that every person, whoever he or she might be, had the right and the power of direct communication, through private prayer, with God. Priests might serve as missionaries and teachers, they might lead congregations in forms of worship, but they should never attempt to stand between the individual and God. Although some of her circle were beginning to express their dissension from the Act of Six Articles, she herself was prudently silent on that subject, though one may infer from her main beliefs that she, too, did not accept the principles which the Act embodied.

For the moment, however, all the women were doves rather than hawks. The connection between religious and political power had not yet dawned on their minds, and if it had, it would have been indignantly rejected. The one woman who might then already have turned them into hawks was the Countess of Hertford, but she was at her home at Sheen near Richmond in Surrey, where, in the middle of August, she gave birth to a son. (Katherine took the King's barge down the Thames from Hampton Court to attend the christening, spending the night at Richmond Palace with Anne of Cleves, who was now apparently quite reconciled to Katherine's position as Queen.) Joan Dudley, Lady Lisle, was also pregnant, giving birth to her child in the following month. Of her principal ladies, therefore, only the Duchess of Suffolk, Katherine's sister, and Joan Denny, would have been present with Katherine at the time of her 'conversion'. It was, in fact, more a dedication than a conversion, for the beliefs that she then went on to support were a direct development of the Humanism with which she had been imbued since childhood: she was never, in spite of popular opinion, a convert to the Protestant religion as it then was.

Meanwhile, the sieges of Boulogne and Montreuil dragged on inconclusively, and it began to look as though Henry would be away much longer than had been expected. On 25 August, Katherine reported to him that the country was as quiet as it had ever been, and a few days later the Earl of Hertford, having seen his wife safely through the birth of their son, crossed the Channel to join the King outside Boulogne. This left only Cranmer with Katherine, since Wriothesley had to remain in London, and Katherine then decided that she, Cranmer, and the rest of the small Court, including the King's children, should go on a short Progress. Both Queen and Archbishop loved riding and hunting; the King would welcome a present of some of his own stags; and the Progress would give a fine opportunity to continue their discussions away from the bustle of Hampton Court. Accordingly, on 1 September, they set off for Woking, having first sent out guides to ensure that the district was free from plague.

Katherine kept in touch with events, as Henry did on his Progresses, through the King's Messengers, and on the day after they arrived in Woking she received reports of further disturbances on the Scottish Borders. The Wardens had done their work well, and the Scots had been driven off without doing any serious damage. Katherine wrote to both men, Sir Thomas Wharton and Sir Ralph Evers, thanking them for their services, and requiring them to pass on her thanks 'in our name' to those that served under them. 'We require you to continue your diligence,' she added 'especially now in the time of their harvest, so as their corn may be wasted as much as may be.'

The use of the royal 'we', the military orders to destroy crops, and the days she then spent in the saddle, hunting with considerable success in the forests of Surrey and Kent, show Katherine in the unusual rôle of the traditional soldier-like Queen, more concerned with the defence of her subjects and her prowess in sport than in her books. It was almost as though she were giving a demonstration of her ability to rule, that she was Queen Regent in fact as well as in name, and that, should the worst befall Henry in France, she was ready and able to continue the regency.

From Hertford's report which he sent back soon after his arrival in France, however, such a contingency seemed less likely than ever. They hoped to be in Boulogne within the next two days, he wrote, and added:

> The King's Majesty hath stayed me here to bring the Queen's Highness good news of this town, which I pray you to show her Grace; and also that, thanks be to God, his Highness is merry and in as good health as I have seen his Grace at any time these seven years.
> from the King's Majesty's camp before Boulogne, 2nd September.

As had so often happened during the campaign, the attack failed for lack of gunpowder, and six days later Henry wrote to Katherine explaining what had happened. They had not yet captured the main castle, but they had won the greater part of the town and the French King was about to send ambassadors to discuss the possibility of peace. The letter (written by Henry's clerk) continued with a reference to a request she had made, and which clearly had a bearing on her new intellectual activities: 'Where she asks his pleasure as to accepting certain ladies into her chamber in lieu of some that are sick, he remits their acceptance to her own choice; and although some that she names are too weak to serve, they may pass the time with her at play.'

Then, with a characteristic display of sudden emotion, wanting Katherine to share his optimism and his success so far, Henry pushed the clerk aside and added the following postscript in his own, almost illegible hand:

> P.S. At the closing up of these our letters this day, the castle before named with the dyke is at our command, and not like to be recovered by the Frenchmen again (as we trust), not doubting, with God's grace, but that the castle and town shall shortly follow the same trade, for as this day, which is the eighth of September, we begin three batteries, and have three more going, besides one which

hath done his execution in shaking and tearing off one of their greatest bulwarks.

No more to you at this time, sweetheart, but for lack of time and great occupation of business, saving we pray you in our name to give our hearty blessings to all our children, and recommendations to our cousin Margaret [Douglas], and the rest of the ladies and gentlewomen, and to our Council also.

Written with the hand of your loving husband,

Henry R[3]

The castle held out for the best part of another week, and it was not until 14 September that the King sent Katherine's brother-in-law, Sir William Herbert, whom he had knighted on the field, to England to tell her that Boulogne had finally capitulated. Herbert did not arrive in Woking until 19 September, and Katherine then ordered devout and general processions to be held in every town and village to give thanks to God 'for this great benefit which He hath heaped upon us'.

The end of her regency was in sight, with, one imagines, some regret on Katherine's part. Henry did not return immediately, however, for Norfolk was still having trouble outside Montreuil, and Katherine decided to move the Court to Eltham in Kent to await the King's arrival from Dover. Messengers had to be sent out daily to check the route and find alternative ways to avoid plague spots, with the result that it took ten days to get from Woking to Eltham. Henry crossed the Channel secretly on the night of 1 October, and on the 3rd he was finally reunited with Katherine and his family at Leeds Castle in Kent.

On 30 September, Katherine had carried out her final act as Regent by revoking the previous restrictions on French visitors, and giving them permission to live and trade once more in England without the need to register their names or to become English subjects.

Henry and Katherine then moved to Greenwich, and there Cranmer took his leave. Except for a short period a year later, Cranmer did not reside at Court again until the end of Henry's reign. The three months he had spent with Katherine during her regency would have to serve for the three years he had spent with Anne Boleyn in Durham Place. But this time there was no Thomas Cromwell to lead a party of hawks; the Council was divided against itself; and the King was too preoccupied with other matters to show more than a passing interest. From Cranmer's point of view, he had shown Katherine the way, and it was now up to her and her ladies to do the rest. He kept in touch with Katherine's royal school at Court – he was Prince Edward's godfather, and he took his duties seriously – but in all the major events in the following two years, he was to keep discreetly and safely in the background.

NOTES

1 Strype, *Ecclesiastical Memorials*.
2 Strype, *Ecclesiastical Memorials*.
3 As transcribed by Agnes Strickland in *Queens of England*.

12 The Queen's Ladies

Katherine Parr had now been Queen for some fifteen months. During that period, her main concern had been to establish herself as a loving and obedient wife, and as an affectionate and industrious stepmother. Her few sorties into politics had all been connected with the King's children, and nothing she had done could be interpreted as having any motive other than the well-being of the royal family. Even the appointment of John Cheke was easily justified on the grounds of his outstanding scholarship, which Gardiner himself could not deny. Her one outside venture had been the offer of her patronage to Cambridge University, but here, too, Gardiner, as Chancellor of the University, could hardly object. Outwardly, her period as Regent had been marked by common sense and a brief display of 'the stomach of a man', and no fault could be found with the few decisions she had had to make. She was now sure of herself and her position, and she could welcome Henry home with a clear conscience.

It was never Katherine's intention, however, to be nothing more than a dutiful wife and model stepmother. These were the foundations on which to build her influence and authority – and the neglect of which had been one of the main causes of the downfall of Anne Boleyn and Catherine Howard – but, in her eyes, God had not called her to the high office of Queen of England simply to look after Henry and his children. Nor did Henry marry her solely for this purpose; his Queen was expected to play her part in public life, to bolster his image as a true Father of his People and, behind the scenes, to support his moves and plans for maintaining his power. It was primarily to give her the experience she needed in Council that he had appointed her Queen Regent and, as he had probably expected, it strengthened her will as well as her authority. It was now time for her to step into the political arena.

Katherine's appreciation of the change in her status was reflected in her clothes. At the entertainment of the Spanish Duke of Najera in February 1544, she had worn her favourite colours – crimson and gold.

The Spanish account of the reception described her dress (quoted by Strickland):

> An open robe of cloth of gold, the sleeves lined with crimson satin, and trimmed with three piled crimson velvet, the train more than two yards long. Suspended from the neck were two crosses, and a jewel of very rich diamonds, and in her headdress were many rich and beautiful ones. Her girdle was of gold, with very large pendants.

But for some months now, as shown by her household accounts, she had changed from crimson to purple, the traditional colour of 'Imperial Majesty'. The crimson clothes were not discarded, and her footmen and pages continued to be dressed in crimson doublets and hose, but from now on, whenever the occasion called for it, she wore purple.

It was an assertion of authority rather than pride. Cranmer and her own inclination towards learning and religion had given her inborn ambition, already encouraged by Henry, a sense of direction. She had become a woman with a purpose in life, and with characteristic determination she concentrated her resources on achieving that purpose. She remained as serene and as tactful as ever, but there was a new firmness in her manner, a more positive approach to her rôle as Queen.

In her self-assigned task, Katherine was helped by the fact that Henry had made a major diplomatic blunder at Boulogne. In the heat of the battle, he had been informed by the Bishop of Arras, whom Charles v had sent as a special messenger that, having obtained his main objectives, the Emperor was planning to make peace with the French, and that Henry was invited to send a delegate to the discussions to take care of English interests. Henry had declined the offer, saying merely that he reserved the right to make his own terms with the French later. The Emperor had then gone ahead with the negotiations, and on 18 September, at Crépy, his delegates agreed terms for a separate peace treaty with Francis I. The result of the treaty was to isolate Henry, and to leave the French free to turn all their forces against England.

It was, therefore, a furious and embittered Henry that returned to England. The siege of Boulogne had lasted twice as long and had cost more than twice as much as had been expected, and now he was not even to be allowed to enjoy his victory in peace. The Dauphin was already marching to the relief of Boulogne, and the Dukes of Suffolk and Norfolk had retired in disorder to Calais. Henry fumed. On 8 October, he wrote to both Dukes, telling them that he could not accept their 'bolstering and unapparent reasons, especially when they enculke a feigned necessity to cloak and maintain their faults too much apparent to indifferent [impartial] eyes'. After itemising their failures, he continued: 'We pray you to seek no more indirect excuses to cloak your ill-favoured retreat, but rather study and be as vigilant to see our honour, herein somewhat touched, redubbed, and if peace follow not, to preserve our pieces and withstand our enemy.'

As it happened, the territory had been so wasted by the previous fighting that the Dauphin could find no supplies to sustain his army and, after burning a few houses and a village, he retreated. Francis then agreed to send an embassy to discuss peace terms. Henry sent the Earl of Hertford and Sir William Paget as his representatives, but after the first few meetings it was clear that the French would accept nothing less than the return of Boulogne to their hands. Hertford was then told to go to Brussels where, together with Gardiner, he was to see the Emperor and insist that the Emperor should renew the fighting with the French on the grounds that they were attacking English possessions, which fact was to be used to invoke the mutual-aid clause of Henry's earlier treaty with the Emperor. It was a hopeless mission. The Emperor was polite but firm. Henry, he pointed out, had been properly invited to take part in the negotiations at Crépy, but had refused; he must now take the consequences of his own actions.

The result of these diplomatic failures was feverish activity in England. War again with France was inevitable, but this time it would be England, not France, which would be on the defensive. Typically, not a single voice of blame or protest was heard. It was inconceivable that Henry had blundered, and from the innermost circles at Court down to the brawling taverns, everyone was utterly convinced that England had been the victim of a dastardly Continental trick. Offers of help from his equally infuriated subjects poured in to Henry. The repayment of the huge loan of 1542 was waived, and new taxes were voted with genuine enthusiasm.

Only Henry seems to have realised how serious a mistake he had made. Chapuys, reporting on a meeting with the King, Katherine, and Princess Mary, three days after Christmas at Greenwich, stated that Henry was short-tempered, muddled in his facts, and not at all his usual self. Katherine, on the other hand, was calm and gracious. Indeed she was Henry's salvation at this stage, cooling him down and persuading him to look at other diplomatic means for averting war. It was almost certainly at her suggestion that her secretary, Walter Bucler, was sent early in January to Germany to try to persuade the Protestant League to come to England's help. It was also most likely Katherine who, at the same time, talked Henry into sending a secret messenger to the Queen of Navarre and Madame d'Estampes the French King's sister and mistress respectively, to get them to bring feminine pressure to bear. The Queen of Navarre and Madame d'Estampes were, like Katherine, very strong supporters of the Humanist cause and, although Katherine had never met them, they were all well known to each other. The use of women's power was fast becoming a key factor in Katherine's work in England, and its extension to the diplomatic field was a natural corollary. It did in fact eventually lead to peace, but not until another year of war had passed.

From Katherine's point of view, however, the main outcome of this feverish activity was to leave her free to pursue her objectives in learning and religion. These objectives were a straightforward development of the Humanist ideals: first, to improve the lot of the common people by the spread of education, and, secondly, to make religion a private matter between the individual and God, with the emphasis on charity to one's neighbours and faith in the power of God (specifically, Jesus Christ) to redeem the individual from sin. Following the examples of Erasmus and Vives, she did not wish, nor at first did she attempt, to upset the Church, but the doctrines of simplicity and direct communion with God, without the intercession of priests, struck at the root of the Church's power. In Katherine's view, the priests were needed as teachers, not intermediaries; they also had a rôle as missionaries to spread the Word of God, but they could not, and should not, claim to be the only sources of the knowledge and power of God.

The methods by which Katherine sought to achieve her objectives were propaganda and satire – the weapons of the doves rather than the hawks, and again following the example of Erasmus and Vives. Her forces were her circle of ladies at Court, supported by a number of scholars who received her patronage or who were employed through her at the royal school. Patronage she bestowed on, among others, Thomas Sternhold, Nicholas Udall, and, at a later stage, Miles Coverdale; and at the royal school she employed such household names of scholarship as Richard Cox, John Cheke, Roger Ascham, William Grindall, and Anthony Cooke. In addition to these, there were the preachers, such men as Hugh Latimer, Nicholas Ridley, Nicholas Shaxton, John Redman and, possibly, Edward Crome, who were regular visitors to her chambers, and who supplied the practical, professional touch.

Katherine's first few moves were innocuous. She persuaded Princess Mary to join the scholars in a general project for the translation of Erasmus' paraphrases of the Gospels, while she herself produced, in English, a mixture of biblical quotations and some original ideas of her own in the form of psalms and simple prayers. The eleven-year-old Princess Elizabeth was also inspired, and gave Katherine a translation from the French of the Queen of Navarre's *Mirror of a Sinful Soul* as a New Year's gift on 31 December 1544. In a fulsome accompanying letter, Elizabeth informed Katherine that as an iron instrument grows rusty if not used, 'even so shall the wit of a man or woman wax dull and unapt to do or understand anything perfectly unless it be always occupied upon some manner of study'. She accordingly offered Katherine the translation as proof of her industry and ability, asking her to correct it where necessary, and stating that until it had been corrected, no one but the Queen should see it.

It is probably just as well that no one else did see it, for it was an extraordinary exercise for a young girl. After a few paragraphs of verbal self-flagellation – 'Is there any hell so profound that is sufficient to punish the tenth part of my sins?' – and so on, Elizabeth continued her translation:

> But thou which hast made separation of my bed and did put false lovers in my place and committed fornication with them; yet for all this thou mayest come unto me again ... O poor soul! to be where thy sin hath put thee; even upon the highways, where thou didst wait and tarried for to beguile them that came by ... Therefore, having fulfilled thy pleasure, thou hast infected with fornication all the earth which was about thee.[1]

In spite of the erotic mysticism, there was nothing in this nor in the work of the Queen or Mary to alarm anybody, but soon after the New Year, the Queen's circle received a visit from Katherine's one-time Lincolnshire protégée, Anne Askew. It will be recalled that Anne had been sent back home from Court in the days of Anne Boleyn to take the place of her sister, who had died, in the marriage contract which her father,

Sir William Askew, had made with one Thomas Kyme. Anne was a sparkling, highly educated woman, and her marriage to a solid, country squire, against her will, had had small hope of success.

In some respects, it is difficult to blame Thomas Kyme for what had happened. A wife was expected to conform with her husband's way of life, and in any case, it would have been far beyond his capability to become a Seymour or a Dudley, the type of man Anne probably preferred. Anne resented the marriage from the beginning, and although she bore Thomas Kyme two children (whose names and descendants are lost to posterity), she seems to have made no effort to make the best of things. Thomas Kyme, on the other hand, may well have tried to make her contented, but he lacked the light touch and intellectual sympathy which alone might have succeeded. To make matters worse, Anne mocked his efforts with not over-subtle irony – she despised all men who could not match her own wit and learning – and in the end, Thomas Kyme drove her from his house.

During the few years which the marriage lasted, Anne had turned to religion for comfort. Since she had been educated in the Humanist tradition, she decided to find out for herself directly from the Bible, rather than from priests, what God had to say to her. At first, she was confined to market-day visits to Lincoln, where she could study the great chained Bible in the cathedral, but later she managed to obtain and keep for her own use a copy of Tyndale's Bible, which was well annotated with comments pointing out passages which differed substantially from the traditional teaching of the Church. Studying apparently entirely on her own, she developed a profound religious belief which was similar, though not identical, to the concepts of Erasmus, and which was wholly opposed to the Old Faith, to which her husband and most of the surrounding district adhered.

Anne's father, having barely escaped Cromwell's clutches for harbouring a priest who was wanted for treason in 1540, had died a year later, and her eldest brother, Sir Francis Askew, who had been knighted at Boulogne, was now the head of the family. It seems likely that Anne appealed to him for help when she was turned out of her home, which was probably in December 1544, and that it was due to him that she was then able to go to London, where she hoped to obtain a divorce from her husband. Once in London, there were other members of her family to help her and, of course, there was the Queen.

Before Anne Askew went to London, however, she stayed nine days in Lincoln, where she spent the time arguing with the Dean and Chapter of the cathedral. It was probably the first time she had been able to indulge in deep, intellectual debate on religious matters, and she thoroughly enjoyed the experience. It proved a fatal mistake, for some of the priests then went to Thomas Kyme and told him that his wife was infringing the Six Articles and could be charged with heresy. It is not clear from the records whether it was Thomas Kyme on his own who laid the information against her, or whether it was done with the help of the priests, but the result was the same, and early in March 1545 Anne was arrested in London.

In the interval between leaving Lincoln and her arrest, Anne had got in touch with Katherine and her ladies. They were delighted by her lively account of her discussions with the priests in Lincoln, and by her as a person. She was then twenty-five years old and, according to Protestant accounts, exceptionally beautiful. She carried off the fervour of her beliefs with a gay, cheerful wit, which greatly endeared her to her audiences, and clearly Katherine and her ladies were convinced that she was in no way to blame for her husband's action in driving her away from her home and children. She was well connected in the City, and she was also one of Katherine's distant relatives from the North; the ladies at Court welcomed her with open arms. Anne's arrest, therefore, came as a considerable shock, and her trial was to be the spark which turned the Queen's circle of doves into a party of hawks.

Anne was examined first by one Christopher Dare, a professional inquisitor, at the Sadler's Hall. The majority of his questions were designed to trap her into a denial of one or more of the Six Articles, but she skilfully evaded the issue and confessed only that she once said she would rather read five lines in the Bible than hear five masses, 'for the one edified her, and the other not at all'. Dare was followed by a priest who demanded to know her opinion about the sacrament of the altar, but she refused to answer, 'perceiving him to be a Papist.'

She was then taken before the Lord Mayor – Sir William Laxton, not Sir Martin Bowes as stated by Strype and Foxe – and he decided to question her himself. Foxe takes up the tale, apparently quoting from a verbatim transcript.[2]

Lord Mayor: Thou foolish woman, sayest thou that the priests cannot make the body of Christ?

195

Anne Askew: I say so, my Lord: for I have read that God made man; but that man can make God, I never yet read, nor, I suppose, ever shall read it.

Lord Mayor: No, thou foolish woman? After the words of consecration, is it not the Lord's body?

Anne Askew: No. It is but consecrated bread, or sacramental bread.

Lord Mayor: What if a mouse eat it after consecration? What shall become of the mouse? What sayest thou, thou foolish woman?

Anne Askew: What say you, my Lord? What shall become of her?

Lord Mayor: I say, that mouse is damned!

Anne Askew: Alack, poor mouse![3]

In her own account of the trial, Anne states that she only smiled when she was asked about the mouse, but the court could not restrain its laughter, and the Lord Mayor abandoned his questioning. Nevertheless, he committed her to the Compter prison to await further examination. No friend was allowed to speak to her for eleven days, but she told a priest that she was willing to go to confession and that she intended to receive the sacrament at Easter. This showed her willingness to comply, outwardly at least, with the Six Articles, and her family then applied for bail. The Lord Mayor refused to grant bail, however, without the agreement of Edmund Bonner, the Bishop of London, who then demanded the right to examine her himself.

The Bishop had her brought to his house on 20 March. She was accompanied by her cousin, Britain, and a lawyer from Gray's Inn, and she was told she might have learned divines to help her as well if she so wished, but she declined the offer. Meanwhile, influence had been brought to bear on the Bishop, and there is little doubt that the source was Katherine Parr, acting through Joan Denny, the wife of Sir Anthony Denny, the King's confidential aide. The Bishop began his examination, therefore, in conciliatory tones. He was very sorry for her trouble, he told her, and that no man should hurt her for whatever she said in his house. He hoped she would follow the advice of her well-wishers and tell him all the things that burdened her conscience, repeating that no advantage would be taken of her. Anne replied that she had nothing to say, for her conscience was not burdened.

Bonner was somewhat taken aback, and changed the subject to the question of the sacramental bread: was it, or was it not, the body of Christ? Anne simply replied, 'I believe as the Scripture doth teach me.' Bonner repeated the question in a number of different forms, but each time she gave the same answer. Eventually, he left her, saying that he thought he knew her mind and that he would write out a confession for her to sign. He returned a little while later with the document, which he read to her and asked her if she agreed. She said, 'I believe so much thereof as the Holy Scripture doth agree unto; wherefore I desire you that ye will add that thereto.' Bonner began to show signs of anger and told her that she should not teach him what he should write. He then went into the main hall and read the document to Anne's friends and a number of other people who were there. They all saw no harm in it and tried to persuade her to sign it. Anne takes up the tale herself:

> Then, said the Bishop, I might thank others and not myself for the favour that I found at his hands; for he considered, he said, that I had good friends, and also that I came of a worshipful [well-born] stock. Then answered one Christopher, a servant unto Mr. Denny, 'rather ought you, my Lord, to have done it in such case for God's sake than for man's. Then my Lord sat down, and took me the writing to set thereto my hand, and I wrote after this manner: 'I, Anne Askew, do believe all manner of things contained in the faith of the Catholic Church.'
>
> Then, because I added 'the Catholic Church', he flung into his chamber in a great fury. My cousin, Britain, followed, desiring him for God's sake to be good Lord to me. He said that I was a woman and he was nothing deceived in me. Then my cousin Britain desired him to take me as a woman, and not to set my weak woman's wit to his Lordship's great wisdom. Then went into him Dr Weston and said the cause why I did write there the Catholic Church was that I understood not the church written before. So, with much ado, they persuaded my Lord to come out again and to take my name and those of my sureties.

Because of difficulties concerning the bonds of the sureties, it was another three days before Anne was released. These had been but preliminary examinations, and she was only released on bail; she still had to stand a formal trial before judge and jury. Her case came up on 13 June 1545, at the Guildhall, where she was arraigned with a man and another woman, all on the same indictment of having infringed the Act of Six Articles. There were no witnesses against her or the other woman (a Mrs Joan Sawtery), however, and the witness against the man was shown to have been acting from malice: 'whereupon twelve honest and substantial men of the City of London were charged (to give their verdict), which found all the said persons not guilty of their indictment; wherefore they were discharged and quit paying their fees.'[4]

The Queen's ladies knew the moment that Anne was released on bail that they had triumphed. Bonner would never have let her go if he had intended to prosecute her seriously in the courts, and her release was the signal for a great upsurge of activity. Anne was encouraged to write a full description of her examination by Bonner and the others, and this was printed and circulated as a pamphlet. The Queen's name was not mentioned, but her sympathy and help was apparent to all, and with Katherine behind them, the believers in the New Faith felt they could safely come out into the open once more. The Six Articles were openly flouted, priests were laughed to scorn, and new copies of the books which had been banned and burnt the year before were procured from Holland and Germany and circulated as freely as they had done in the days of Anne Boleyn.

Bishops Gardiner and Bonner, and the rest of the Papists on the Council, looked on in impotent fury. So long as the King was not prepared to act, there was nothing they could do. And they knew that whether he wished to act or not, Henry's hands were tied – not so much by Katherine, but by the diplomatic situation abroad. Even while Bonner was questioning Anne Askew, a messenger had returned from the Queen of Navarre bringing hopes of support from her and her Humanist colleagues to persuade Francis I to call off his campaign against England. The Queen's secretary, Walter Bucler, had also sent encouraging news from Germany, where the Protestant League had offered to help by a combination of threats against the French and offers of mediation between Henry and Francis. With so much Humanist and Protestant sympathy being rallied to his cause abroad, Henry could not, and would not, lift a finger against the Humanists and Protestants at home.

To cap it all, the husbands of the Queen's principal ladies, all now open believers in the New Faith, were the popular heroes of the day. They were everywhere and anywhere where the Kingdom was being threatened. Early in February, the Earl of Hertford and Lord Lisle routed a French attack on Boulogne; then, after the defeat and slaughter of Sir Ralph Evers and his men by the Scots at Ancrum Moor at the end of February, Hertford sped to the North to take command, while Lisle returned to sea and swept the Channel clear of French ships. Hertford's brother, Thomas Seymour, took over as Warden of the Cinque Ports, and the Duke of Suffolk hastened south to organise defences round Portsmouth, where an intercepted letter from the Emperor's ambassador in Paris had shown that the main French attack was to be made. For the Hertford faction, therefore, it was action, action, all the way, while all that Norfolk and Gardiner could offer was a check of corn supplies, which threatened to become scarce, and a review of the defences of East Anglia, both of which were important, but neither of which was likely to catch popular imagination.

In these circumstances, Katherine and her ladies had everything their own way. The Duchess of Suffolk named her pet spaniel 'Gardiner', and won a cheap laugh every time she called the dog to heel. She also gave a big dinner at which, in a party game, she named the Bishop as the man she loved least. As she was later to say when Gardiner was imprisoned during the reign of Edward vi, 'It was merry with the lambs when the wolf was shut up.'

On a more serious note, Katherine Parr extended her religious propaganda activities to include a full-length book, setting out a detailed statement of her own beliefs. The book, called by the forbidding, but in those days popular, title of *The Lamentation of A Sinner*, was not actually published until after Henry's death, but references in the book itself and its mention in Gardiner's correspondence, indicate that copies of the first draft were circulating at Court by November 1545. She must, therefore, have started writing it soon after the first trial of Anne Askew. During this period Katherine also gave further encouragement to preachers of the New Faith, and they were now frequent visitors at Court, while in May Henry gave permission for the publication of a book of ordinary prayers in English, known as *The King's Primer*.

Most of the prayers were probably written by Cranmer, but Henry wrote the preface himself. Considering the necessity of intelligent prayer, he wrote, we have given our subjects a form of praying in their own mother tongue. The book was to be used by schoolmasters, 'next after their A.B.C. now by us also set forth', to teach the young. (*The A.B.C. set forth by the King's Majesty*, which was also published at this time, was one of Henry's most notable achievements in the field of education, and is a model of its kind.) Still hugging the middle of the road, however, Henry concluded his preface with the statement that those who understood Latin and who thought they could pray more fervently in Latin, might continue to use the Latin tongue, provided they adhered to the form of Latin prayers which were also included in the *Primer*. It is not known whether Katherine had a hand in either the *Primer* or the *A.B.C.*, but she would have seen drafts of both books, and the strong Humanist trend in them is an indication of her possible influence.

It is indeed remarkable that Henry had time for such matters during this stage of his kingdom's affairs. Defence preparations at home and diplomatic activity abroad had reached a new peak of intensity, and every possibility of improving England's position was rigorously examined.

At home, the intelligence report that the French intended to attempt a landing on or near the Isle of Wight was confirmed. Further information indicated that the attack would take place about the middle of July, and Henry decided he would join the Duke of Suffolk at Portsmouth. To avoid revealing how much was known about French plans, the King's journey was disguised as a summer Progress to start at Greenwich, with some uncertainty about the route the King intended to take. Meanwhile, Lisle was ordered to have the Fleet in readiness off the Isle of Wight by the end of June.

Abroad, further attempts were made to get the Emperor to honour his obligations under the mutual-aid clause of his treaty with Henry. Here, Katherine and Princess Mary had a part to play, for on 9 May, Chapuys reported that the Queen and Princess had had a long talk with him as he was passing through the gardens of St James' Palace. Katherine had told him, he said, how much she hoped that the Emperor would continue his friendship, and how affectionately she wished to be remembered to the Emperor's sister, the Queen Regent in Brussels. In a separate letter to the Queen Regent, Chapuys added that he refrained 'from detailing the complimentary expressions used by the Queen of England towards her, knowing she [the Queen Regent] has no appetite for such things', but nevertheless Katherine was playing her part with some skill, for her affectionate messages to the leading Catholic woman in Europe were clearly designed to appease the Emperor's fears that Henry might be binding himself too strongly to the Protestants.

Meanwhile, the political situation which the religious activities of Katherine and her ladies had created cried out for a Cromwell to seize the initiative in the Council, and Sir William Paget, one of the two Principal Secretaries, saw himself in the part. With most of the leading members of the Council away on military duties, it was an excellent opportunity for him to strengthen his hand and, remembering perhaps how Cromwell had used women to gain a hold over their husbands, he began by seeking the favour of the Countess of Hertford. Paget, however, lacked Cromwell's subtle ruthlessness, and his first efforts fell on stony ground. He wrote to the Earl of Hertford, who was then in Darlington building up his army, with some comment on the Earl's failure to write to his wife. Hertford's reply was acid:

> P.S. I perceive ye find fault with me for that I have written two times and send never a letter to my wife, as though you would be noted a good husband and that no such fault could be found in you. I would advise you to leave off such quarrels, or else I will tell my Lady [Paget's wife] such tales of you as you will repent the beginning.

But Paget then adopted another of Cromwell's tactics, and arranged matters so that all communications with the King had to be channelled through him. This enabled him gradually to set himself up as an arbiter of what should or should not go through, and some weeks later, at the end of June, Hertford was obliged to ask his help in a suit to the King for a grant of a religious college which was being dissolved in Yorkshire. Paget held up the request but, again lacking Cromwell's ruthlessness, he did not dare offend Hertford, and a fortnight later he was humbly seeking Hertford's advice on the best way to raise more funds for the King.

Since Katherine saw Paget every day, there was no need for any correspondence between them during this period, and hence, unfortunately, no record of their relationship. All that is known is that Katherine trusted him sufficiently to let him read a draft copy of her *The Lamentation of a Sinner*, but otherwise there is nothing to show that he made any headway with her, or came anywhere near establishing the sort of relationship which existed between Cromwell and Anne Boleyn. In this respect, therefore, his bid to be a second Cromwell failed, but he did eventually succeed, towards the end of Henry's reign, in achieving a key position in the Council's power-game.

On 1 July 1545, Henry and Katherine, having sent Princess Elizabeth and Prince Edward to Ampthill for safety, set off from Greenwich on what they hoped would seem to spies to be a normal summer Progress. On 5 July, they stayed at Nonesuch; on the 9th, they were at Guildford, and then they switched suddenly south, arriving at Farnham on the 13th, and eventually at Portsmouth on the 15th. Four days later, the French Fleet, consisting of some three hundred ships, was anchored off the Isle of Wight. The new Spanish Ambassador, van der Delft, who had replaced Chapuys, and who was present with the King and Queen on the Progress, gives an eye-witness account:

Next day, Sunday [19th July], while the King was at dinner on the flagship [the *Great Harry*], the French fleet appeared. The King hurriedly left the flagship and the English sailed to encounter the French, shooting at the galleys, of which five had entered the harbour while the English could not get out for want of wind. Towards evening, the ship *Mary Rose* of Vice-Admiral George Carew foundered, all the 500 men being drowned save about 25 or 30 servants, sailors and the like. Was told by a Fleming among the survivors that when she heeled over with the wind, the water entered by the lowest row of gun-ports which had been left open after firing. They expect to recover the ship and guns. On Monday, firing on both sides lasted all day and at nightfall one of the French galleys was damaged ... On Tuesday, the French landed on the Isle of Wight and burnt 10 or 12 small houses; but they were ultimately driven to take refuge in a small earthwork fort, and a large force, 8,000, is now opposed to them. Yesterday, Wednesday, and the previous night, nothing could be heard but artillery firing, and it was rumoured that the French would land elsewhere ...

On Saturday, 25 July, the French Fleet withdrew and sailed up the coast towards Dover. Lisle was becalmed and could do nothing but watch them sail away. Three days later the French returned and landed a force of some fifteen hundred men near Dover, but they were driven back to their ships with the loss of about a hundred men by the local defence forces. The landing marked the end of the French invasion attempt, and they then retired to their own waters. There was one more short engagement in the middle of August which Lisle successfully repulsed, and on 20 August he reported that he had received intelligence that the French Fleet had retired fully to the Seine mouth and was unlikely to put to sea again 'this year'. He added that French fishermen said 'there never was a journey so costly to France as this had been, nor more shame spoken of amongst themselves'.

Henry was now ready to talk peace to the French, but he was determined to treat sword in hand, and Lisle was ordered to teach the French a lesson by carrying out two or three raids on the French coast. At the same time, Hertford was ordered to destroy the Scottish harvest in the Lowlands as a reprisal for their dealings with the French and in order to secure the Borders against any further invasions. Lisle carried out his orders early in September with conspicuous success, destroying the town of Tréport and a number of Normandy villages without loss to his own forces, and on 18 September Hertford reported that they had sacked Kelso, Jedburgh, and some fourteen other towns, estimating that they had done twice as much damage as they did during the sack of Edinburgh in 1544. Henry now felt secure, and both fleet and army were recalled and disbanded.

Throughout these events, Henry and Katherine had continued their Progress, hunting and banqueting in their customary manner in order to show the world their contempt for the French forces lined up against them. On 23 August, however, the Duke of Suffolk, who was with Henry on the Progress, suddenly sickened and died. His death affected Henry greatly. The Progress was cut short, and the Court returned quickly to Windsor where Henry ordered a state funeral for the immensely popular Duke. One other result of the Duke's death was that it brought the Duchess of Suffolk, now very much alone in the world, even closer to the Queen than she had been, and the friendship between the two women became an inseparable bond.

The peace moves which Henry now set in hand showed that he had fully recovered his old diplomatic skill. He accepted the offers of both the Emperor and of the German Protestants to act as mediators between him and Francis i, and two separate sets of negotiations were arranged, both to be carried out at the same time. The first, for which Henry selected Gardiner to be his chief delegate, was to take place in Brussels under the direct eye of the Emperor, and the second, for which Tunstall and Paget were selected as delegates, was to take place outside Calais under the chairmanship of the Germans. Francis willingly entered into Henry's game, appreciating that by these means they could keep the Emperor guessing as to their real intentions – whether they meant peace, or whether they meant to form a new military alliance against the Emperor – and thereby each would be able to squeeze concessions out of Charles v which both needed for the future welfare of their kingdoms. (Henry needed a guarantee of peaceful trade with Flanders; Francis needed a guarantee of his existing frontiers.)

The return to peace also meant a renewal of the struggle between the reformers and the Gardiner/Norfolk faction.Gardiner had become increasingly alarmed at the progress the reformers had made, and he felt bitter about the insults which the Queen's ladies and others had hurled at him, so much so that he refused to see Katherine before his departure to Brussels, telling Paget to make his excuses to her for him. Moreover,

Gardiner had been led to believe that the negotiations he was to conduct were the principal ones, and that those under the Protestant mediation were intended merely as a smoke-screen. This meant that Henry would no longer be under any obligation to support the Humanists, and that he, Gardiner, could now safely renew his campaign against them.

Gardiner began with a scathing attack on Cranmer. Passing through Canterbury on his way to take ship at Dover, Gardiner had been present when Cranmer had held a trial of a band of demobilised soldiers who had gone on a rampage in the precincts of the cathedral, menacing the people and reciting a bawdy parody of some biblical texts. Cranmer had tried and convicted them in the morning, but that same afternoon he had set them free. This, said Gardiner in a letter to Paget on 21 October, was proof that Cranmer was a coward, implying that he was unfit to be Archbishop.

Gardiner arrived in Brussels at the end of October. Paget then enclosed with a letter of further instructions a number of pamphlets which were circulating in London, and what appears to have been a draft copy of Katherine's *Lamentation*. One of the pamphlets, called *The Complaint of Roderick Mors*, was a Protestant plea for the redress of wrongs suffered by the common people. In a very long letter, written to Paget on 5 November, Gardiner offered his comments. The pamphlet, he said, would do nothing but promote trouble among the people. The author was well named, for his work would mean the death of his body and the damnation of his soul. The pamphlet contained personal attacks on Gardiner, and therefore Gardiner had decided that he would write a 'book' in reply. He continued:

How many books and scrolls have been cast abroad in London within this year and the offender never found out, so many priests searched and put from their goods for a time, so openly done and the offenders never found out. These be common open matters. As for private attacks, there have been a great many, and such particular tales blown abroad as cannot be sown but of the devil.

Paget had suggested that he should despise such things, but he could not disregard the 'wealth of the realm'. He did not fear these malicious follies during the King's life, but if those who were now young despised religion and conceived another opinion of God than what was true, what would happen? The example of Germany had already shown that the

204

result would be the breakdown of obedience to princes and the Emperor, 'who, whatsoever he be, is their superior'.

After a few more pages in the same vein, Gardiner turned to Katherine's book: 'That book [his reply to Roderick Mors] I write to the world, but to the book of *Lamentation* which you sent, I only answer lamentably to you, digesting in these letters the displeasure received in reading this most abominable book.'

He concluded:

> This is my best pastime here, and this letter may be read at leisure or not at all, for it is no pain for me to write and I never wrote so much in a month as I have done in this, and I look so lustily, thanks be to God, that I talk shamefastly of any sickness by the way. God make all that be sick, either in body or soul, whole.

But if Gardiner thought the country was disintegrating into Protestant anarchy, the Protestants thought otherwise. Writing a few weeks later, John Hooper, an ardent supporter of the New Faith, told Henry Bullinger in Germany:

> The news from England is that idolatory is nowhere stronger. Our King has destroyed the Pope, but not popery; he has expelled all the monks and nuns, and pulled down the monasteries; he has caused all their possessions to be transferred into his Exchequer, and yet they are bound, even the frail female sex, by the King's command to perpetual chastity. England has at this time at least 10,000 nuns, not one of whom is allowed to marry. The impious mass, the most shameful celibacy of the clergy, the invocation of saints, auricular confession, superstitious abstinence from meats, and purgatory, were never before held by the people in greater esteem than at the present moment...
> The chief supporters of the Gospel in England are dying every hour. Within these two years are dead Lord Chancellor Audeley, the Duke of Suffolk, Sir Edward Baynton [the Queen's First Lord of the Bedchamber], Poynings, the King's deputy at Boulogne, Sir Thomas Wyatt, known throughout the world for his noble qualities, a most zealous defender of yours and Christ's religion, Dr Butts, the King's physician: all these were of the Privy Council[5] and all died of the plague and fever; so that the country is now left altogether to the bishops and those who despise God and all true religion...

The situation was in fact much more evenly balanced than John Hooper had reported, and it was 'the frail female sex' in the person of the Queen and her ladies who were holding the bishops at bay. Towards the end of the year Katherine published her book of prayers, with Henry's permission, and Cranmer, with Katherine's help, obtained Henry's approval for a further injunction to priests to pull down saint's images, which, to give Hooper his due, were being newly erected in many churches. At the same time, a number of other 'superstitious' acts, such as creeping to the Cross, and prayers for help to the saints, were abolished. The Six Articles, however, remained very much in force, giving Gardiner and his fellow bishops the weapon they needed with which to suppress the Gospellers, and causing confusion and violent emotions among the people.

It was in these circumstances that, on 23 November 1545, Parliament assembled at Westminster for what was to be its last session in Henry's reign. Among the Bills they were asked to approve was one for the further dissolution of religious institutions, such as colleges, chantries, and stipendiary priests (for the King's need for funds was now greater than it had ever been), and another for the banning of religious books of the New Faith. Without Cromwell to control it, and with both Gardiner and Paget absent abroad on diplomatic missions, Parliament for once reflected the conflict among the people they represented. The debates were angry, bitter, and prolonged, and it was by no means certain that they would agree to the requests of the King's ministers. So great was the bitterness that on Christmas Eve, when Parliament was due to be prorogued, Henry came down and gave the prorogation speech in person. After exchanging compliments with his faithful subjects, Henry developed his main theme:

> Yet, although I wish you, and you wish me, to be in this perfect love and concord, this friendly amity cannot continue, except both you, my Lords Temporal and my Lords Spiritual, and you, my loving subjects, study and take pains to amend one thing, which surely is amiss and far out of order; to the which I most heartily require you. Which is that Charity and Concord is not amongst you, but Discord and Dissension beareth rule in every place. Saint Paul saith to the Corinthians, the thirteenth chapter, 'Charity is gentle, Charity is not envious, Charity is not proud,' and so forth. Behold then, what love and charity is amongst you, when one calleth another heretic and anabaptist, and he calleth him back papist, hypocrite and Pharisee? Be these tokens of Charity amongst you? Are these signs of fraternal love amongst you?

After rebuking the proponents of both the Old and the New Faiths, he went on:

> I am very sorry to know and to hear how unreverently that most precious jewel,

the Word of God, is disputed, rhymed, sung, and jangled in every ale-house and tavern ... And yet I am even as much sorry that the readers of the same [the Word of God] follow it in doing so faintly and coldly. For of this I am sure, that charity was never so faint among you, and virtuous and godly living was never less used, nor God Himself among Christians was never less reverenced, honoured, or served.

Then came his final exhortation to a House now humble and contrite as never before, and in an atmosphere so charged with emotion that many were openly weeping:

Therefore, as I said before, be in charity with one another like brother and brother; love, dread, and serve God; to which I, as your Supreme Head and Sovereign Lord, exhort and require you; and then I doubt not but that love and league, that I spake of in the beginning, shall never be dissolved or broke betwixt us.[6]

The youthful Sir William Petre, recently promoted to share with Paget the task of being one of the two Principal Secretaries to King and Council, reported the speech in full to Paget who was now in Calais. The King spoke, he wrote:

So sententiously, so Kingly, or rather fatherly, as peradventure to you that hath been used to his daily talks should have been no great wonder (and yet saw I some that hear him often enough largely water their plants), but to us, that have not heard him often, was such a joy and marvellous comfort as I reckon this day one of the happiest of my life.

On the actual work of Parliament, Petre told Paget:

The Bill of Books, albeit it was at the beginning set earnestly forward, is finally dashed in the Common House, as are divers others, whereat I hear not that His Majesty is much discontented. The book of colleges, etc., escaped narrowly and was driven over to the last hour, and yet then passed only by division of the House.

These actions of the Commons showed that the supporters of Humanism and the New Faith were once more finding their strength. There were also social as well as religious grievances to be redressed, and it was to the new men – the Seymours, Dudleys, Parrs, Dennys, and Herberts – that the people now looked for help. But the King's power was absolute, more so now than ever before, and no one either wished or dared to challenge it. Unless the new men could win the King's support, there was nothing they could do. And it was now obvious to all that the key to winning that support lay in the hands of Katherine and her ladies. 'If the King favours these stirrers of heresy,' Chapuys wrote in an analysis some time later, '. . . it is because the Queen, instigated by the Duchess of Suffolk, Countess of Hertford, and the Admiral's wife [Joan Dudley, Lady Lisle], shows herself infected . . .' In spite of her discretion and careful avoidance of publicity, it was now on Katherine that both factions began to focus their attention.

During the year, Katherine had moved more and more towards the radical Humanists, and by January 1546 it was clear that her support was now wholeheartedly on the side of the Hertford faction, though she was still far from being the Protestant to which the extremists sought to convert her. In the power-game, therefore, it was a question for the Gardiner/Norfolk faction more of how to eliminate her influence with the King than of trying to win her support. On the other hand, her ladies, not content with her political and moderate religious support, and going further perhaps than their husbands thought wise, wanted her to appreciate the iniquity of the Act of Six Articles and to fight for its abolition. Without the Act, Gardiner and the Papists would be deprived of the greater part of their legal power, and the ladies, with the help of their husbands, could then proceed freely with the social and religious reforms so dear to their hearts.

Katherine thus now became subject to two sets of activities: the Papists began to plot her downfall, and her ladies began to step up their religious activities. Katherine's initial attitude to the situation is shown, indirectly, in the famous letter which she wrote to the University of Cambridge in answer to their appeal to her to save them from the consequences of the new law which would enable the King and his ministers to seize much of the University's property. The appeal had been written to her in Latin to show the respect of the Fellows for her learning. Katherine replied:

Your letters I have received, presented on all your behalfs by Mr. Dr. Smith, your discrete and learned advocate. And as they be Latinly written (which is so signified unto me by those that be learned in the Latin tongue), so I know you could have uttered your desires and opinions familiarly in our vulgar tongue, aptest for my intelligence, albeit you seem to have conceived, rather partially than truly, a favourable estimation both of my going forward and dedication to learning.

After further modest disclaimers, Katherine states that she thankfully accepts their document, and continues:

And for as much as I do well understand all kind of learning doth flourish amongst you in this age, as it did amongst the Greeks at Athens long ago, I require and desire you all not so to hunger for the exquisite knowledge of profane learning that it may be thought the Greek's university was but transposed, or now in England again revived, forgetting our Christianity; since their excellence only did attain to moral and natural things: but rather I gently exhort you to study and apply those doctrines as means and apt degrees to the attaining and setting forth the better Christ's reverend and most sacred doctrine, that it may not be laid in evidence against you at the tribunal seat of God how ye were ashamed of Christ's doctrine. For this Latin lesson I am taught to say by Saint Paul, 'Non me pudet evangelii.' The sincere setting forth whereof I trust universally in all your vocations and ministeries you will apply and conform your sundry gifts, arts, and studies, to such end and sort, that Cambridge may be accounted rather an university of divine philosophy than of natural or moral, as Athens was.

Upon the confidence of your accomplishment of which to my expectation, zeal, and request, I, according to your desires, attempted [approached] my Lord the King's Majesty for the stay of your possessions. In which, notwithstanding His Majesty's property and interest through the consent of the High Court of Parliament, His Highness, being such a patron of good learning, he will rather advance and erect new occasion therefor, than confound those your colleges: so that learning may hereafter ascribe her very original, whole conservation and sure stay to our Sovereign Lord, his only defence and worthy ornament; the prosperous estate and princely government of whom long to preserve, I doubt not but everyone of you will with daily invocation call upon Him, whom alone and only can dispose all to every creature.[7]

The subtlety of this involved letter lies in the sop thrown to Gardiner, the Chancellor of the University, in the request to play down the Humanist studies of the ancient philosophers and modern science, of which Gardiner disapproved, while at the same time directing their attention to the application of their learning to the New rather than the Old Faith, a sentiment which will have mollified the apparent denial of Humanism.

But the hardest course to follow in politics and religion is the middle of the road. Henry managed it by a combination of force and consummate Machiavellian skill in manipulating the opposing parties, but Katherine either could not, or would not, use the same tactics. In any case, she had already moved too close to the Hertford faction for there to be any longer any hope of deceiving Gardiner. The letter to Cambridge was written on 26 February 1546, and within a week the first signs of the plot against Katherine began to appear.

The initial moves were directed at an attempt to set Katherine and her ladies against each other. This was done by circulating rumours that Henry was beginning to tire of Katherine in favour of the widowed Duchess of Suffolk. Van der Delft, the Emperor's ambassador, reporting the rumours, stated: 'Some attribute it to the sterility of the present Queen, while others say that there will be no change during the present war. Madame Suffolk is much talked about and in great favour, but the King shows no alteration in his demeanour to the Queen, although she is said to be annoyed at the rumour.'

Then came word from Stephen Vaughan, the King's factor in Antwerp, who, writing to Wriothesley and Paget, reported:

> This day came to my lodging a High Dutch, a merchant of this town, saying that he had dined with certain friends, one of whom offered to lay a wager with him that the King's Majesty would have another wife; and he prayed me to show him the truth. He would not tell me who offered the wager, and I said that I never heard of any such thing, and that there was no such thing. Many folks talk of this matter, and from whence it comes I cannot learn.

This letter was written from Antwerp on 7 March, and it is significant that Gardiner was in Antwerp on that day, on his way back from the negotiations with the Emperor which had been moved from Brussels to Utrecht. This story was followed by another, also from Flanders, that Anne of Cleves, who had stayed at Court much longer than usual after the New Year festivities, was to be Katherine's successor and that she had already borne the King two sons, a story which was wholly untrue.

These tactics irritated rather than frightened Katherine and her ladies, and strengthened rather than weakened the bond between them. Their reaction was to increase their reforming activities. Anne Askew once more became a frequent visitor at Court, and Katherine arranged that throughout Lent Hugh Latimer and other preachers of the New Faith should come to her chambers every afternoon and expound the Gospels to her and her ladies. At the same time, she began to engage the

King more and more in religious discussions, playing on his fondness for intellectual debate gradually to persuade him to drop the Act of Six Articles.

Katherine may also have been further encouraged by the new follies of the Earl of Surrey, the weak link of the Gardiner/Norfolk faction. Early in February, a senseless act of bravado outside Boulogne[8] had led to the loss of some five hundred men in a skirmish with Oudart du Bies. This was followed in the middle of March by a report from another of the King's agents, John Dymock, who stated that he had been told by Flemish merchants that supplies destined for the garrison at Boulogne were falling into wrong hands. The report continued:

> I asked whether they [the embezzlers] were English, Dutch, or Italians; and he answered, 'It may chance both of yours and ours, and more you get not of me, but let your governors look substantially upon the affairs of Boulogne, whom that they do put in trust there, for the King's Majesty, your master, is deceived in every way.'

Surrey was recalled for questioning. His accounts were found to be in such disorder that they could not be deciphered, and that, coupled with his military foolhardiness, led to his dismissal from his post at Boulogne and from Court. Hertford, who had already been alerted to take a force of three thousand men to Calais to redeem Surrey's blunder, then crossed the Channel and took overall command of the area.

Instead of being encouraged by these events, however, Katherine should have paid more attention to the diplomatic situation abroad which, as always, played a major part in Henry's decisions concerning religion. Both sets of negotiations with the French, that at Calais and that under the Emperor's aegis, had failed. On the other hand, both Gardiner and the French delegate had succeeded in winning the concessions they wanted from the Emperor. The result was that Henry was once more in close alliance with the Catholics, and this in turn meant that Gardiner would again be allowed to direct his whole attention to the persecution of 'heretics', foremost among whom were the Queen and her ladies. The Hertford faction were trying to counter Gardiner's diplomatic success with one of their own, and Lisle, probably as a result of the efforts of the Queen of Navarre, had established secret contact through a Venetian merchant with his opposite member of the French Council, Admiral d'Annebault, in a renewed attempt to make a treaty with the French. But these negotiations were bound to take time, and meanwhile Gardiner and Norfolk had the field to themselves.

Following the same pattern as that of their attempt to bring down Cromwell and Anne of Cleves, Gardiner and Norfolk developed their attack on two fronts. On the one hand, the King's fancy was to be caught by a suitable replacement from the Howard family who could step into Katherine's shoes, and on the other, proof was to be found that Katherine had infringed the Act of Six Articles.

The person nominated to take Katherine's place was the Duke of Norfolk's daughter, the Duchess of Richmond, the widow of the King's illegitimate son. To avoid rousing suspicion, a complex plot was worked out by which Norfolk would pretend to be trying to heal the breach between the Howards and Seymours by offering his daughter in marriage to the Earl of Hertford's brother, Sir Thomas Seymour. To add verisimilitude to the plot, other cross-marriages between Surrey's sons and Hertford's daughters were also to be proposed. The Duchess of Richmond was then to set out to win Henry's favour and either marry the King instead of Seymour, or, if Katherine survived the plot, to marry Seymour and become the King's mistress. 'Which,' her brother, the Earl of Surrey told her, 'should not only be a means to help herself, but all her friends should receive a commodity by the same.'

It is pleasing to report that Sir Gawen Carew, giving this evidence which he said was told him by the Duchess of Richmond herself, went on to say: 'Whereupon she defied her brother, and said that all they [the Howards] should perish, and she would cut her own throat rather than that she would consent to such villainy.'

This part of the plot, however, was of minor importance. Someone else could easily be found to take the Duchess of Richmond's place, and the main attack was on the religious front. Again, the approach was elaborate. Gardiner, with the help of his main supporters on the Council, Wriothesley, Riche, and Norfolk, obtained the King's agreement for a renewal of inquisitions into heresy in Essex and Suffolk, to be conducted by Bishop Bonner. This was then followed, on 7 May, by an examination of Norfolk's younger son, Lord Thomas Howard, by the Privy Council. A summary of the interrogation states:

Lord Thomas Howard appeared and was assured of the King's clemency if he would frankly confess what he said in disproof of the sermons preached in Court

212

last Lent and his other talk in the Queen's chamber and elsewhere in the Court concerning scripture; but as, although acknowledging his fault, he did not confess the particulars which the Council would have him confess, he was remanded.

Hugh Latimer was then sent for, and the bishops were instructed to 'fish out the bottom of his stomach', but this also revealed nothing other than that he had preached before the Queen. The Council now turned into the Court itself, and there they unearthed one John Lassels (possibly the same man who had given evidence against Catherine Howard). He was accused of being an associate of a Dr Crome who had at first maintained, but then later recanted, his heresy concerning the sacrament. But Lassels refused to answer their questions on the grounds that he might incriminate himself. This was more promising material, and Lassels was arrested pending further inquiries.

At this point, it seems that Gardiner, prompted possibly by Bonner, remembered Anne Askew. Although she had been set free after her trial a year before, her evidence had clearly shown that she denied the first and principal article of the Six Articles, that which affirmed that the sacramental bread was the true body of Christ. It was known that she had been a frequent visitor at Court, and her character was such that it was most unlikely that she would have changed her opinions about the sacrament. Accordingly, on 24 May, the Council sent for her and her husband. Thomas Kyme, to appear before them within fourteen days.

Meanwhile, Lisle, having finally completed and signed an agreement for 'an honourable peace forever' with the French Admiral, returned to London and found the Court in a state of tension. Another courtier, George Blagge, whom Henry called affectionately 'My Pig', had been arrested, Nicholas Shaxton, the former Bishop of Salisbury, had been pulled in, together with a man called White from the City of London, and no one knew whose turn would be next. No move had yet been made, however, against the Queen or her ladies, and, according to Foxe, Katherine continued her regular discussions on religion with the King. She may have hoped, through him, to stop Gardiner's activities, or she may have been simply unaware of the fact that she was the main target, but it was clear to Lisle and to Katherine's brother, the Earl of Essex, that Gardiner, for the moment, held the whip hand, and that they must at least appear to acquiesce in his proceedings if they were to save their own necks.

213

It was in these circumstances that, on 19 June, Anne Askew and her husband, whom Anne had not seen for nearly two years, came before the Privy Council at Greenwich. Anne began by objecting to the presence of Thomas Kyme, who, she declared, was no longer her husband. The Council thereupon sent him away and began questioning Anne on her own. The Lord Chancellor, Wriothesley, opened the inquiry by saying that it was the King's wish that she should give the Council her honest opinions and tell them all that she knew. Anne refused. She said that if the King wished to hear what she had to say, she would prefer to tell him herself. Wriothesley retorted that 'it was not meet the King should be troubled with her', to which she replied that Solomon, who was the wisest King that ever lived, had not objected to listening to two common women. Wriothesley quickly changed the subject, and for the next five hours, he and Gardiner cross-examined Anne on her beliefs. As she had done at her examination a year before, Anne evaded the main issue of the sacrament, and exasperated Gardiner with her dialectics. Eventually, they sent her away in the custody of a gentlewoman of the Court.

Next day, she was brought before the Council again, but she insisted that she had already said all she had to say. In a letter which she is believed to have smuggled out to a friend, Anne continues the story:

> Then after divers words they bade me go by. Then came my Lord Lisle, my Lord of Essex, and the Bishop of Winchester [Gardiner], requiring me earnestly that I should confess the sacrament to be flesh, blood, and bone. Then said I to my Lord Parr and my Lord Lisle that it was great shame for them to counsel contrary to their knowledge. Whereunto, in few words, they did say that they would gladly all things were well.

Gardiner then asked to speak to her alone, but she refused, and Wriothesley took up the questioning once more. However he, too, had to admit defeat. 'Then came Master Paget to me with many glorious words, and desired me to speak my mind unto him. I might, he said, deny it again if need were. I said that I would not deny the truth.'

Paget was foolish enough to try to cap her quotations from the Bible, but by now Anne must have known both the Old and New Testaments by heart and easily out-classed him. Realising that he was out-matched, Paget persuaded her to debate the matter with a wiser man than he, and he called in Dr Cox, Prince Edward's senior tutor. It was a clever move, for Cox was a supporter of the New Faith, and if anyone could persuade her to resolve her conscience about the Six Articles, as he himself had done, he was the man. But he, too, was confounded by her knowledge of the scriptures. Anne's letter continues: 'Then on the Sunday I was sore sick, thinking no less than to die. Therefore I desired to speak with Latimer. It would not be. Then was I sent to Newgate in my extremity of sickness, for in all my life afore was I never in such pain. Thus the Lord strengthen you in the truth. Pray, pray, pray.'

So far, on the surface at least, Gardiner and Wriothesley had seemed to be making a genuine effort to persuade her to admit that the sacrament was the real body and blood of Christ. If she were to do so they implied, everyone would be happy, and she would be released. In little more than a week, however, they changed their tactics drastically, and at her next examination, on 29 June, the questioning took a very different turn.

The events which caused this change are described by Foxe in his *Acts and Monuments*, which was written some fifteen or twenty years later. Foxe does not date these events as precisely as they are here, but their occurrence during this last week in June would account fully for what followed later.

According to Foxe, Henry's leg worsened, and in his pain, he began to be irritated by Katherine's religious discussions. By chance, Gardiner happened to be present at the end of one of her talks with the King, and after she had left the room, Henry commented in Gardiner's presence: 'A good hearing it is, when women become such clerks [i.e., scholars], and a thing much to my comfort to come in mine old days to be taught by my wife!' Gardiner seized the opportunity, and agreed whole-heartedly with Henry that the Queen was wrong to argue with him, especially since one of the King's rare virtues 'was his learned judgment in religion, above not only princes of that and other ages, but also above doctors professed in divinity'. With further flattering remarks, Gardiner went on to insinuate that the Queen was not at all what she seemed to be, and that she encouraged others to oppose the King's efforts to establish religious uniformity in the kingdom. Henry was all attention, and he finally agreed that, provided they could find sufficient evidence of their allegations, Gardiner and his fellow Councillors might go ahead and draw up articles condemning Katherine.

Gardiner then consulted with Wriothesley, Norfolk, and Riche and they decided to proceed first against the Queen's ladies, beginning with her sister (Lady Herbert), Elizabeth, Lady Tyrwhitt, one of the 'professional' Ladies-in-Waiting who had been at Court since the days of Catharine of Aragon, and the Queen's cousin, Matilda, Lady Lane. After indicting them, they would then proceed against the Duchess of Suffolk, Countess of Hertford, Lady Lisle, and their friends, and then finally against the Queen herself. And the best witness to prove their case was undoubtedly Anne Askew, whose association with the Queen and her ladies was well established, and who was herself now on trial.

In papers which were again smuggled out of prison, Anne relates what then took place:

Then Master Riche sent me to the Tower, where I remained until 3 o'clock, when Riche and one of the Council came, charging me upon my obedience to show them if I knew any man or woman of my sect. Answered that I knew none. Then they asked me of my Lady of Suffolk, my Lady of Sussex, my Lady of Hertford, my Lady Denny and my Lady Fitzwilliam. Answered that if I could pronounce anything against them, I could not prove it. Then they said the King was informed that I could name, if I would, a great number of my sect. Answered that the King was as well deceived in that behalf as dissembled with in other matters. Then they bade me show how I was maintained in the Compter, and who willed me to stick to my opinion. I said that there was no creature that therein did strengthen me, and as for the help that I had in the Compter, it was by means of my maid, who as she went abroad in the street, made moan to the prentices, and they by her did send the money; but who they were I never knew. Then they said that there were divers ladies that had sent me money. I answered that there was a man in a blue coat who delivered me 10s and said that my Lady of Hertford sent it me; and another in a violet coat gave me 8s, and said my Lady Denny sent it me; whether it were true or no, I cannot tell, for I am not sure who sent it me, but as the maid did say. Then they said there were of the Council that did maintain me, and I said no.

There seemed no hope to Wriothesley, who had now joined Riche in the Tower, of getting anything more out of her by this means of interrogation. The few admissions she had so far made were evidence only of the sympathy of the Queen's ladies, not complicity. Wriothesley and Riche thereupon decided to resort to torture, and they ordered the Lieutenant of the Tower to place her on the rack, telling her that she would remain there until she had made a full confession of the names of all the ladies and gentlewomen who shared her views.

Anne did not know how long she was on the rack, only that it was 'a long time', but she lay still and did not cry out or say anything. Wriothesley and Riche then seemed to have lost control of themselves. Accusing the Lieutenant of being too lenient with her, they pushed him aside and, taking off their coats, proceeded to turn the screws themselves with a sadistic violence that almost killed her. The horrified Lieutenant could not stand it, and he insisted that she should be released. Anne continues her account:

> Incontinently, I swooned, and then they recovered me again. After that I sat two long hours reasoning with my Lord Chancellor upon the bare floor; where he with many flattering words persuaded me to leave my opinion. But my Lord God (I thank His everlasting goodness) gave me grace to persevere, and will do, I hope, to the very end. Then was I brought to a house and laid in a bed, with as weary and painful bones as ever had patient Job. I thank my Lord God therefor. Then my Lord Chancellor sent me word, if I would leave my opinion, I should want nothing: if I would not, I should forthwith to Newgate, and so be burned. I sent him again word that I would rather die than break my faith.

Wriothesley and Riche had got little out of her, but with that little and, possibly playing on the fear of those who will not have known what Anne might have said under torture, with other evidence they claimed to have, they drew up a list of charges against Katherine and her ladies.

The work of drawing up the charges was probably completed by 4 July, for on that day the Privy Council ordered the Queen's auditors to produce the account books for her estates, ostensibly to check whether they were up to date, but more probably to sort out who was going to get what as soon as she was attained. According to Foxe, the King was shown the charges and signed them, indicating his approval that they should start proceedings as soon as everything was ready. This is supported by a report from the Emperor's ambassador, written on 6 July, in which he stated that he had heard from a secret source that 'the King continued melancholy'. He had not gone to Mass, nor into his gardens as he usually did in summer.

On 8 July, the proclamation banning heretical books was repeated, presumably to ensure that charges of possessing such books could be sustained in law.

Then, two things happened: first, Henry, either from remorse, or, as Foxe maintains, as part of a deliberate scheme, told his physician, Dr Wendy, what was in store for Katherine; secondly, a copy of the charges against the Queen was dropped by one of the Councillors 'accidentally' in the passage outside the Queen's chambers, where it was found and brought to Katherine.

The events of the previous week, the torture of Anne Askew, the examination of Lassels, Latimer, and Shaxton, the search for heretical books, had already brought Katherine's nerves to breaking point, and when she read the document of the charges against her, she collapsed and took to her bed. Dr Wendy came to attend her, and told her what the King had told him. He added his opinion that the King still loved her very much, and that if she begged his forgiveness and submitted as humbly as possible to his wishes, Henry would save her from her enemies.

Dr Wendy must then have told the King that Katherine had collapsed, for later that day, Henry came to see her. 'She uttered her grief, fearing lest His Majesty had taken displeasure with her, and had utterly forsaken her. He, like a loving husband with sweet and comfortable words, so refreshed and appeased her careful mind that she began to recover' (Foxe).

This was a hopeful sign, but Katherine was by no means out of danger, and she spent the whole of the following day working out the best tactics for regaining the King's confidence in her. In spite of what Dr Wendy had suggested, it would not be enough simply to throw herself on Henry's mercy and hope that he would pardon her. These had been the tactics of both Anne Boleyn and Catherine Howard and had not helped either of them at all. Instead, she must somehow convince the King that she had done nothing wrong, that there was in fact nothing to forgive. And this must be done as soon as possible, before she was arrested, for, as she well knew, as soon as she should be imprisoned in the Tower, she would be powerless to help herself.

That night, probably 13 July, after supper, she acted. Accompanied only by her sister and her cousin, Lady Lane, who carried the candle before her, she visited the King in his bedchamber. She found him with a small company of gentlemen among whom, fortunately, were none of the Gardiner faction. The King interrupted the discussion which was going on and gave her a friendly welcome, inquiring courteously after her health. Then, assuming the air of a student seeking knowledge, he turned the talk to religion and asked Katherine if she could resolve some doubts he had on an obscure point which he had raised.

218

Previously, Katherine would have jumped into such a discussion with lively pleasure, but she had anticipated the situation, and now she modestly declined the offer to take part. She was but a silly, poor woman, she said, so much inferior to the King, that she could not understand why he should now, 'in such diffuse causes of religion', require her judgment. If she did say anything, she continued, yet she must and would still refer her judgment 'in this, and in all other cases, to Your Majesty's wisdom, as my only anchor, supreme head, and governor here on earth, next under God, to lean unto.'

'Not so, by St Mary!' Henry exclaimed. 'You are become a doctor, Kate, to instruct us (as we take it), and not to be instructed or directed by us.'

'If your Majesty take it so,' Katherine replied, 'then hath your Majesty very much mistaken me.' She had always thought, she went on, that it was unseemly and preposterous for a woman to attempt to teach her husband; rather she must be taught by him. 'And whereas I have, with your Majesty's leave, heretofore been bold to hold talk with your Majesty, wherein sometimes in opinions there hath seemed some difference, I have not done it so much to maintain opinion, but rather to minister talk.' She had hoped by these means, she said, to distract and entertain him, to ease his suffering and to take his mind off the pain in his leg. But she had also encouraged the discussions, 'that I, hearing your Majesty's learned discourse, might myself receive profit thereby; wherein, I assure your Majesty, I have not missed any desire in that behalf, always referring myself in all such matters to your Majesty, as by ordinance of nature it is convenient [right] for me to do.'

This was Katherine at her best: humble, flattering, but speaking with such conviction that no one could disbelieve her. Most important of all, it was an explanation, not an excuse. She did not ask forgiveness, for clearly there was nothing to be forgiven. Henry was delighted with her. He could not have made a better reply himself. 'And is it even so, sweetheart?' he cooed with pleasure. 'And tended your arguments to no worse end? Then perfect friends we are now again, as ever at any time heretofore.'

The relief among the company in the King's bedchamber was immense. Henry gathered Katherine into his arms, embracing and kissing her, and telling her that her words had done him more good than if someone had given him £100,000. Never again would he mistake her intentions, he told her, and 'with great signs and tokens of marvellous joy and liking', he kept the party going far into the night before he gave her leave to return to her chambers.

No one told Gardiner, Wriothesley, or any of their faction, what had happened, and the next afternoon the King went into his garden and summoned Katherine and her ladies to come and join him: 'He was as pleasant as ever he was in all his life before,' Foxe relates, 'when suddenly, in the midst of their mirth, in cometh the Lord Chancellor [Wriothesley] with 40 of the King's guards at his heels, on purpose to take the Queen and her ladies.' Henry stopped him and, taking him aside, demanded an explanation. Wriothesley whispered something which the ladies could not hear, and then Henry shouted at him, 'Knave! Arrant knave! Beast! Fool!' and ordered him to 'avaunt out of his presence'.

As soon as he had gone, Henry returned to the Queen, still muttering with anger. Katherine tried to calm him down, saying that she did not know what Wriothesley had done to offend him, but perhaps it was through ignorance rather than ill-will. 'Ah, poor soul,' Henry replied, 'thou little knowest how evil he deserveth this grace at thy hands. O, my word, sweetheart! He hath been towards thee an arrant knave, and so let him go.'

The date of this incident was almost certainly 14 July, for on that day, the French Ambassador reported that the King had quite recovered from his indisposition and was his old self again. It was two days before Anne Askew was due to be burnt as a heretic. Katherine had saved herself and the rest of her ladies; it now remained to be seen what could be done to save Anne.

The situation was difficult, delicate, and complex: difficult, because Henry had been told, and now firmly believed that Anne Askew was the main cause of the religious 'revolt' at Court, and he never looked kindly upon anyone, sacramentary or Papist, who sought to upset his policy of religious uniformity; delicate, because a wrong move at this stage would once more put Katherine and her ladies in jeopardy; complex, because, although there was enormous public sympathy for Anne as a result of her torture in the Tower, and hence no one on the Council, not even Gardiner, wished to proceed with her execution, Anne herself was now determined to be a martyr.

Anne does not give the appearance of a woman with a well-developed political sense, but she may have realised that until someone in whom the People (in the widest meaning of the word) wholly believed made a dramatic stand against the superstition and corruption of the Old Faith, religion would never be reformed. Be that as it may, she had now assumed a state of beatitude, utterly convinced of God's grace, impervious to pain, and looking forward with unfeigned cheerfulness to her death. Praying and smiling, 'with an angel's countenance', she exhorted her fellow prisoners — John Lassels, Nicholas Belenian (a priest), and John Adams (a tailor) — who were condemned to die with her, to remain firm in their faith.

In the face of such determination, Katherine's task was hopeless. Without some gesture from Anne, some wish to compromise with the King's uniformity, however slight, a pardon was impossible. On the day of her execution, 16 July 1546, Anne, unable to stand because of the torture she had suffered on the rack, was carried in a chair to Smithfield, where she was bound, still in her chair, to a stake between the stakes of her fellow prisoners. She listened attentively to the sermon, preached by Shaxton who had recanted, nodding her head when she agreed with him and, when she disagreed, saying, 'He misseth, and speaketh without the Book,' smiling cheerfully at the vast crowd which had gathered to witness the burning. Then, just as the sermon ended, a messenger came from the King, offering her his pardon if she would recant. She turned her eyes away from him, and said that she had not come thither to deny her Lord and Master. Helplessly the Lord Mayor, Sir Martin Bowes, gave the order for the fires to be lit. John Loud, an eyewitness, is quoted by Strype:

And afore God, at the first putting to of fire, there fell a little dew, or a few pleasant drops, upon us that stood by, and a pleasant cracking from heaven, God knows whether I may truly term it a thunder crack, as the people did in the Gospel, or an angel, or rather God's own voice. But to leave every man to his own judgment, methought it seemed rather that the angels in heaven rejoiced to receive their souls into bliss, whose bodies their Popish tormentors had cast into the fire.

In reality, the 'thunder crack' was probably the explosion of a charge of gunpowder which it was customary to conceal among the faggots in order to bring the suffering of the victims to a quick end, but the people who were there, were intensely moved by the event. The sight of a young woman, so obviously holy, so obviously innocent of any real crime, steadfastly praying and smiling while the flames leaped up around her, shocked the London crowd as it had seldom been shocked before. There was no immediate revolt, but the strength and bitterness of the emotions of the people were dangerously similar to those which had been aroused by the execution of Sir Thomas More and the Carthusian monks. But then it had been Anne Boleyn and Cromwell whose blood the people had sought; now it was on Gardiner, Bonner, and their fellow bishops that their hatred was turned.

The failure to rescue Anne Askew filled the Queen and her ladies with remorse, but her death had given them the power and the right political circumstances they had been seeking. They went into action at once. Humanists to the core, their first objective was that there should be an immediate end to all religious persecutions, of Papists as well as sacramentaries. Henry, moved perhaps as much by the angry mood of his subjects as by Katherine's persuasions, agreed and, on the day after Anne's execution, George Blagge and Christopher White, who were waiting their turn in the Tower, were pardoned and released. (In his letter of thanks to the King, Blagge dryly remarked that it was as well he was free, for otherwise 'your pig would have been well roasted'.) In the following few weeks, all others, in various parts of the country, who were awaiting trial or execution under the Act of Six Articles, were released, and for the rest of Henry's reign there were no more executions on the grounds of religion. Anne Askew, indeed, was the last person to be executed under the infamous Act. The Queen and her ladies had ensured that she had not died in vain.

Next, the women sought to establish the New Faith as the principal faith of the kingdom. It needs to be repeated, perhaps, that this faith was not the Lutheran Protestant doctrine or the Calvinist creed of predetermination, but the Humanist and Erasmian doctrine of simplicity, charity and gentleness. Until Cranmer had completed his own cherished project of a Book of Common Prayer, only the Bible (in English) and the translations of Erasmus' paraphrases of the Gospels, for which Princess Mary and also, perhaps, Katherine were partly responsible, were to be used in the churches. On the question of the sacrament of the altar, they agreed with Anne Askew's interpretation: it should not be abolished, but it should be taken as a Holy Communion of worshippers, gathered together in reverent memory of the Last Supper and Christ's Passion, and not as some mystical, pagan rite. Both the bread and the wine should be served to those who wished to receive it, but there should be no more superstitious nonsense about the bread and the wine being the flesh and blood of Christ.

In this objective, the Queen and her ladies were also largely successful. Cranmer, who for years had been in two minds on the subject of the sacrament, now came wholly over to their point of view. He later claimed that it was Ridley who converted him, but as his modern biographer, Professor J. Ridley, has pointed out, he had heard Ridley's arguments many times before this date, and his conversion must have been due to other causes – the most likely of which are the martyrdom of Anne Askew, in which he played no part, and the arguments of the Queen.

But the greatest triumph, for which Katherine must take the credit, was the conversion of Henry himself. His swing away from the middle of the road towards the New Faith became apparent at a banquet which was given for the French Admiral d'Annebault on 24 August. The Admiral had come to England earlier in the month to receive Henry's ratification of the treaty which Lisle and the Admiral had thrashed out in June. Earlier Lisle had gone to Paris to receive Francis' ratification and had been given a royal welcome. Not to be outdone by his old rival, Henry had decided to give the French Admiral an even more magnificent reception. Wriothesley (the chronicler, not the Chancellor) described the event:

> The 24th day of August, he [d'Annebault] was brought to the King's presence, and dined that day at the King's board, and so remained in the Court, with banquetting and hunting, and rich masques every night with the Queen and ladies, with dancing in two new banquetting houses, which were richly hanged, and had rich cupboards of gold plate, and set with rich stones and pearls, which shone richly; and the 28th day, he took his leave of the King and Queen, and so came to London again.

At the first banquet, Henry, supported by Cranmer, rose from his seat and took the Admiral on one side. Leaning heavily on the shoulders of the two men, for he could now barely stand without help, Henry asked the Admiral to suggest to the French King that the Mass should be abolished in both their countries and be replaced by a communion service. Francis should then repudiate the Pope, and then both Henry and Francis would be in a position to force the Emperor to follow suit.

Francis did not accept the proposal, but Cranmer was astonished at the evidence that Henry's offer gave of his decision to establish what Cranmer called 'a sincere religion' in England. That this was in truth Henry's intention was later confirmed in a letter from Hertford to Princess Mary shortly after Henry's death. It was the summit of Katherine's achievement during her reign as Queen.

In their final objective, however, Katherine and her friends could not, and did not, succeed. This was to eliminate the use of religion as a means for obtaining political power. The concept that religion was a private matter, a direct communication, as it were, between the individual and God, and that priests should be teachers rather than intermediaries, was a fine ideal, but it was one that would only be possible among a people whose intelligence and learning were equal to Katherine's own. Much could be done, and was done, to eliminate the elements of superstition and fear of the priest's power from the New Faith, but religion always means power – and often wealth – to those who control and exploit it, and all that was achieved was to transfer that power from one set of hands to another. This other set of hands was that of the Hertford faction, who, initially at least, used that power carefully and to the benefit of the people, but they too, eventually succumbed to intolerance and malice, and it was not until the reign of Elizabeth that a degree of religious peace and tolerance was achieved.

Had Henry survived another few years, it might have been a different story. With his experience and Machiavellian statecraft to guide them, the Queen and her ladies might have been able to retain control long enough to fan the little spark of Humanism into a national ideal which would have swamped the seekers after religious power. As it was, however, the King was now a very sick man. It was obvious to all that he had not long to live, and the Hertford faction concentrated its efforts on ensuring that they would have the government of the country in their hands when the King died.

The account of their success is too well known to need repeating in detail here. As Chapuys wrote in an analysis the day after Henry's death, but before he, Chapuys, knew he was dead, Hertford and Lisle were the only two men of real ability in the country, and there was no one who could withstand them. At the end of November, the Bishop of Winchester (Gardiner) was dismissed from the Council. In the second week of December, the Duke of Norfolk and his son, the Earl of Surrey, were arrested for treason. At the end of December, the King was persuaded to make his will, to which Hertford, Paget, Denny, and Herbert were the principal witnesses, and in which Denny, Herbert, and Hertford's brother, Sir Thomas Seymour, were added to the Council which Henry nominated for Edward's minority. On 19 January 1547 Surrey was executed, and on the evening of 27 January, the King, warned by Denny that his hour had come, sent for Cranmer. By the time Cranmer arrived, an hour or so after midnight, the King had lost the power of speech, but he was able to grasp Cranmer's hand, and for the next hour Cranmer sat by him, praying for him and comforting him. Finally, at about two in the morning, pressing Cranmer's hand to show that he had made his peace with God, Henry died. His death saved the Duke of Norfolk who was due to be executed later that day, but meanwhile Hertford and Paget, pacing the gallery while they waited for their King to die, had completed their arrangements for securing control of the government. When it was at last sure that the King was dead, Hertford galloped off in the darkness to bring the nine-year-old boy, who was now King Edward VI, to London.

The last time that Katherine saw Henry alive would seem to have been 24 December, when Henry sent her and Princess Mary to Greenwich while he went to Westminster to deal with the Duke of Norfolk and his son. Katherine was back at Westminster on 10 January, when she wrote a letter, in Latin, to Prince Edward, praising him for his studies. According to a report from the French Ambassador, however, she was not allowed to see the King, whose illness by then had probably reached the stage at which he would have been loath to let any woman see him.

There is no report of Katherine's reactions when she was told he was dead, but it seems likely that the formal display of sorrow was genuine. She had depended on him for protection and friendship ever since her early childhood, and he had taken good care of her, as well as of her brother and sister. Katherine had given, perhaps, as much as she had received, but her relief at being released from her burdens was coloured by a deep regret at losing a source of strength and comfort the equal of which she was never likely to find again.

NOTES

1 J. E. Neale, *Queen Elizabeth*.
2 Written up by John Loud, a noted reformer who may well have been present.

3 Quoted by Strype from Foxe's MSS.

4 Wriothesley's *Chronicle*: Foxe, Strype, and other early historians omit this first trial of Anne Askew and run the evidence of these examinations together with those which took place a year later in May/June 1546. From the documents in *Letters & Papers*, however, and from Wriothesley's *Chronicle*, which, during this period, is faultlessly accurate concerning the dates and names which it records, there is no doubt at all that this trial took place at this time and quite separately from the other more famous trial of Anne Askew in the following year. The second trial (see p. 213) is also recorded by Wriothesley and documented in *Letters & Papers*.

5 Only the first two named were in fact Privy Councillors.

6 Quoted by Foxe, Pollard and others.

7 Strype, *Ecclesiastical Memorials*.

8 Surrey had relieved Poynings as Governor of Boulogne towards the end of the previous summer.

13　Lady Seymour of Sudeley

From the deaths of her two former husbands, Katherine Parr had inherited enough to make her a very wealthy woman: from the death of her third husband, Henry VIII, she hoped, according to one of her earlier biographers (Leti), to inherit a kingdom. If this is true, she was disappointed. In spite of Henry's obvious fondness for her and his admiration of her political skill, he did not name her as Regent in his will, nor as having any particular function in the Government he had nominated for Edward VI's minority. Either he doubted her ability to control Hertford and Lisle, who would clearly dominate the new Council now that Gardiner and Norfolk had been removed, or he was persuaded by Hertford that such a step was not necessary. On the other hand, he did not forget Katherine:

> And for the great love, obedience, chastity of life, and wisdom being in our forenamed wife and Queen, we bequeath unto her for her proper life, and as it shall please her to order it, three thousand pounds in plate, jewels, and stuff of household goods, and such apparel as it shall please her to take as we have already. And further, we give unto her one thousand pounds in money, and the amount of her dower and jointure according to our grant in Parliament.

The £4,000 worth of plate and money (equal today to about £100,000) was not excessive, but her dower and jointure made her as wealthy as any person could hope to be. Apart from a life interest in the very extensive lands bestowed on her by Parliament, Katherine was the outright owner of the Palace of Chelsea, her favourite residence, and the great manors of Wimbledon and Hanworth. She had a personal train of a hundred and twenty yeomen in her own livery, who, together with the rest of the servants and women in her household, made up a staff of more than two hundred people to take care of her. From the material point of view, therefore, she had no grounds for complaint, but she would have felt a certain emptiness in her new life. As Queen Dowager, she no longer had any direct connection with politics: no favours to bestow, no counsel to give, no schemes to make or break. Of her circle of ladies, the Countess of Hertford and the Lady Lisle were now in the key positions, and neither seemed disposed any longer to seek her help or advice. Nor was there any real need for her intervention, for Hertford, now styled the Duke of Somerset, had taken over the leadership of the Council as Protector, and from the first he showed himself more than willing to carry out the social reforms which had been complementary to the religious reforms which Katherine and her ladies had planned.

There was some consolation for Katherine in the fact that when Hertford had arranged for himself to be created Protector and Duke of Somerset, he had also arranged for Katherine's brother to be raised to the next rank to a Duke, so that Lord William Parr, Earl of Essex, was now the Marquis of Northampton, second in the Council only to the Protector himself. At the same time, John Dudley, Lord Lisle, was created Earl of Warwick, handing over his office of Lord High Admiral to the Protector's brother, Sir Thomas Seymour, who, in turn, was created Baron Seymour of Sudeley in Gloucestershire. The opposition was pacified by giving Wriothesley the Earldom of Southampton, and Riche was made a Baron. It was all neatly and quickly done, and two days after Henry's funeral, the reforming party had the boy King and the government of the country firmly under its control. It was all as Katherine herself would have wished to see, but it left nothing more for her to do.

Then, a month or so after Henry's death, the new Admiral, Thomas Seymour, burst into Katherine's life. He seems, almost literally, to have swept her off her feet, and the once so prudent Queen became an adoring, love-sick woman, with no more control over her emotions than a fourteen-year-old girl. She did not drool or lose her dignity, for it was an adult affair, and she retained some of her former sense of caution, but from now on, she fell wholly under Seymour's spell, ready to do whatever he wished. Disdaining the Council's permission, she accepted Seymour's offer of marriage probably early in March, stating only that there should be a decent period of mourning for the late King before the wedding itself took place. She wrote in reply to a note from Seymour:

My Lord, as I gather by your letter, delivered to my brother [-in-law] Herbert, ye are in some fear how to frame my Lord your brother to speak in your favour. The denial of your request shall make his folly more manifest to the world, which will more grieve me than the want of his speaking. I would not wish you to importune for his good-will, if it come not frankly at the first. It shall be sufficient once to require it, and then to cease. I would desire you might obtain the King's letters in your favour, and also the aid and furtherance of the most notable of the Council, such as ye shall think convenient; which thing obtained shall be no small shame to your brother and loving sister [-in-law], in case they do not the like.

My Lord, whereas ye charge me with a promise, written with mine own hand, to change the two years into two months, I think ye have no such plain sentence written with my hand. I know not whether ye be a paraphraser or not. If ye be learned in that science, it is possible ye may of one word make a whole sentence, and yet not at all times alter the true meaning of the writer; as it appeareth by this your exposition upon my writing.

When it shall be your pleasure to repair hither, ye must take some pain to come early in the morning, that ye may be gone again by seven o'clock; and so I suppose ye may come without suspect. I pray you let me have knowledge overnight at what hour ye will come, that your portress may wait at the gate to the fields for you.

And thus, with my most humble and hearty commendations, I take my leave of you for this time, giving you like thanks for your coming to Court when I was there.

from Chelsea.

P.S. I will keep in store till I speak with you my Lord's large offer of Fausterne,[1] at which time I shall be glad to know your further pleasure therein.

By her that is, and shall be, your humble, true and loving wife during her life,
Katherine the Queen, K.P.

Committing herself on paper in this way was most unlike Katherine, but there was more to come. A little while later, she felt the need to explain herself to her lover. She wrote:

My Lord, I send you my most humble and hearty commendations, being desirous to know how ye have done since I saw you. I pray you be not offended with me in that I send sooner to you than I said I would, for my promise was but once in a fortnight. Howbeit, the time is well abbreviated, by what means I know not, except weeks be shorter in Chelsea than in other places.

My Lord your brother hath deferred answering such requests as I made to him till his coming hither, which he saith shall be immediately after the term. This is not the first promise I have received of his coming, and yet unperformed. I think my Lady hath taught him that lesson; for it is her custom to promise many comings to her friends, and to perform none. I trust in greater matters she is more circumspect.

229

And thus, my Lord, I make my end, bidding you most heartily farewell, wishing you the good I would myself.

from Chelsea.

P.S. I would not have you think that this mine honest goodwill toward you to proceed of any sudden motion of passion; for, as truly as God is God, my mind was fully bent, the other time I was at liberty, to marry you before any man I know. Howbeit God withstood my will therein most vehemently for a time, and through His grace and goodness made that possible which seemed to me most impossible; that was, made me renounce utterly mine own will, and to follow His will most willingly. It were long to write all the process of this matter. If I live, I shall declare it to you myself. I can say nothing but as my Lady of Suffolk saith, 'God is a marvellous man.'

By her that is yours to serve and obey during her life,

Katherine the Queen, K.P.

It seems unlikely that Seymour would have appreciated Katherine's brand of irony, but he more than made up for it with a combination of compelling charm and boisterous self-confidence which seemed to have blinded Katherine to his serious defects of character. He had an over-riding passion for power and wealth, but with no other objective than his own self-aggrandisement. At the same time, his judgment of situations, of the continually shifting pattern of the power-game, was appallingly bad: he saw complex plots in simple actions, and dismissed as unimportant moves which were designed to bring him down. As a result, he was devious when he should have been straightforward, direct when he should have been circumspect. Worst of all he was consumed with jealousy for his brother, and, although he later strongly denied the allegation, there is little doubt that his prime motive in seeking Katherine as a bride was to supplant his brother as Protector. The historian, Heylyn, contrasted the characters of the two brothers as follows:

The Duke [was] mild, affable, free, and open; more easy to be wrought on, but in no way malicious, and honoured by the common people, as the Admiral was more generally esteemed among the nobles. The Protector was more to be desired for a friend, and the other more to be feared as an enemy. The defects of each being taken away, their virtues united would have made one excellent man.[2]

As it was, Thomas Seymour's continual undermining of the power of his brother brought about not only his own downfall, but eventually the ruin of his brother as well.

But for the moment, Katherine and the Admiral were mainly concerned with winning approval for their marriage, and they sought to enlist the help of the boy King. To this end, Seymour bribed one John Fowler, who was Edward's personal attendant, to intercede for him. Giving evidence at Seymour's trial nearly two years later, John Fowler deposed that, after inquiring after Edward's health, Seymour had asked him if the young King did not sometimes ask about him. Fowler continued:

Then I demanded of him, 'What question should his Majesty ask of you?' 'Nay, nothing (said he), only sometimes his Highness would ask why I married not.' 'I never heard him ask any such questions,' quoth I. Then my Lord paused awhile, and after said to me, 'Mr Fowler, I pray you, if you have any communication with the King's Majesty soon, or tomorrow, ask his Highness whether he would be content I should marry or not; and if he says he will be content, I pray you ask his Grace whom he would have to be my wife?' I said I would; and that night, his Highness being alone, I said to his Majesty, 'And please your Grace, I marvel my Lord Admiral marrieth not.' His Highness saying nothing to it, I said again, 'Could your Grace be contented he should marry?' His Grace said, 'Yea, very well.' Then I asked his Majesty whom his Grace would that he should marry? His Highness said, 'My Lady Anne of Cleves,' and so pausing awhile, said after, 'Nay, nay, wot you what? I would he married my sister Mary, to turn her opinions.' His Highness went his ways, and said no more at that time.

These were not at all the answers that Seymour sought, and when he heard Fowler's story on the following day, he told Fowler to ask Edward outright if he would have any objections if he and Katherine were to marry. He added that if Edward approved, would he ask the King to be a suitor for him in his cause. Katherine had also written to Edward and, though the letters have not been found, it is clear from the young King's replies that he was still as fond of her as ever. In the first of her letters, dated 30 May 1547, he acknowledged some general expressions of goodwill and love on Katherine's part, and exhorted her: 'Cease not to love and read the Scriptures, but persevere in always reading them; for in the first you shew the duty of a good wife [widow] and a good subject, and in the second, the warmth of your friendship, and in the third your piety to God.'

This was followed by further letters from Katherine (which, again, unfortunately have not survived) and further conversations conducted through Fowler until eventually Edward was brought to understand what was required of him. His reply, written on 25 June, was all that Katherine and the Admiral could have desired, so much so, in fact, that there is a strong suspicion that Seymour might well have dictated, or at least indicated, the wording:

> To the Queen's Grace:
> We thank you heartily, not only for the gentle acceptation of our suit unto you, but also for the loving accomplishing of the same, wherein you have declared, not only a desire to gratify us, but to declare the goodwill, likewise, that we bear to you in all your requests. Wherefore ye shall not need to fear any grief to come or to suspect lack of aid in need, seeing that he, being my uncle, is of so good a nature that he will not be troublesome any means unto you, and I of such mind, that for divers just causes I must favour you. But even as without cause you merely require help against him whom you have put in trust with the carriage of these letters, so may I merely return the same request unto you, to provide that he may live with you also without grief, which hath given him wholly unto you; and I will so provide for you both, that if hereafter any grief befall, I shall be a sufficient succour in your Godly or praiseable enterprises.
> Fare ye well, with much increase of honour and virtue in Christ.
> From St James, the five-and-twenty day of June,
>
> Edward[3]

However, this letter, an incredible effort for a nine-year-old boy, was written at least a month after the event it recommends, for, as appears from another letter written by the Admiral to Katherine on 17 May, they were by then already married. As quoted by Agnes Strickland, he wrote:

> Yesternight, I supped at my brother [-in-law] Herbert's, of whom, for your sake besides mine own, I received good cheer; and after the same, I received from your Highness, by my sister Herbert, your commendations, which were more welcome than they were sent. And after the same, she waded further with me touching my lodging with your Highness at Chelsea, which I denied, but that indeed I went by the garden as I went to the Bishop of London's house, and at this point stood with her a long time, till at last she told me by further tokens, which made me change colour, who, like a false wench, took me with the manner; then remembering what she was, and knowing how well ye trusted her, examined whether those things came from your Highness or were feigned. She answered 'that they came from your Highness, and he [Lord Herbert] knew it to be true,' for the which I render unto your Highness my most humble and hearty thanks, for by her company, in default of yours, I shall shorten the weeks in these parts, which heretofore were four days longer in every one of them than they were under the plummet at Chelsea.

The rest of the letter goes on to assure Katherine of the caution with which he, Seymour, was proceeding with the Council, and concludes with further declarations of his affection for her. The subscription reads:

> From him whom ye have bound to honour, love, and in all lawful things obey,
>
> T. Seymour, &c.

When the marriage eventually became public, probably about July, the Protector showed his anger at his brother's presumption, but nevertheless gave his reluctant consent. The Protector's wife, the Duchess of Somerset, however, seized her opportunity. Claiming that Katherine had forfeited her rights as Queen Dowager by a marriage so far beneath her station, she demanded that she should now have precedence over Katherine. The friendship between the two women had never been particularly strong, and open hostility now broke out between them. The Duchess refused to bear Katherine's train at Court, and even tried to push her, physically, out of her place at the head of their entrances and exits at Court. Heylyn writes that the Duchess was reported to have said:

> Did not Henry VIII marry Katherine Parr in his doting days, when he had brought himself so low by his lust and cruelty that no lady that stood on her honour would venture on him? And shall I now give place to her, who, in her former estate, was but Latimer's widow, and is now fain to cast herself for support on a younger brother? If Master Admiral teach his wife no better manners, I am she that will.

Katherine won the battle by invoking the Act of Succession which clearly stated that she had precedence over all ladies in the realm, that after her came the Princesses Mary and Elizabeth, after them, Anne of Cleves, and only then came the Duchess of Somerset. But the quarrel was the end of Katherine's circle of ladies, and thereafter each went her own way. The Duchess of Suffolk remained her close friend, Lady Tyrwhitt continued in her service, nor did her sister desert her, but they were no longer a political force. Individual women were to continue to obtain high office and great power, but it was to be several centuries before women once more combined together to present a united front to obtain their objectives.

In the months that followed, Katherine became more and more embroiled in the intrigues of her husband. His main efforts were directed at getting control of the King and at building up his strength at sea and in the West Country, where he had a certain amount of local influence, but at the same time he lost no opportunity to stir up trouble for his brother. The Protector's high-handed action in letting Katherine's property to a friend, a Mr Long, was blown up into a major incident, and Katherine found herself involved in a bitter dispute, which, in earlier days, she would have circumvented by more diplomatic means. She wrote to her husband to tell him what had happened:

My Lord,

This shall be to advertise you that my Lord your brother hath this afternoon made me a little warm. It was fortunate we were so much distant; for I suppose else I should have bitten him. What cause have they to fear having such a wife? Tomorrow, or else upon Saturday, at three o'clock in the afternoon, I will see the King, when I intend to utter all my choler to my Lord your brother, if you shall not give me advice to the contrary; for I would be loth to do anything to hinder your matter. I will declare to you how my Lord hath used me concerning Fausterne; and after I shall most humbly desire you to direct mine answer to him in that behalf. It liked him today to send my chancellor to me, willing him to declare to me that he had brought Mr Long's lease, and that he doubted not but I would let him enjoy the same to his commodity, wherein I should do to his succession no small pleasure, nothing considering his honour, which this matter toucheth not a little, for so much as I at sundry times declared unto him that only cause of my repair into those parts was for the commodity of the park, which else I would not have done. He, notwithstanding, hath so used the matter, with giving Mr Long such courage, that he refuseth to receive such cattle as are brought here for the provision of my house; and so in the meantime I am forced to commit them to farmers. My Lord, I beseech you send me word with speed how I shall order myself with my new brother.

And thus I take my leave with my most humble and hearty commendations, wishing you all your Godly desires, and so well to do as I would myself, and better.

from Chelsea, in great haste.

By your humble, true, and loving wife in her heart,
Katherine the Queen, K.P.

Then came the matter of certain jewels which Henry had let Katherine have on certain state occasions. Seymour claimed that these had been given, not lent, to Katherine, and that they should now be restored to her. He went to great lengths to get legal opinions to support his case, and once more tried to invoke the young King's aid, but this time without success.

The person most disturbed by Katherine's marriage was Princess Mary. She had looked on Katherine not only as a much-loved friend, but also as an ideal of virtue, learning, and prudence, which, religion apart, was an example for all women to follow. Even on religious questions, the basic Humanism of their common education was a powerful bond, and Mary had been more than willing to co-operate with Katherine in the promulgation of the works of Erasmus, contenting herself with the fact that Erasmus was, after all, still a member of the Roman Catholic Church. But now she was profoundly shocked by Katherine's behaviour. Katherine's marriage so soon after Henry's death, her descent into sordid squabbles with the Duchess of Somerset, her willingness to be degraded by Thomas Seymour into little more than a conniving wife of an adventurer, shattered the picture she had built up of Katherine, and she felt once more alone and friendless in a hostile world. She made some attempt to persuade Princess Elizabeth to join her in breaking their relationship with Katherine, but Elizabeth, while agreeing that Katherine's behaviour might not have been all that it should have been, advised caution. There was nothing that either of them could do to change the situation, and for herself, Elizabeth wrote, 'the Queen having shown me so great affection, and done me so many kind offices, I must use much tact in manoeuvring with her, for fear of appearing ungrateful for her benefits'.

Mary accepted her half-sister's advice, and there was no open breach with Katherine, but neither was there any resumption of the close friendship of former years. She turned more and more towards the Roman Catholic Church and the sympathy of her Spanish cousins, and before long the bitterness, which Katherine had tried so hard to eradicate, returned – with consequences which were to make her reign the most abhorred of the Tudor age.

Elizabeth's attitude was very different. Her mention of the need to use tact with Katherine was no more than a sop to Mary's feelings, and Katherine was still as much her heroine as ever before. She had been overjoyed when, shortly after Henry's death, Katherine had invited her to join her household at Chelsea. She was then thirteen years old, and she was a lively witness to Thomas Seymour's courtship of Katherine. She thoroughly approved of the match; it was no more than Katherine deserved after all those years of servitude to elderly men, and for all his defects, the Admiral was as gay, bold, and as handsome as any woman could wish her lover to be. When he chose, the Admiral was capable of a great open-hearted friendship, and he transformed Katherine's demure household into a rollicking setting for high spirits and good cheer.

Elizabeth was delighted by the change. She found that although Katherine remained her usual serene self, she was more relaxed and much more willing to talk about world affairs. Elizabeth was now Katherine's only pupil, and the whole of Katherine's exceptional talent for teaching was lavished upon her. The young Princess lapped it up. Her main tutor throughout 1547 was William Grindall. He died of the plague in January 1548, and Roger Ascham then took over. But from Grindall and Ascham, Elizabeth could only learn the Humanities; from Katherine, she could learn what mattered most to her, the art of politics. There is also little doubt that Katherine stimulated her latent sense of destiny and encouraged her to see herself not as a neglected Tudor orphan, but as a young woman who, one day, might well control the fate of a nation. And Katherine sought to ensure that, when that day came, Elizabeth would use her power in the highest ideals of the generations of Humanist women who had paved the way for her.

But the seventeen months that Elizabeth spent with Katherine were not all taken up with lessons and eager discussions. The Admiral interrupted them constantly with his demands for amusement and his boisterous, good-humoured teasing. Mistress Ashley, Elizabeth's governess, later gave a graphic description of their frolics:

> At Chelsea, after my Lord Thomas Seymour was married to the Queen, he would come many mornings into the said Lady Elizabeth's chamber before she were ready, and sometimes before she did rise, and if she were up, he would bid her good morrow, and ask how she did, and strike her on the back or buttocks familiarly, and so go forth to his chamber, and sometimes go through to her maidens and play with them. And if the Princess were in bed, he would put open the curtains and bid her good morrow, and she would go further into the bed. And one morning he tried to kiss the Princess in her bed, and this deponent was there, and bade him go away for shame.

The frolics seemed innocent enough, but Elizabeth was no longer a child and, to stop the gossip, Katherine decided to accompany her husband on his visits. She also decided that it would be best to move further into the country to one of her other manors at Hanworth in Middlesex. Mistress Ashley continued to appear to be shocked:

> At Hanworth, for two mornings, the Queen was with him, and they both tickled my Lady Elizabeth in bed. Another time at Hanworth, he romped with her in the garden, and cut her gown, being black cloth, into a hundred pieces, and when this deponent came up and chid Lady Elizabeth, she answered that she could not strive withal, for the Queen held her while the Lord Admiral cut the dress.

The Admiral was told that his conduct was slandering the good name of the Princess. 'God's precious soul!' he swore, 'I will tell my Lord Protector how I am slandered; and I will not leave off, for I mean no evil.'

But the situation began to get out of hand. Elizabeth's adolescent urges were roused, and Seymour was not the sort of man to resist temptation. Elizabeth later told her cofferer, Parry, 'that she feared the Admiral loved her but too well, and that the Queen was jealous of them both; and that, suspecting the frequent access of the Admiral to her, she came suddenly upon them when they were alone, he having her in his arms.'

The incident was too much for Katherine, and the week after Whitsun in 1548, she sent Elizabeth back to her own establishment at Cheshunt. Then, to the delight of all Katherine's friends, it became certain that Katherine was pregnant. After all the barren years with her three previous husbands, she had not believed the first early symptoms, but now she could feel the quickening child stirring within her. The event restored her former good humour, and within a month she was writing to Elizabeth again as amicably as if nothing had ever happened to disturb their friendship. She wished, she wrote, that Elizabeth could be with her now at Sudeley Castle in Gloucestershire, which Seymour had finally rebuilt to his satisfaction, and to which he had at last brought Katherine as her future home with him. Elizabeth acknowledged her news with pleasure, and she, too, replied as though nothing had come between them (quoted by Agnes Strickland):

> I much rejoice at your health, with the well liking of the country, with my humble thanks that your Grace wished me with you till I were weary of that country. Your Highness were like to be cumbered if I should not depart till I were

237

weary of being with you; although it were the worst soil in the world, your presence would make it pleasant.

If she were to be present at the child's birth, she would, she wrote, see him beaten, for the trouble he had put her to. (Katherine had complained of not being well.) Elizabeth also had news of some old friends:

Master Denny and my Lady, with humble thanks, prayeth most entirely for your Grace, praying the Almighty God to send you a most lucky deliverance.

After further commendations, she concluded:

Written with very little leisure, this last day of July,

Your humble daughter,
Elizabeth

Meanwhile, Seymour continued with his schemes against his brother. Through John Fowler, he kept in touch with Edward vi, sending him pocket money, and doing all he could to win the boy King's affection. At the same time, prompted perhaps by Katherine, he embarked on a project to obtain the wardship of Lady Jane Grey, then eleven years old and the daughter of one of Katherine's childhood companions, the French Queen's daughter, Lady Frances Brandon, now the wife of the Marquis of Dorset. The Lady Jane was Edward's cousin, but Seymour considered that she would make a most suitable bride for the young King when both should come of age, and he persuaded the Marquis of Dorset that he, Seymour, would be able to make the match. It would, of course, also enable Seymour to strengthen his hold on the Crown, but that was not the concern of the Marquis. The bargain was struck, and Seymour obtained the young girl's wardship for £500. Lady Jane was then brought to Sudeley and joined Katherine's household.

In spite of the intrigue surrounding the arrangement, the following months were to be the happiest in the unfortunate Lady Jane Grey's short life. In Katherine, she found a woman who encouraged and shared her love of learning and religion, while, from Katherine's point of view, the prematurely learned girl, though not to be compared with Elizabeth, proved a pleasant and interesting companion. Together, they passed the last few cumbersome and tiring months of Katherine's pregnancy in friendly discussions and the quiet content of reading the classical and Humanist books both loved so much.

The baby was born on 30 August 1548, at Sudeley Castle. Somewhat to Seymour's disappointment it was a girl, but it proved that Katherine, contrary to expectations, could conceive and successfully bear children. She was then only in her thirty-sixth year, and Seymour confidently hoped that his daughter would be followed by sons in due course. The birth also gave Seymour's brother an opportunity to make a conciliatory gesture. The Protector wrote (as quoted by Agnes Strickland):

> After our hearty commendations, we are right glad to understand, by your letters, that the Queen, your bedfellow, hath a happy hour; and, escaping all danger, hath made you the father of so pretty a daughter. And although (if it had pleased God) it would have been to both of us [his wife and himself] and we suppose also to you, a more joy and comfort if it had, this the first-born, been a son, yet the escape of the danger, and the prophesy and good hansell [omen] of this, to a great sort of happy sons, which (as you write) we trust no less than to be true, is no small joy and comfort to us, as we are sure it is to you and to her Grace also, to whom you shall make again our hearty commendations with no less gratulation of such good success.
>
> Thus we bid you heartily farewell from Sion, the 1st of Sept., 1548.
>
> Your loving brother,
>
> E. Somerset

Katherine, however, had not 'escaped danger'. Puerperal fever set in, and within a few days, she became delirious. Elizabeth Tyrwhitt, who was with her, later made a statement in which she described the bedside scenes (again quoted by Agnes Strickland):

> Two days before the death of the Queen, at my coming to her in the morning, she asked me where I had been so long, and said unto me that she did fear such things in herself that she was sure she could not live. I answered, as I thought, that I saw no likelihood of death in her. She then, having my Lord Admiral by the hand, and divers others standing by, spake these words, partly, as I took, idly [in delirium]: 'My Lady Tyrwhitt, I am not well handled, for those that be about me care not for me, but stand laughing at my grief, and the more good I will them, the less good they will to me.' Whereunto my Lord Admiral answered, 'Why, sweetheart, I would you no hurt.' And she said to him again, aloud, 'No, my Lord, I think so'; and immediately she said to him in his ear, 'but my Lord you have given me many shrewd taunts.' These words I perceived she spake with good memory, and very sharply and earnestly; for her mind was sore disquieted. My Lord Admiral, perceiving that I heard it, called me aside, and asked what she said, and I declared it plainly to him. Then he consulted with me that he would lie down on the bed with her, to look if he could pacify her unquietness with gentle communication, whereunto I agreed; and by the time that he had spoken

239

three or four words to her she answered him roundly and sharply, saying, 'My Lord, I would have given a thousand marks to have had my full talk with Huick [her doctor] the first day I was delivered, but I durst not for displeasing you.' And I, hearing that, perceived her trouble to be so great that my heart would serve me to hear no more. Such like communications she had with him the space of an hour, which they did hear that sat by her bedside.

The fever worsened. There was now no hope of recovery and, between two and three o'clock in the morning of 5 September 1548, Katherine Parr died. Shortly before she died, she regained her senses and dictated her will to Dr Huick and her chaplain, John Parkhurst, who were keeping watch over her. The will was short and to the point. The document (quoted by Strickland) deposes: 'That she, then lying on her death-bed, sick of body, but of good mind and perfect memory and discretion, being persuaded, and perceiving the extremity of death to approach her, gives all to her married spouse and husband, wishing them to be a thousand times more in value than they were or been.'

There were no minor legacies, and the will was not signed, but the death-bed declaration, attested by doctor and chaplain, was considered good in law, and the will was accepted and proved on 6 December 1548.

Save for the fact that Katherine's body was embalmed and encased in a lead coffin to preserve it from destruction, her funeral was conducted according to the simple doctrine of the New Faith. Lady Jane Grey was the chief mourner, and Miles Coverdale, whom Katherine had brought back from his exile in Germany, and to whom she had given the post of being her almoner, preached the funeral sermon. In it, he declared to the congregation 'how that they should none there think, say, or spread abroad, that the offering [of alms] which was there done was done anything to benefit the dead, but for the poor only; and also the lights [candles], which were carried and stood about the corpse, were for the honour of the person, and for none other intent or purpose.'

Katherine's own view of death was summed up in a letter she wrote to Lady Wriothesley on the death of her only son. After expressing her sympathy, Katherine continued (as quoted by Strype):

Therefore amongst other discrete and Godly consolations given unto you, as well by my Lord your husband, as other your wise friends, I have thought with mine own hand to recommend unto you my simple counsel and advice: desiring you

240

not so to utter your natural affection by inordinate sorrow that God have cause to take you as a murmurer against his appointments and ordinances. For what is excessive sorrow but a plain evidence against you that your inward mind doth repine against God's doings, and a declaration that you are not contented that God hath put your son by nature, but His by adoption, in possession of the heavenly kingdom? Such as have doubted of the everlasting life to come, doth sorrow and bewail the departure hence: but those which be persuaded that to die here is life again, do rather hunger for death and count it a felicity than to bewail it as an utter destruction.

For a time there was some talk that Thomas Seymour had hastened Katherine's death, a charge which was later made against him at his trial, but it is clear from the confusion into which his affairs were then thrown that he had neither anticipated nor expected it. 'I was so amazed [stunned],' he wrote to the Marquis of Dorset a month later, 'that I had small regard either to myself or my doings, and partly then thinking that my great loss must presently have constrained me to have dissolved my whole house, I offered to send my Lady Jane unto you whensoever ye would send for her.' But he had now recovered himself. His aged mother was coming from Wolf Hall to take care of his household, and he begged the Marquis to allow the Lady Jane to remain at Sudeley.

It was probably also at this time that Thomas Seymour decided to speed up his plans for taking over the government of the young King. He brushed aside his brother's offers of peace, and for the next two months he rushed from place to place in the West Country, organising the ships under his command (which for long had been engaged, with his encouragement, in open piracy), and striving to win support from the local gentry. By January, the Council felt they could ignore him no longer, and on 17 January 1549, he was arrested and sent to the Tower. At first, he refused to answer the charges which were made against him, saying that he was the King's uncle and that he had every right to do what he had done. He was left in the Tower for a month to reconsider his attitude, but he again refused to answer the charges. The Council then took the extraordinary step of appealing to the young King who was now only eleven years old.

Edward listened attentively to the charges, and then, without being prompted, gave his decision. 'We do perceive,' he announced, 'that there is great things which be objected and laid to my Lord Admiral mine uncle; and they tend to treason: and we perceive that you require but

241

justice to be done. We think it reasonable, and we will well that you proceed according to your request.'

'With these words,' the report in the Council register ends, 'coming so suddenly from his Grace's mouth of his own motion, as the Lords might well perceive, the said Lords and the rest of the Council were marvellously rejoiced, and gave his Highness most hearty praise and thanks.'

The Act of Attainder was finally passed in Parliament on 5 March, and on the 10th, Edward had no hesitation in agreeing with the verdict. The Protector signed the death warrant, and Sir Thomas Seymour was duly executed on Tower Hill on 20 March, having an hour or so before his death written notes to both Princess Mary and Princess Elizabeth, urging them to take steps to overthrow the government. He died, said Hugh Latimer, 'very dangerously, irksomely, horribly'.

Katherine's daughter, who had been christened Mary, was taken in for a time by the Duchess of Somerset, but she soon tired of her charge, and the Duchess of Suffolk then took the baby with her to Grimsthorpe on the understanding that the Protector would defray the costs. Several months went past, however, without the Duchess of Suffolk receiving either the silver plate, furniture, and clothes, which belonged to Katherine's daughter, or the money for her upkeep. The costs were considerable, since, as the Queen Dowager's daughter, the Lady Mary was expected to have a retinue of nurses and servants appropriate to her rank, which was almost that of a royal child. After several attempts to persuade the Duchess of Somerset to honour her promises, the Duchess of Suffolk wrote to William Cecil, who was then employed as an administrator on the Protector's staff (as quoted by Strype):

It is said that the best means of remedy to the sick is first plainly to confess and disclose the disease wherefore lieth for remedy; and again, for that my disease is so strong that it will not be hidden, I will disclose me unto you. First, I will (as it were under *benedicite* and in high secrecy) declare unto you that all the world knoweth, though I go never so covertly in my net, what a very beggar I am. This sickness, as I have said, I promise you, increaseth mightily upon me. Amongst other causes whereof is, you will understand not the least, the Queen's child hath lain, and yet doth lie at my house, with her company about her, wholly at my charges. I have written to my Lady Somerset at large; which was the letter I wrote (note this) with mine own hand unto you; and among other things for the child, that there may be some pension allotted unto her according to my Lord Grace's promise.

242

Now, good Cecil, help at a pinch all that you may help. My Lady also sent me word at Whitsuntide last by Bartue [Richard Bertie, the Duchess of Suffolk's steward, whom she later married], that my Lord's Grace, at her suit, had granted certain nursery plate and stuff as was there in the nursery. I send you here enclosed [a list] of all parcels as were appointed out for the child's use; and that ye may the better understand that I cry not before I am pricked, I send you Mistress Eglonby's letter unto me, who, with the maids, nurses, and others, daily call on me for their wages, whose voices mine ears may hardly bear, but my coffers much worse. Wherefore I cease, and commit me and my sickness to your diligent care, with my hearty commendations to your wife.

at my manor of Grimsthorpe, the 27th August.

Your assured loving friend,
K. Suffolk

The Duchess of Suffolk's troubles came to an end a few months later when Parliament restored Katherine's daughter to her father's lands and property. Since nothing more was ever noted in the records concerning the Lady Mary Seymour, the historian Strype concludes that she must have died in childhood. Miss Strickland, however, believes that she lived to become a wife and mother, marrying a Sir Edward Bushel, by whom she had a daughter through whom her fortune and pedigree eventually descended to the Lawson family who originally came from Westmorland and Cumberland. But the evidence for this rests on family legend, and the absence of documentary proof makes it impossible to establish the truth or otherwise of the claim.

Of the rest of Katherine's family, her sister's husband, William Herbert, was created Earl of Pembroke, and Wilton Abbey in Wiltshire has remained in the Herbert family down to the present day. Katherine's brother, Lord Parr, Marquis of Northampton, led a chequered political career, forfeiting his lands under Queen Mary, only to have them partially restored again by Queen Elizabeth. The Marquis married twice more after his divorce from Anne Bourchier, but he left no descendants. He died in October 1571, a comparatively poor man, and Queen Elizabeth paid for his funeral.

Katherine's uncle, Lord Parr of Horton, had died in 1547, also without heirs, so with the death of the Marquis, the Parr line came to an end. It had taken six generations to build up to the pinnacle which Katherine Parr reached, and few families can boast of so fine a result of their struggles. It is, I believe, no exaggeration to say that without Katherine Parr, Queen Elizabeth would not have been the woman she was, nor her reign the epic it became. It was to Katherine that Elizabeth owed her rescue from oblivion and her right to succeed to the Throne of England. Above all, it was from Katherine that Elizabeth acquired the learning and political skill which enabled her to dominate the power-game and to lead a high-spirited, almost ungovernable nation to fame and fortune.

NOTES

1 One of Katherine's properties which Somerset wished her to rent to a friend.
2 Quoted by Nichols in *Literary Remains of Edward VI*.
3 Nichols in *Literary Remains of Edward VI*, and others.

Epilogue

Nearly two hundred and fifty years after Katherine Parr's death, in the summer of 1782, a Mr John Lucas discovered the coffin of Katherine Parr amid the ruins of the chapel at Sudeley Castle. With morbid curiosity, he ripped open the top of the coffin and found her body wrapped in six or seven seer cloths. The body was entire and uncorrupted, and, cutting through the seer cloths, he found the flesh of one of her arms to be still white and moist. He took a few locks of hair, which was auburn in colour, and returned the coffin to its grave.

The event was reported locally, and during the next ten years the coffin was unearthed and opened on three separate occasions, on the last of which, in 1792, it was roughly buried, upside down, by a party of drunken men. In response to public demand, a search for it was again made in 1817. It was eventually found, but by then nothing but her skeleton remained. The roots of the ivy which covered the ruined walls of the chapel had penetrated the coffin and filled the greater part of it. The coffin was reconstructed from the badly damaged original lead casing, and was found to measure 5ft 10in in length, indicating that Katherine Parr was a much taller woman than had been generally supposed. The reconstructed coffin was then placed between two stone slabs in the vault alongside the tomb of Lord Chandos, whose family then owned Sudeley Castle.

The castle was subsequently used as a public house, but in 1837, John and William Dent bought it in order to save it from ruin. Among other renovations, they employed Sir John Gilbert Scott, a famous architect of his day, to direct the rebuilding of the chapel. A new and magnificent altar-tomb was erected for Katherine Parr's last resting place, and her effigy, 'rendered as correctly as it could be from the portraits which are extant', now rests upon the altar which contains her coffin. Before the coffin was walled up in the tomb, it was thoroughly cleaned, and in the process, the original inscription came to light. As Sir Frederick Garnett, CB, wrote in *Queen Katherine Parr and Sudeley Castle* (1893), it reads:

KP
Here lyethe Quene
Kateryn wife to Kyng
Henry the VIII And
last the wife of Thomas
Lord of Sudeley high
Admirall of England
And onkle to Kyng
Edward the VI
dyed
f September
MCCCCC
XLVIII

Katherine would have smiled at this honour done in her name, for she strongly believed that money spent on tombs and funerals would be far better spent on the relief of the poor. Nevertheless, it was a fitting monument to this Queen of England whose own cautious policy of modest self-effacement has largely contributed to the ignorance of later generations of how much she did for the peace and welfare of the English people.

INDEX

247

249

251

Throgmorton, Sir George, 23n, 109–10, 111, 123, 124–5, 126
Tunstall family, 24
Tunstall, Cuthbert, 27, 29–30, 43, 49, 64, 66, 123, 124, 125, 129, 133, 135, 146, 151, 160, 164, 165–6, 203
Tyrwhitt, Lady Elizabeth, 215, 233, 239
Tyrwhitt, Sir Robert, 87, 170

Udall, Nicholas, 192
Ughtred, Elizabeth, 105, 128n

Vaughan, Stephen, 174, 210
Vaux of Harrowden, Lord Nicholas, 26
Vere, Dorothy de, 66
Vives, Juan Luys, 31–6, 48, 50, 52–3, 55, 151, 153, 166, 192

Wallop, Sir John, 169, 170, 171
Warham, Archbishop of Canterbury, 63

Warwick, Earl of see Lisle, John Dudley, Lord
Watkins, Richard, 158, 159
Wendy, Dr, 217, 218
Westmorland, Countess of, 102
Westmorland, Earl of, 80, 89, 95
Wharton, Sir Thomas, 100, 148–9, 185
White, Christopher, 222
Willoughby, Katherine see Suffolk, Katherine, Duchess of
Willoughby, Lady Mary, 15, 16, 17, 28, 30, 51, 53, 71, 79
Willoughby, Lord William, 16
Wolsey, Cardinal, 18, 22, 31, 56, 60, 61, 62, 126, 128, 131, 174
Worcester, Countess of, 75
Wotton, Nicholas, 121
Wriothesley (chronicler), 81, 223, 225–6n
Wriothesley, Lady, 240
Wriothesley, Sir Thomas, 124, 156, 160, 167, 174, 177, 178, 185, 210, 212, 214, 215, 216–17, 219–20, 228
Wyatt, Sir Thomas, 106, 116, 146, 205

HENRY VIII AND HIS COURT

NEVILLE WILLIAMS

A magnificent evocation of the English court in the early sixteenth century, dominated by its colossus, Henry Tudor. Neville Williams sets the scene by describing the royal palaces, the organisation of the King's Household and the daily ritual of court life. Against this background, he introduces the six queens of Henry VIII, the succession of royal ministers, from the overnightly prelate Cardinal Thomas Wolsey, to the scheming temporal lord, Edward Seymour, Duke of Somerset, and the circle of princes of blood and courtiers who surrounded the King. Yet, above all, Henry remains the central character – his personality and his style of kingship producing a court of unsurpassed brilliance.

The text is enriched by the many illustrations which vividly recreate Henry's daily life, and that of his family, friends and courtiers.

£1·95 Illustrated

THE TOWER OF LONDON
In the History of the Nation

A. L. ROWSE

The Tower of London is a unique historic institution: royal palace, fortress for the City and state prison, and originally the nation's record office and zoo. In these capacities it offers a mirror through which English history may be seen – in the White Tower Richard II abdicated his throne to his cousin Henry Bolingbroke; the Garden Tower, now called the Bloody Tower, was probably the scene of the murder of the little Princes; on the scaffold of Tower Green two of Henry VIII's Queens met their deaths; through Traitors' Gate so many political prisoners passed, including Elizabeth I when she was a princess. Yet the Tower has its lighter side too – up to the reign of James II, monarchs stayed in the Tower on the eve of their coronation, passing to the Abbey at Westminster on the following day; in 1671 there occurred the comic episode of Captain Blood's attempt to steal the Crown Jewels, and after the doomed Jacobite rebellion of 1715 the Earl of Nithsdale succeeded in escaping from the Tower in the clothing of his Countess.

A. L. Rowse, one of our greatest living historians, tells the story of this incomparable building with all the mastery of narrative, the imagination, poetry and irony at his command.

£2·50 Illustrated

All Sphere Books are available at your bookshop or newsagent, or can be ordered from the following address:

Sphere Books, Cash Sales Department,
P.O. Box 11, Falmouth, Cornwall.

Please send cheque or postal order (no currency), and allow 15p for the first book plus 5p per copy for each additional book ordered up to a maximum of 50p in U.K. or Eire. Overseas customers and B.F.P.O. please allow 20p for the first book and 10p per copy for each additional book.